The Changing British Political System: Into the 1990s

The Changing British Political System:
Into the 1990s

Ian Budge, David McKay, Rod Rhodes, David Robertson, David Sanders, Martin Slater, Graham Wilson with the collaboration of David Marsh for Chapter 3

second edition

LONGMAN
London and New York

Longman Group UK Limited,
Longman House, Burnt Mill, Harlow,
Essex CM20 2JE, England
and Associated Companies throughout the world

Published in the United States of America
by Longman Inc., New York

First published 1983
Revised edition 1985
Second edition 1988
Third impression 1990

British Library Cataloguing in Publication Data

The changing British political system: into
   the 1990s. – 2nd ed.
   1. Great Britain – Politics and government
   – 1979–
   I. Budge, Ian   II. The new British political
  system
   320.941   JN231
   ISBN 0-582-02041-7

Library of Congress Cataloging-in-Publication Data

The changing British political system: into the 1990s.

   Rev. ed. of: The new British political system.
   Bibliography: p.
   Includes index.
   1. Great Britain – Politics and government – 20th
century.   2. Great Britain – Economic policy.   I. Budge,
Ian.   II. New British political system.
JN231.C386   1988   320.941   87–16969
ISBN 0–582–02041–7

Set in 10/12 Linotron 202 Baskerville Roman

Produced by Longman Group (FE) Limited
Printed in Hong Kong

Contents

Preface

When we looked at our first attempt to explain contemporary British politics, written in 1982 with the experience of the Callaghan and first Thatcher Governments in mind, we were pleased to find so many forecasts confirmed and interpretations still valid in 1987. Political fragmentation remained the central problem for Conservatives in the late eighties, as the government tried, with mixed success, to impose itself on trade unions and local authorities, the two major centres of resistance to public expenditure cuts and deregulation.

The economic and social problems which beset all British governments do, however, increasingly compel change. They make it unlikely that political processes and institutions will continue unaltered, even over a short period of time. Although, for example, we originally emphasised the growing political role of courts and judges, this has expanded so fast, both through government legislation (particularly on trade unions) and through judges' own interpretations of law, that a complete rewriting is required. The same is true of the police, which the Thatcher governments have used in an increasingly political and coercive role.

Where events have overtaken us, we have totally rewritten the relevant chapters of this volume. In these areas the second edition provides an original new treatment, very up-to-the-minute in its assessment of events and personalities. Where there are continuities, or where our interpretations and forecasts have anticipated, rather than been displaced by, events, we have carefully weighed and updated what was written before. In general, we have aimed to provide a rounded assessment of the first and second Thatcher administrations of the early and mid 1980s. We have also added two totally new chapters, on the mass media and the British world role, which seemed essential to a full account of national politics at the present time.

What we aim to provide, therefore, is a complete, new, analysis of British politics, firmly based on the experience of the 1980s. Where it carries on from the first edition is in its treatment of the underlying social continuities and national and international constraints on government action; above all, the fragmentation of British politics and society, and the decline of the economic base.

The overpowering pressures for change prevent us from concentrating on the major features of political institutions in the confidence that they will remain largely as they are. Such a description would not be applicable long. What we provide instead is a self-contained and comprehensive account of contemporary British politics and of their relations with economy and society, which is as up to date as possible while identifying tendencies likely to alter the present situation quite radically. We have deliberately emphasised neglected institutions such as the European Community, legal system, quangos, and police, who hardly figure at all in traditional accounts. This is because their power and influence have increased markedly in the 1980s, will increase further and are bound to alter the established balance.

Political changes in post-war Britain have followed economic developments. We therefore start with the major economic challenges which have faced governments over the last fifty years, and their varied attempts to meet them. In explaining the relative failure of these, we consider the internal dynamics of government and Civil Service, and their relationships with societal groups, in Chapter 2; and the relevance of Parliament in Chapter 3. Parliamentary procedures inevitably involve the political parties, both at the level of leaders and activists and in their relationships with electors (Ch. 4). An important question from the viewpoint of representative democracy in Britain is what electors want, and how they relate this to voting decisions in favour of one political party or another. This involves some consideration of the influence of the media – the press, radio and television (Ch. 5).

Of course, the central government is not the only elected authority – even less the only administrative authority – in Britain. There exists an incredibly diverse range of local and regional governments active both in servicing their constituents and supporting or opposing central government, and which we consider in Chapter 6. An important question here is how far Thatcherite attempts to impose central authority on the localities have succeeded in permanently changing relationships. European bodies also exercise authority in Britain by virtue of various treaties – most important, those setting up the European Community. Community institutions increasingly affect life in Britain, so we examine their activities in Chapter 7. As political disputes become more difficult to resolve, the only bodies left in many cases to make even interim decisions are the courts, to which both supporters and opponents of Thatcherite government have had increasing recourse. We examine their expanding powers in Chapter 8. The Conservative Government, faced with trade union resistance and increasing urban disorder, has placed unusual reliance on the police to impose social and political control. As protest becomes more common in response to economic and social hardship, the role of police and military assumes greater significance. Usually ignored because of the traditional law-abidingness of the population, the question of the internal use of coercive forces is considered in Chapter 9. As Britain becomes increasingly enmeshed in the American and European alliances, her international role impinges more heavily on domestic politics, especially as the two major parties now disagree about it. Chapter 10 summarises the background to this debate and presents the foreign and defence options now available. Chapter 11 draws together our conclusions on the nature of British policy-making, its prospects for overcoming current economic and social problems (which are intimately related to the ways it can adapt and change) and its ability to meet the desires and needs of the population. We end with a brief assessment of the features which distinguish the new politics of the 1980s and which will underlie the politics of the early 1990s.

Each chapter in the book has been prepared by a specialist. However, owing to the authors' daily association, the overall themes have been considered as a whole, and each chapter closely related both to the overall analysis and to the other chapters. The result is an account which combines authoritative, detailed treatment of each topic with a clear overview of general developments. We hope that this avoids the weaknesses, and combines the strengths, of single-author treatments on the one hand, and collections of specialised papers on the other. If it does, this is due to the congenial atmosphere of the Essex Department of Government, and the frequent opportunities it provides for the meeting of like (and sometimes unlike!) minds.

Obviously, the book draws on a vast range of discussions and analyses of British politics. The use we make of them is our own and we retain responsibility for any errors of interpretation or fact. (But we trust these are limited!) Bearing in mind the need for a free-running and uncluttered discussion, we have forborne the use of footnotes and references except where discussion has relied exclusively on one source for a particular area or where sources for detailed figures are being cited. The references and bibliography list major references and make suggestions for further reading.

List of figures and tables

Chapter 1
Economic difficulties and government response 1931–1987

Wherever we look in contemporary Britain, we see evidence of increasing political and administrative activity. From social security to defence expenditure, from land-use planning to police surveillance, no one would dispute that governments now are more active than at almost any other time in our history.

The extent and nature of government involvement has been the dominant issue for British politics in the post-war period. To understand why this is so, and to appreciate why all governments, whether they wanted to or not, have been forced to expand their role, requires some appreciation of modern economic developments and political reactions to them.

British politics and government intervention 1931–87

1931–45 The rise of intervention

Contrary to usual belief, central economic management became firmly established not during the Second World War but following the world crisis of 1931. World economic dislocation exposed the weakness of major British industries such as steel-making, coal-mining, shipbuilding and textile manufacture, radically increased the numbers of unemployed to a quarter or a third of the workforce in many regions, and forced the abandonment of the gold standard, that is, the link between the value of the pound and the price of gold, symbolic of the unquestioned integrity and value of the currency.

The National (basically Conservative) Government of the ensuing eight years reacted to these alarming developments with a new economic strategy. Although this fell short of modern economic planning, it did represent a fundamental break from the essentially liberal traditions which had dominated policies until then. The new policy was inspired by the need to protect weak British industry and agriculture from foreign competition. To achieve this it was necessary both to raise tariffs on imports and to encourage the reconstruction of ailing industries. A contemporary comment by Neville Chamberlain on the introduction of the Import Duties Bill shows how interventionist the new policy was:

[The Bill] does provide us with such a lever as has never been possessed before by any government for inducing, or if you like, forcing industry to set its house in order. I have in my mind particularly iron and steel and cotton; and my belief in the advantages of protection is not so fanatical as to close my eyes to the vital importance of a thorough reorganisation of such industries as these, if they are even to keep their heads above water in the future (Beer 1965: 293).

During the 1930s the National Governments encouraged reorganisation in the basic industries (mainly through the creation of cartels), provided central marketing schemes for agricultural products (the marketing boards) and began a policy of regional revival (via the Special Areas Acts of 1935, 1936 and 1937). The Government also pursued a low interest rate policy of monetary expansionism – although the motivations here were probably as much a desire to reduce the national debt as to fuel economic expansion. However, it would be misleading to characterise the National Government as benevolent in relation either to industrial recovery or to social policy. By modern standards it was neither, and on the social side cut welfare and unemployment benefits and applied means tests; but the protection of industry from foreign competition combined with reorganisation was a radical change. There was no indicative planning in the sense of pointing the general direction in which economic and social change should go, and administrative innovations were few and far between (the marketing boards being the main exception). But a regulative framework for unsystematic, special purpose developments was laid down, and for the first time applied to industrial protection.

Towards the end of the decade, support for more comprehensive regulation and planning was mounting steadily and manifested itself in a number of policy areas. In land use, the Government legislated to control urban sprawl in the still prosperous Midlands and South East. More significantly, it set up the Barlow Commission on the Distribution of the Industrial Population which in 1940 recommended a two-pronged attack on the twin problems of regional unemployment and population drift to London and the Midlands. Growth in the prosperous cities should be contained with rigid controls on industrial location, while industry should be given incentives to locate in the distressed North and West. These were radical proposals indeed, and clearly demanded some central coordinating authority if they were to be effectively implemented.

Between 1937 and 1942 a number of other commissions provided recommendations on New Towns (Reith Report), land values (Uthwatt Report), land utilisation in rural areas and national parks (Dower and Hobhouse Report) and social security (Beveridge Report). Many of the commissions were concerned with the physical environment – reflecting the growing influence of the town-planning lobby during the 1930s. Beveridge was given a very wide brief – all income maintenance (unemployment benefit, pensions, national assistance), welfare services and health – as was Barlow. But it is notable that no commission on the reorganisation of industry or industrial relations was created. We can sum up the growth of state intervention in the 1930s in terms of two major developments. First, an acceptance by the Government of a role in regulating industrial and agricultural production, and second the beginnings of a planning movement with some recognition that the problems of society and economy could be solved only through increased government action. There is no doubt that these changes came about in response to the near collapse of international capitalism in the 1930s. But, crucially, recovery was seen in terms of reviving old industries (iron and steel, mining, textiles, shipbuilding) and regions which were assumed to be victims of international forces. Little thought was devoted to restructuring or to channelling investment into high productivity, high growth industries. Physical planning apart, the enhanced state role was perceived solely in terms of how to help declining traditional industries and, in embryo form at least, how to ameliorate the social evils of industrial decline. Within the Labour Party the same issues dominated – although the more draconian solutions were adopted of government ownership and control of industry, together with state support of comprehensive welfare and health services.

Between 1936 and 1945 attitudes towards state intervention among political leaders and public alike were transformed by two events – the acceptance of Keynesian economics and the total modification of the economy during the Second World War. The monetarist orthodoxy accepted by the National Governments of the 1930s held that industrial development could take place only if there was general confidence in the currency, maintained by government budgets in which revenues equalled or surpassed expenditures. Keynes showed that the economy could function for long periods well below the level of production it might potentially attain with full use of available resources. Since one underused resource was labour, this implied long-term unemployment for large sections of the workforce. Governments could, however, raise the equilibrium to nearly full capacity by increasing government expenditure and therefore stimulating demand. The war seemed to confirm the validity of this assumption. Massively increased expenditure on armaments started during the late 1930s; by June 1943 only 60,000 people were registered as unemployed. By 1945 few political leaders disputed the need for at least partial acceptance of Keynesian demand management. The war also gave planning an enormous boost – both in theory and in practice. Prices, incomes, industrial relations and production were all strictly controlled by central committees. Not before or since has the British economy been so rigidly disciplined.

Being both authoritarian and comprehensive, wartime controls were always seen by civil servants and many politicians as temporary – a fact reflected by the *ad hoc* nature of the administrative reforms of the period. The old pre-war ministries remained intact ready to resume their traditional roles once hostilities ceased. Labour politicians were much less antipathetic to controls, but as the post-war period was to confirm, even they were highly ambivalent about centralised planning of the positive variety, where the state took all important economic decisions leaving only a residual role to the market.

The Keynesian Revolution and the war destroyed for ever the minimal state spending policies of the previous eras. Towards the war's end the major earlier Reports plus further White Papers on employment and education laid foundations for greatly increased state spending in social and economic policy. This accepted, state planning through a central planning agency was rejected by the Conservatives and had won little sympathy among Labour politicians.

Moreover, neither party had devoted much intellectual energy to the question of industrial reorganisation and planned industrial investment.

Labour and the new order 1945–51

The Labour Government elected in 1945 passed a remarkable volume of legislation. Basic industries were nationalised, the welfare state created, regional policy strengthened dramatically and physical planning by local authorities established as mandatory. All these policies remain with us today – indeed they still constitute the core of state intervention in British society. Conservative governments have tinkered with the basic framework but only in the case of nationalisation have they dismantled an essential part of it.

Post-war policy was dominated by a driving desire to re-establish full employment. Keynesian demand management, nationalisation and regional policy were either primarily or partly designed to achieve this end, and in combination with a favourable international trading position after 1945, successfully produced full employment until 1951. Industry readapted to peacetime conditions very efficiently and Britain's share of world trade actually increased during these years. If full employment and industrial recovery were achieved quickly, little progress was made in the field of economic policy. Various wartime reports had, in fact, pleaded for a close co-ordination of industrial location and industrial policy (Barlow) and for full-blown positive economic planning (Beveridge 1944, in his 'unofficial' report on employment). Neither were to transpire, however, in part because of opposition from established bureaucracies – and in particular the Treasury – to a new central planning agency. (There was even opposition to calling the new Ministry of Town and Country Planning just plain 'planning' for fear it might assume a more comprehensive planning role.)

But probably more important was the absence of a coherent policy towards economic policy within the Labour Government. In the first year after the war there was much talk about the need for a national plan plus all the administrative machinery necessary to implement it, but instead the Government opted to retain the wartime planning machinery. The 1947 fuel crisis came as a rude shock bringing severe shortages of coal and other raw materials. In response, the Government created a Central Economic Planning Staff (CEPS) who would implement an annual economic survey or short-term plan for manpower resources and economic growth.

Under the guidance of Stafford Cripps a limited and short-term form of planning actually prevailed during 1947 and 1948. Some reassertion of direct control over labour, and an effective wage freeze were part of the strategy, as was voluntary restraint on prices by manufacturers. From late 1948 onwards, however, enthusiasm for planning declined and was effectively abandoned by 1950. Reasons for its demise are varied. The unions objected to wage restraint, the new austerity of 1947–48 was electorally unpopular. Perhaps more important, the administrative innovations were never more than *ad hoc* in nature. Existing departments continued much as before, the economic surveys were for one year only, and opposition to yet more controls and planning from within the Cabinet was mounting.

But we should be wary of underestimating the scope of Labour's efforts during these years. In social policy a truly comprehensive welfare state had been created providing free health care and secondary education, public housing, and a wide range of income maintenance payments for the disadvantaged. Similarly in land-use planning a comprehensive approach had been adopted – although there was no attempt to co-ordinate physical with economic planning. In the economic area, indeed, Labour's efforts depended more on improvisation and persuasion than on radical reforms:

... Labour leaders quite failed to see the possibilities of using the new public sector as a way of steering the whole economy in the direction they desired. They behaved as if, while carrying through their plans for nationalisation, they had no understanding of the real meaning of what they had done. Ownership changed; power did not. It had long since ceased to be true, if indeed it ever was, that the shareholders in industries like the mines and railways exercised any real power over them (Leruez 1975: 76).

And in economic affairs, nationalisation was the only legacy left by Labour to successive governments. Keynesian demand management had already been accepted by the late 1930s, and was continued through to the late 1970s. When the Conservatives came to power in 1951, the basic relationships between government and unions and government and industry were almost unchanged from the pre-war years. The unions played no integrated role in economic or industrial policy and although big business was quite happy to accept a regulative government role, especially in foreign trade, they too were largely excluded from central economic policy-making. Administrative changes were largely confined to the creation of new bureaucracies to implement the programmes of a burgeoning welfare state. So while the public sector had been expanded enormously, the basic tools available to governments to guide and control the public sector had changed very little.

The Conservatives and the state 1951–64

The Conservatives fought the 1951 election on the twin themes of preservation of the welfare state and the decontrol of the economy. Decontrol meant lower income and purchase taxes (in 1951 they remained very high), an end to rationing (especially of building and other materials), abolition of the prohibitive tax (100 per cent) on land development profits, relaxation of exchange controls and the denationalisation of certain industries (notably road transport and steel). All of these were achieved by 1959, and decontrol almost certainly contributed to the growing prosperity of the 1950s.

The Conservatives also preserved the essentials of the welfare state for which there was considerable public support throughout the 1950s. Some small changes were made, mainly by tinkering with some services (notably housing and charges for health services) so as to make their free availability somewhat more selective. But the changes were quite small.

5

If the Conservatives did not dismantle the welfare state or other, by then fairly substantial, parts of the public sector, what part did they play in controlling or guiding public intervention? To answer this we have to divide the period into two parts. Until about 1960, government intervention in industry was minimal but Keynesian demand management continued. After 1960 Keynesian methods were combined with incomes policy and some embryonic planning devices both to control inflation and to achieve a higher rate of economic growth. The transition from the minimalist role to something approaching indicative planning, with government stipulation of general goals and priorities, was inspired by an increasing disenchantment with Britain's economic performance, which was falling behind that of its main competitors.

Using fiscal and monetary policy to stimulate or depress economic activity in the Keynesian fashion, the Government soon found itself in a vicious 'stop-go' cycle. The fundamental problem was perceived as a need to defend the value of sterling by avoiding recurring balance of payments deficits (an imbalance of imports over exports which affected confidence in sterling). As the economy expanded, so imports increased, the trade deficit widened and the Bank of England was forced to buy more pounds with its foreign currency reserves to maintain exchange rates at their declared values. With reserves falling and the deficit continuing, governments felt obliged to depress economic activity by raising taxes and restricting credit in order to reduce imports and solve the balance of payments crises. But this brought a rise in unemployment and a fall in output causing governments once more to inflate the economy thus precipitating yet another sterling crisis. Such 'stop-go' tactics became common between 1953 and 1970. A related problem was inflation which accelerated during 'go' periods and declined during 'stop' periods. In today's terms both the inflation and unemployment rates were very low (Table 1.1); but, crucially, Britain was losing out to her main economic competitors. Indeed, as the decade wore on the fundamental problem with the economy was increasingly defined as a failure to achieve a rate of economic growth comparable to other major industrial countries. Measured by almost any criteria – industrial investment, productivity, gross national product *per capita* – Britain was being outstripped by other countries and in particular by Germany and France.

By the late 1950s sympathy for more state intervention in industry and the economy generally was mounting within the Conservative Government and, infatuated with the French experience, Selwyn Lloyd, the Chancellor of the Exchequer and Harold Macmillan, the Prime Minister, launched a limited form of indicative planning in 1961. Their main planning device was the National Economic Development Council (NEDC or Neddy) which comprised members of government, industry and the unions and whose main function would be to identify the obstacles to faster growth and then recommend ways in which these could be removed.

In its first report, Neddy estimated that an annual growth rate of 4 per cent per annum between 1961 and 1966 was possible *if* there was a change in the relationship between government and industry, *if* public expenditure could be projected ahead accurately over the five years, and *if* prices and incomes could be held down and thus balance of payments crises avoided. There is little

Table 1.1 Unemployment and inflation, UK 1953–87

Year	Unemployment %[*]	Change in retail prices[†]
1956	1.0	2.0
1957	1.3	3.7
1958	1.9	3.0
1959	2.0	0.6
1960	1.5	1.0
1961	1.3	3.4
1962	1.8	2.6
1963	2.2	2.1
1964	1.6	3.3
1965	1.3	4.8
1966	1.4	3.9
1967	2.2	2.5
1968	2.3	4.7
1969	2.3	5.4
1970	2.5	6.4
1971	3.3	9.4
1972	3.6	7.1
1973	2.6	9.2
1974	2.5	16.1
1975	3.9	24.2
1976	5.2	16.5
1977	5.7	15.8
1978	5.6	8.2
1979	5.3	13.4
1980	7.1	15.0
1981	10.1	12.0
1982	12.3	8.6
1983	12.3	5.3
1984	12.9	4.6
1985	13.2	5.5
1986	11.3++	3.9
1987	10.0 (to September)	4.2 (to September)

Sources: *British Labour Statistics, Historical Abstract*, HMSO; *Department of Employment Gazette*, HMSO; *The Economist, Economic Indicators* (1985 and 1986)

Notes
* Wholly unemployed, Great Britain, excluding school-leavers and adult students.
† Twelve monthly change in weekly rates from December of previous year.
++ New series, August 1986. Underlying trend remained upwards.

doubt that Neddy's recommendations in this and in subsequent reports were both sensible and carefully worked out. However, in spite of the fact that the Government accepted the 4 per cent target, few of the recommendations were implemented in full. Relations with industry were to be fostered via a number of Economic Development Councils or 'little Neddies', whose job was to improve the flow of information between a range of key industries and the Government. However, as with similar experiments under Cripps in 1945, these were more talking shops dominated by industry spokesmen than genuine policy instruments designed to fix targets and then set about meeting them.

Neddy also had to compete with the Treasury – a key government department largely antipathetic to planning and eager to defend sterling and pursue monetary orthodoxy. To be fair, the Government did go so far as to reorganise the Treasury in 1962 and create a new section on the National Economy, whose job would be to liaise with Neddy. Also, for a short period between 1962 and 1964, Neddy did constitute a real rival to the Treasury and with the Chancellor (by then Reginald Maudling) on its side, led the way towards economic expansion. What Neddy and the Chancellor were unable to do was to control prices, wages and, perhaps most importantly, public expenditure. Failure with prices and incomes was understandable given the absence of a long-term legislative framework to control either (although Selwyn Lloyd had introduced a 'pay pause' during the sterling crisis in 1961). As the economy expanded so labour became scarcer and unions were better able to bargain for higher wages and to oppose more efficient, but disruptive, work practices.

Public expenditure was viewed in a way dramatically different from today. As pointed out earlier, the growth of the welfare state and nationalisation had been accompanied by remarkably few administrative reforms. The system of control over expenditure in the 1950s was largely unchanged since the mid nineteenth century. In sum it was approved annually in the budget, never surveyed systematically and never planned more than one year ahead. With the publication of the Plowden Report in 1961 (*Control of Public Expenditure*, Cmnd 1432) and Neddy's call for five-year expenditure planning, the Government at last accepted the need for expenditure surveys which eventually became a regular annual affair in 1969 (known as the Public Expenditure Survey Committee or PESC). But in the early 1960s, when the prevailing view was that the Government could spend its way out of trouble, very few systematic controls on expenditure existed.

In sum then, the later Tory years were characterised by a new enthusiasm for economic planning, and by some quite ambitious experiments in that direction, but also by failure to institute detailed changes needed to make planning work. On the production side, targets were of the broadest macro variety, planning within specific sectors of industry being quite primitive. Incomes, prices and expenditure were at least partly beyond the Government's control: thus as expansion set in, inflation and trade deficits were aggravated yet again.

Labour and planning 1964–70

Serious overheating of the economy together with the usual sterling crisis appeared before the 1964 general election, so on coming to power Labour inherited a difficult economic position. As a Labour Government emerging from thirteen years in Opposition, Harold Wilson and his Cabinet were eager to pursue reforms in social policy (mainly in housing, pensions, education and transport) all of which were expensive; to renationalise steel (also expensive) as well as to continue the Conservative policy of rapid economic growth.

Significantly, however, Labour's ideas about how to produce growth had developed very little in Opposition. Their main innovation, the creation of the Department of Economic Affairs (DEA) in 1965, was inspired by a deep mistrust of the Treasury and a perception that Neddy's role was by necessity limited because it was outside the main machinery of government. Hence the DEA was a full-blown government department assigned the job of long-term economic planning, the Treasury being confined to its traditional role as short-term expenditure controller. The DEA's brief was extensive: to devise a longer-term national plan, to revitalise industry and improve efficiency (working partly through the 'little Neddies'); to work out a prices and incomes policy and to reorganise regional policy. As it turned out this most radical administrative change lasted just four years, and as an effective policy institution the DEA was operational for less than two. Two major reasons for its failure can be identified. First and foremost was the accelerating rate of economic crisis during the 1965–67 period. Britain's competitive position had been deteriorating for some years, balance of payments deficits were slowly increasing, and sterling was clearly overvalued. Committed to economic growth and the expansion of public services, the Labour government found it impossible to reconcile its policy objectives with economic reality. In historical perspective it is clear that a bad situation was aggravated by the Government's deference to the official Treasury line of giving priority to the value of sterling. So when in 1966 a serious payments' crisis and a crippling seamen's strike coincided to induce investors to sell pounds, the Government opted to abandon national planning and safeguard the currency by restricting credit. Indeed, the second reason for the DEA's demise was precisely its organisational isolation from that institution, the Treasury, responsible for providing immediate advice in crisis situations.

. . . The structure (of the DEA) was such as to reinforce the Treasury's traditional weaknesses: a low concern for growth among economic priorities, a lack of knowledge of and interest in the working of industry (including the impact on industry of fiscal and monetary policies), and an overriding concern for the defence of sterling. Thus as the balance of power within Whitehall tilted away from the DEA and towards the Treasury, the ills which Labour in Opposition had diagnosed and sought to cure became embedded deeper and deeper in the structure of government (Shanks 1977: 34–5).

It is crucial to understand that deflation in order to defend sterling was not the only policy option open to Harold Wilson in 1966. He could have devalued and solved the immediate crisis – an option actually taken a year later in 1967. He could have cut public expenditure, but with Keynesian economics still very much alive and a host of election commitments to honour, this was never a realistic alternative. Finally, he could have frozen prices and incomes in order to cut costs, improve industry's productivity and reduce inflation. In fact prices and incomes policy was gaining in popularity as a possible solution to the country's problems. In 1965 a new independent body, the National Board for Prices and Incomes (NBPI), had been created to investigate income and price increases and arbitrate on their fairness. But a total wage and price freeze would have been unpopular with the unions as well as with industry and was avoided, at least for the time being.

Economic planning was effectively laid to rest after 1967. The DEA together with the institutions it fostered fell into disuse. So the Industrial Reorganisation Corporation, which had been set up to provide loans to industry to speed efficiency, found it could not operate in the absence of a secure and predictable economic climate. The NBPI and an incomes policy were also effectively abandoned. Instead, under the guidance of the new Chancellor, Roy Jenkins, economic policy reverted almost to a pre-Keynesian strategy: some government expenditure was cut (mainly in defence), foreign loans repaid and taxes increased. Interestingly, the Jenkins deflation was not so damaging to employment as might have been expected (Table 1.1), largely because the 1967 devaluation did produce something of an investment boom.

Labour's six years in office were characterised by continual economic crises. The reconstruction of industry and achievement of a high growth rate eluded the Government. In fact, Britain's share of world trade fell from 13.9 per cent to 10.8 per cent during these years. In spite of this, some important reforms and election pledges were carried through. Comprehensive education was launched, and public transport and physical planning reorganised. Public expenditure also increased, notably in education, health and local government; but in comparison with the 1945–50 period, Labour had hardly been a radical reforming government. Taxation increased quite dramatically from 32 per cent of gross domestic product in 1965 to 43 per cent in 1970. Moreover, within the Labour movement the seeds of disquiet at the Government's failure to redistribute income and wealth had been sown. It was clear that the failure of economic planning had prevented the government from instituting major social reforms.

The 1970s: plus ça change . . .?

If the 1960s were years of periodic crises, the 1970s were years of unremitting economic crisis. For present purposes we can divide the period into four quite distinct sections, each representing a sharp change in the role of the state in economy and society.

1970–72: Conservative expansionism The first thing the new Conservative Government of Edward Heath did on coming unexpectedly to office in 1970 was to dismantle the NBPI and the Industrial Reorganisation Corporation, therefore apparently disavowing both income policy and a strong state role in guiding industry. The Government was also intent on reforming industrial relations (primarily to render the introduction of more efficient working practices easier) by imposing a more rigid framework of law oh union activity. What transpired was the 1971 Industrial Relations Act which sought to make unions accept certain legal restrictions on their activities, notably on their right to strike, and to submit themselves to a special court. From its inception this inspired the fiercest hostility from the unions.

In the absence of an incomes policy and industrial strategy, how were inflation and payments crises to be solved? Strangely, and in spite of some reforms in the control of public expenditure, *not* by reducing expenditure. Instead, a policy of economic expansion via reduced taxation and increased public expenditure was followed. With no controls on income and expenditure, inflation took off, soaring from 6.4 per cent in 1970 to 9.4 per cent in 1971 – easily the highest figure since 1950 (Table 1.1). This situation could not last long as the rapid increase in prices and expenditure was bound to undermine the balance of payments and Britain's trading position. In a famous about-turn in November 1972, Heath announced a prices and incomes freeze.

1972–74: incomes policy and confrontation Phase I of the Heath freeze lasted until March 1973 when under phase II all employees were to be subject to an annual increase of £1.00 a week plus 4 per cent *per annum*. The new system was to be policed by a Pay Board, and price increases were also to be carefully controlled by a newly established Price Commission. Phase II represented a highly significant break with past Conservative principles. Machinery was created to control prices and incomes for a minimum of three years, implying the acceptance of a permanent incomes policy. This indicated Conservative endorsement of a highly interventionist economic policy.

Although opposed by the unions, phase II was generally adhered to. Not so with phase III, however, which provoked confrontation by the unions and eventually brought down the Government. In fact phase III was really quite flexible, permitting a maximum of 7 per cent increase plus extra amounts for productivity payments and working unsocial hours. The miners demanded more than the norm on the grounds that they were a special case. Faced with extensive picketing not only of collieries but of power stations and other energy supplies, hardship and short-time working throughout the country, with the addition of a railway strike and public disenchantment with statutory wages policy (by October 1973, only 37 per cent of the public considered phase III fair – *Financial Times*, 16 November 1973), Heath decided to call a general election.

The Government's 'U-turn' on incomes policy in 1972 was accompanied by another *volte face* on industrial policy. In spite of the liberalism and minimal state intervention which apparently prevailed in 1970, Heath very soon began to indulge in a range of policies to aid, succour and guide industrial recovery. Bankrupt companies (Rolls Royce, Upper Clyde Shipbuilders) were bailed out, regional incentives and development grants were strengthened, a Minister for Industrial Development attached to the new Department of Trade and Industry, and manpower retraining reorganised and greatly strengthened. All this did not amount to planning in the sense of economic targets being set over a fixed time period, but it did represent a new corporatism involving close liaison between government and industry.

Finally, the Government was pledged after 1972 to cut public expenditure.

Table 1.2 Total government expenditure as a percentage of GNP, selected years 1970–85

Year	1970	1971	1972	1974	1976	1978	1979	1980	1981	1982	1983	1984	1985
%	40.5	40.6	41.2	46.6	46.8	44.1	44.0	47.6	48.0	47.4	47.1	46.8	45.3

Source: *National Accounts*, OECD, various years

However, by 1973 the pressures to increase expenditure (partly to compensate for the effects of incomes policy) were mounting and when they left office, the Conservatives were actually presiding over a larger public sector than in 1970 (in terms of the government share of gross national product, and number of enterprises owned by government – see Table 1.2). This is crucial because it demonstrates how much the Heath Government was relying on incomes policy to harness inflation; talk of controlling the money supply, which dominated the policy agenda in the late seventies, was almost completely absent.

1974–75: a return to planning?   While in opposition, the Left wing of the Labour Party converted its disenchantment with the 1964–70 period into a set of alternative policies. Eventually published as the *Labour Programme 1973*, these called for a dominant role for the state in the British economy. Britain's industrial recovery, so the programme asserted, could be facilitated only by further nationalisation, the creation of a National Enterprise Board (NEB), the introduction of planning agreements between government and individual industries, a new deal for workers in industrial relations and the management of firms, and the protection of vulnerable industries from foreign competition.

Many of these ideas formed the basis of the 1974 Manifesto and on coming to power, the Labour Government set about implementing at least some of them. The Industrial Relations Act was repealed, a National Enterprise Board whose job would be to act as a state holding company to encourage investment and improve productivity was created, and a system of planning agreements between industries and the state established. In incomes policy, a new social contract would bind both government and unions to moderation on incomes matters. In fact, the social contract resulted in anything but moderation, weekly wage increases jumping from 12.2 per cent a year in 1973 to 29.4 per cent in 1974. Inflation too bounded ahead, reaching 16.1 per cent in 1974 and a staggering 24.2 per cent in 1975 (Table 1.1). Finally, the Conservatives' quite generous public expenditure targets for 1974 and 1975 were met in full.

Nineteen seventy-four was a bad year for all the developed countries; the quadrupling of oil prices by the Organisation of Petroleum Exporting Countries (OPEC) in late 1973 had precipitated a sharp downturn in world trade and an acceleration of inflation everywhere. A good part of the 1974–75 inflation must be attributed to these international forces. But Britain suffered from additional problems peculiar to her. British industrial competitiveness continued to decline and British unions were more successful than those in many other countries in keeping wage rates up to or beyond the rate of inflation. In fact up to the end of the 1970s, in spite of general economic difficulties, the majority of the British population enjoyed growing prosperity and a rising standard of living – a striking phenomenon whose effects are explored in Chapter 4. From a general economic and business point of view, however, the combination of a falling national income, accelerating rates of inflation and wages, and a high level of public expenditure could not go on. Moreover, unemployment was rising fast. The assumptions of Keynesian demand management seemed no longer to apply. According to Keynesian orthodoxy, unemployment or under-capacity occurred only when prices and interest rates were low. Inflation was a product of rapid growth and labour shortages. Now, however, most countries experienced both inflation and high rates of unemployment at the same time. This fact, above all others, was responsible for the revival both of incomes policies and, crucially, of traditional monetary policies.

1975–79: monetarism and incomes policy The Labour Left's policies for radical surgery on the British economy came to very little. Surgery there was, but it was of the conservative rather than socialist variety. The first change came in July 1975 when a Government now dominated by the Labour Right announced a new incomes policy granting £6 a week for all workers earning up to £8,500 and nothing for those earning over this figure. This was not a statutory policy but an agreement worked out between the Government and the Trades Union Congress (TUC). It was remarkably successful (strikes fell to a twenty-two-year low during the £6 a week period) and demonstrated the growing strength of the TUC. This informal agreement was renewed in July 1976 when a 5 per cent limit to all increases was agreed, and again in 1977 when a 10 per cent limit was accepted. Five per cent was proposed in 1978 but effectively rejected by the unions. Their resentment at government imposition of this 'ceiling' was shown by widespread transport and public service strikes in the 'winter of discontent' (1978–79) which almost certainly lost Labour the May 1979 election.

As important was the conversion of the Government to a limited form of monetarism. During 1976 investors' selling of sterling reached panic proportions. Fixed exchange rates (the Bank of England commitment to buying sterling for fixed sums in other currencies) had been abandoned in 1971 and the pound left free to fall – and fall the pound did, to a low of $1.57 at one point. Britain was approaching the point where the Government could not meet immediate payments on outstanding debts. In exchange for massive loans from the International Monetary Fund (IMF), Denis Healey, the Chancellor, agreed to new controls on the money supply. Interest rates rose to a record 15.5 per cent and public expenditure was cut. After complex negotiations, the IMF and the Treasury agreed that the Public Sector Borrowing Requirement (the amount needed by the Government to cover the gap between projected resources and expenditure) should be trimmed by £3 billion over two years. In fact, public spending did not fall quite as rapidly as planned (see Table 1.2) but the very idea of using public sector spending as *the* major instrument of economic policy was new (notwithstanding Roy Jenkins's more limited efforts in this direction between 1968 and 1970).

The combination of income policy and public expenditure cuts together with stabilising oil prices reduced inflation quite quickly to a low of around 8 per cent between 1978 and 1979 (Table 1.1). However, unemployment remained stubbornly high and Labour's plans both for industrial reorganisation and for social reform were seriously circumscribed by the spending cuts. As with most of its predecessors managing decline rather than implementing programmes of social reform became the Government's overriding preoccupation.

13

The 1980s: Thatcherism and the free market

The early 1980s, with an overall decline of economic activity and a drastic shrinkage of the manufacturing base, seemed a continuation of the late 1970s. Propelled by the general recovery of world trade after 1981, however, the service and financial sectors of the British economy (heavily concentrated in London and South-East England) made particular advances in the middle of the decade, while the reduced manufacturing sector showed itself more internationally competitive. Contrasts between prosperous centre and declining periphery, between expanding suburbs and decaying inner cities, between employed and unemployed, became much more obvious however, and were defined as the major political problem towards the end of the decade. Corresponding to these different economic situations, government policies can also be divided into three phases – all distinguished however by a much stronger belief in the efficacy of the free market and a more pronounced avoidance of overall planning than had been evident since the National Government of the 1930s.

1979–83: intensified monetarism   The new Conservative government was determined to avoid the expediency and fragmentation of the Heath Administration. With a change of personnel (the leadership plus all the key economic posts), the Conservatives were pledged to solve Britain's economic problems not by planning or incomes policies, but through rigid adherence to monetarist orthodoxy. Within a stable operating climate (low inflation and taxes), the market would be given full rein to bring about recovery. Government's role in industrial revival would be minimal.

To achieve a low rate of inflation the money supply and public expenditure would have to be carefully controlled. So on coming to office the Conservatives attempted to cut projected expenditure quite dramatically and raised interest rates to record levels. In order to finance lower income taxes, the indirect tax on sales (VAT: Value Added Tax) was also raised – a fact which partly accounted for a quickly *rising* rate of inflation during 1979–80. Unleashed from incomes policy, wage rates also increased rapidly, although little higher than the rate of inflation.

Reducing the money supply in combination with the world depression between 1978 and 1981 quickly lowered the level of activity in the British economy, and unemployment increased from an already high 5.3 per cent in 1979 to over 12 per cent in 1982. While it would be over simple to claim that the Government's main strategy was to use unemployment to reduce wage rates and therefore inflation, there is no doubt that this was partly its intention.

On the industrial front the NEB, while not disbanded, was quickly reduced in resources and status, and the nationalised industries were required to operate strictly according to commercial criteria. Any idea of social planning or reform involving increased expenditure was put into cold storage to await economic recovery. Unfortunately this was not even faintly visible until 1982.

As a strategy for rapid and extensive revitalisation of British industry, the new policy was as unsuccessful as its predecessors. It is important to stress, however, that at least one component (a policy of high interest rates and expenditure cuts) had been pioneered by the Labour Government between 1976 and 1979. The major change was a new devotion to market principles which naturally meant rejection of a prices and incomes policy. But from 1981 this came creeping back in various forms, notably cash limits on what government departments, public authorities and nationalised industries were allowed to offer to their employees. The need for some kind of incomes policy was in line with developments under previous governments. Similarly, in the field of industrial policy, even during its first year of office, the Thatcher Government was prepared to continue support for lame duck industries (British Leyland, British Steel) and it actually strengthened the industrial retraining and manpower programmes inherited from Labour. This, together with increasing state payments to the unemployed, prevented the Government from reducing public expenditure as a percentage of GNP (Table 1.2).

1983–87: Privatisation and deregulation

Until 1983 the Thatcher government favoured monetarism – a belief that control of the amount of money circulating in the economy would alone improve general economic efficiency. From 1983, however, monetary targets were rarely met and ministers became less and less dependent on the theory. They did not, however, abandon their free market philosophy. Denationalisation (or privatisation), reducing trade union power, and increasing economic incentives in the public sector, all remained central to government policy. The British National Oil Corporation, Jaguar Cars, British Telecom, the Trustee Savings Bank, British Gas and British Airways, Rolls Royce and many council-owned homes were sold. By 1987 plans were being made for selling water companies and other 'natural monopolies' traditionally within the public sector.

Major legislation in 1980, 1982 and 1984 all but transformed industrial relations law. 'Closed shops' i.e. factories where all the workforce have to join a union, had to be approved in a secret ballot by 4/5ths of the workers; secondary picketing (i.e. the picketing of firms not themselves party to an industrial dispute) was outlawed; secret ballots were introduced to approve industrial action, to elect top union officials, and to approve the collection of union political funds. These laws, together with continuing high unemployment, substantially weakened trade unions. They were further debilitated by the costly and often violent miners' strike of 1984/85, which ended with a split in the NUM and an effective victory for the Government.

Unemployment and the incessant decline of Britain's industrial base remained the Thatcher Government's Achille's Heel. By 1987 the number and scope of youth employment schemes, retraining programmes and other employment creation devices had increased considerably. Through all of this, however, the Government never entertained the possibility of a return to an official incomes policy or to an overtly interventionist industrial policy, let alone anything that could be called economic planning. By 1987, although the world price of oil had declined, so reducing vital revenue from North Sea oil, the economy began to show the first real signs of recovery. However, only time will tell if this is a temporary improvement or not.

The late 1980s: free markets and social problems In spite of its overwhelming victory in the General Election of June 1987, the third Thatcher Administration was acutely aware of the political dangers from those left out of free-market prosperity, above all minority ethnic groups, inner city residents, and particularly members of these groups living in the Midlands and North. All these had suffered more than anyone else from the accumulated problems of 19th and 20th century industrialisation, and from accelerated de-industrialisation in the 1980s. Intervention in these areas had traditionally involved heavy use of controls and physical planning, with central government relying on locally elected councils to effect its policies. The Conservatives, in line with their free-market philosophy, sought instead to remove what they saw as the dead hand of Labour-dominated local government through various measures tried out in the mid-eighties and now intensified. The centrally controlled Youth Training Scheme, channelling the energies of the young unemployed, was extended and made semi-compulsory: enterprise zones with suspension of normal planning regulations were set up under nominated boards; council house sales continued and private renting of houses was encouraged. State schools were given greater autonomy and the ability to opt entirely out of local authority control. Meanwhile moral and administrative pressure was applied to those receiving unemployment benefit to take any form of work available, however low-paid and unattractive. Vigorous attempts were also initiated to break away from national pay settlements, so that firms operating in areas of high unemployment could pay less.

By such means the Government hoped to render the depressed areas more attractive to private enterprise by capitalising on their potential reserves of cheap labour. Paradoxically, however, this attempt to free the local economy involved the use of considerable coercive power by central government, particularly in regard to local government and trade unions, the major centres of opposition to its policies (Ch. 6). Central direction also extended to individuals, particularly the young and the unemployed. To a considerable extent Conservative policies can be seen as changing the forms and focus of government intervention, rather than reducing the extent of intervention overall.

On a more general level, the attempt to get government out of the economy appeared by the end of the eighties to have had real but limited success. In areas of traditional strength – finance and services centred on South-East England – free-enterprise policies had strengthened Britain's competitive position in an era of growing interdependence and internationalisation of markets. They had not averted the industrial decline of the outlying areas, but then no previous policies had done that either. What remained problematical was how far the recovery was temporary and linked to special conditions such as the recovery in world trade in the mid-eighties and above all the peaking of oil revenues, which would have freed any government from the balance of payment problems which had dogged previous economic initiatives. Oil receipts had financed the Falklands expedition abroad, and confrontation with unions at home, and thus put the government in a more favourable position to assert their authority. Whether this could continue as oil prices dropped and the oil reserves themselves contracted in the 1990s remained to be seen, but obviously renewed pressures of this type could render the Conservative achievements of the 1980s extremely fragile.

An overview of post-war events

Table 1.3 gives a chronology of the main post-war developments described above, together with a brief description of international as well as of non-economic domestic events which impinged on politics. During some periods attention was deflected from the imperfections of economic policy to alarming foreign developments and the danger of nuclear war. In the 1950s, when the economy enjoyed a modest post-war boom and trade unions could be placated with a share of increasing profits, both the Korean War and a successful disengagement from most remaining territories of the pre-war colonial empire preoccupied successive Conservative Governments. With diminishing commitments elsewhere, entry to the European Community seemed increasingly attractive as a cure for the ills of British industry, by opening wider markets and intensifying domestic competition. After ignoring the actual formation of the Community in 1956, abortive negotiations for entry occurred in 1962 and 1968, before they succeeded under Heath in 1972, only to be revised by Labour in 1974–75.

The eruption of communal strife in Northern Ireland and intensified demands for some form of autonomy in Wales and Scotland also took up considerable political energy in the 1970s. By the end of that decade, however, even these movements were being seen as tensions generated by economic malaise. As membership of the Community failed to exert any visible economic effects and governments took increasingly far-ranging action to reverse economic decline, they stimulated more extensive reactions against their policies. Thus the moderate Labour Government of Callaghan, with its muted interventionist policy, fired radical left-wing demands for control over the parliamentary leadership to ensure the enactment of social reforms and supporting measures of government economic control. Their success in getting such demands accepted in the Labour Party after 1979 prompted a secession by some established leaders and MPs to form the Social Democratic Party, which in alliance with the Liberals had just over a quarter of the votes in the general election of 1983 and over one fifth in 1987.

Labour support for more extensive intervention prompted the Conservative reaction just described with attempts to get government out of business and industrial relations altogether. Even so, the unions felt the Government was responsible for the three million unemployed and must be forced to help them through subsidies and programmes for job creation. 'Non-intervention' was almost as much a recipe for political confrontation in the industrial field as earlier governments' positive intervention had been.

The overall consequence of a declining industrial base, harsher social conditions and uneven prosperity was an intensification of political conflict at all levels of society. At the bottom, violent rioting in many urban centres in 1981 and 1985 warned that socially deprived groups could not be left to bear the consequences of unemployment on their own. And while the unions have been weakened by legislation and unemployment, the 1984–85 miners' strike, a bitter teachers' dispute in 1985–86, and violent picketing of News International's Wapping plant in 1986–87, showed that serious industrial problems were never far from the

Table 1.3 Governments, policies and events, 1945–87

Labour Governments 1945–51 (Attlee)

National Health Service Act 1946	German surrender 1945
National Insurance Act 1946	Japanese surrender 1945
State ownership of coal industry, gas, electricity, transport and steel	
Town and Country Planning Act 1947	Dislocation of international trade after Second World War
Full employment policy; wage and dividends freeze; control of production in many areas; rationing	
Independence of India, Pakistan, Burma and Ceylon 1948	Berlin crisis 1948–49 marks start of cold war with Soviet Union and intensification of Western alliance

Conservative Governments 1951–59 (Churchill, Eden, Macmillan)

Deregulation of trade and financial controls	Korean War 1950–53
Limited denationalisation of iron and steel industry, and road transport	World economic growth Formation of European Community
Invasion of Suez 1956	1956

Conservative Governments 1959–64 (Macmillan, Home)

Independence of most African colonies 1959–64	
Wage and price freeze 1962–63	*Détente* with Soviet Union 1960–79
Unsuccessful application to join EC 1962	Relaxation of cold war and arms race

Labour Governments 1964–70 (Wilson)

Balance of payments crisis 1964–65	
National economic plan effectively abandoned 1966–67	
Increasing credit, wage and dividend restrictions 1966–69	
Devaluation of £ sterling 1967	Vietnam War 1964–73
Unsuccessful application to join EC 1968	
Plan to regulate trade union and industrial relations 1969–70 (revealed in Green Paper *In Place of Strife* 1969) – defeated by trade union and internal Labour opposition	
Intervention of British troops in Northern Ireland 1969	

Conservative Government 1970–74 (Heath)

Floating exchange rate for £ sterling 1971	
Industrial Relations Act 1971 (legal regulation of trade unions)	
'U-turn' from not interfering in industry or wage negotiations to restrictions on wage and salary increases from 1972–74	Discovery of oil in British North Sea Rise in world oil prices 1973–74
Suspension of Northern Ireland Parliament and Direct Rule 1972	
Reorganisation into larger local government units 1972–75	
Entry to EC 1973	
Easy credit and high inflation 1973–74	
Successful strikes by National Union of Mineworkers 1972 and 1974, which disrupt entire country	

Labour Governments 1974–79 (Mostly in minority) (Wilson, Callaghan)

Major election gains by Scottish and Welsh Nationalists 1974–77

High inflation 1974 onwards

Social Contract with trade unions, whereby limits on prices and incomes and legal concessions 1975–78

Referendum for continuing membership of EC 1975

Balance of payments crisis 1976

Severe credit restrictions and increasing cuts in projected government expenditure 1976 onwards

High and increasing unemployment 1975 onwards

'Winter of discontent' 1979 (strikes by numerous groups of workers including transport strike)

Defeat of government proposals for Scottish and Welsh devolution 1979

Continued rise in world oil prices

British oil revenues from North Sea equal payments for foreign oil

---

Conservative Governments 1979 – (Thatcher)

Policy of restricting stock of money to bring down inflation involves further cuts in government expenditure 1979–82 and central restrictions on local government expenditure

Legal restrictions on unions' rights to picket during strikes and to extend scope of stoppage

Falling inflation and greatly increasing unemployment 1980–82

Savage and extensive urban riots 1981

Foundation of Social Democratic Party and leadership defections from Labour 1981

Electoral alliance of Social Democrats with Liberals produces sweeping by-election and local election successes 1981–82

Re-election of Conservatives with large majority, Alliance comes close to Labour in terms of votes but not seats, 1983

Miners' strike 1984–85 most bitter industrial dispute since war

Renewed urban riots, 1985

Unemployment reaches 13 per cent, then begins to fall

Renewed balance of payments problems with drop in oil revenues

'Privatisation' of many nationalised industries including gas

Re-election of Conservatives with large majority 1987, Labour fails to recover and Alliance fails to break through.

Increasing friction between Soviet Union and West from 1979

World economic depression intensifying up to 1981

Falklands War 1982

World economic recovery 1982–86

Oil and other commodity prices fall 1986

Relaxation of Soviet–Western relations 1986–87, serious disarmament negotiations between the USSR and US

---

surface, even if masked and to some extent deflected by increased prosperity among those in work.

Since the major political problems follow directly from government's diagnosis of the economic situation and their reactions to it, the most relevant question with which to start an overall assessment of British politics is why governments have intervened in the ways they have? What forces explain the particular forms of British government intervention in comparison with those adopted by other national governments? And why have they had such mixed success? Much of the book will be indirectly concerned with these points, but we consider them explicitly in the rest of this chapter.

The British experience in perspective

The usual explanation of the variations in economic policy is in terms of competing political traditions. Differences in the stance of successive Conservative Governments, for example, can be related to the contrasting traditions of Liberalism (minimal state intervention) and Toryism (paternalistic intervention to solve particular problems), both of which are combined in the modern Conservative Party (see Ch. 4). Certainly such an analysis has validity. The contrast in Conservative approaches between, on the one hand 1951–59, 1970–71 and 1979–87 and on the other 1960–64 and 1972–74, conforms nicely to the two traditions. Similarly, contrasting traditions on the left of the political spectrum could be invoked to explain the Labour experience. Although in recent years social democratic policies have prevailed in government over more interventionist socialist policies, the latter were officially adopted as the programme for the 1983 general election.

While accepting that an explanation in terms of differing traditions is plausible – and also acknowledging that these traditions are in no way static but are constantly changing – it is only of limited analytic value. It does not, for example, enable us to compare the British experience with that of other countries. One way in which this can be achieved is to identify common characteristics over time and thus judge whether state intervention in Britain, whatever the government responsible for it, has certain peculiar characteristics which can be contrasted with those of, for example, West Germany, France and Japan. From our historical summary we can trace the continuities described below.

Structural economic decline

Indisputably this has dominated the policy agenda over the last fifty years. While some of the issues may have changed (from protectionism to payments deficits, to sterling balances, to regional policy, to the reorganisation of industry), competitiveness has been declining. Scholars and politicians have laboured long and hard to explain the decline, but even today the true causes are uncertain. They relate to such basic factors as the provision for technical education, investment habits, and the institutionalised relationships between industry, finance and trade unions. Whatever they are, the preoccupation with managing decline has been a consistent theme in recent British politics. The fact of secular decline does not in itself tell us very much. But politics in such a context are likely to be different from politics in countries where the economy has experienced high rates of growth. A declining economy results in a shortage of resources and consequent cutbacks in government provision which create the social and political tensions already noted. Specific political and social arrangements may also have contributed to economic decline. Indeed, there are some who see Britain's economic malaise primarily in such terms, particularly in the pressures put on governments by strong groups such as trade unions or the financial interests of the City of London.

Fragmented policy-making

Every political system is characterised by conflicts, anomalies and inefficiencies in its policy-making processes. In some, these problems are sufficiently serious to cause revolutions or frequent outbreaks of political violence. While Britain's system is generally secure from such threats (apart from Northern Ireland where separate causes operate), there is increasing evidence that policy-making arrangements are under serious stress. Later chapters will show in detail how this appears in particular institutions and processes. But from the preceding summary it clearly applies to the key areas of economic policy-making and planning. The most popular and also the crudest way to explain these stresses is to point to the increasing 'overloading' of governments, and in particular to the growing power of trade unions and other groups external to representative institutions. There is no doubt something to this thesis, but again it is analytically limited. Union power may have seriously circumscribed policy makers in the 1970s, but it can hardly account for the failure of the National Plan or of Macmillan's attempts at indicative planning

There are more fundamental reasons for policy failure, many of which relate to the strangely fragmented nature of the British policy-making system. This is strange because in a highly centralised state with a skilled and loyal civil service, one would expect fragmentation to be the least of the problems. Fragmentation occurs at two levels: within government, and between government and key economic interests. Both have related causes. The history of economic policy graphically illustrates how institutionally fragmented the British system is. In spite of acquiring vast new government responsibilities during and after the war, the central administrative machine changed very little. New departments were created and others merged, but, the Treasury apart, remarkably little co-ordinating or planning machinery was established. This remains true today, although institutional controls over public expenditure have been strengthened. The British system has never acquired guiding bureaucracies like the French Commissariat Général du Plan (CGP) or Délegation à l'Amenagement du Territoire (DATAR), which have been crucial in co-ordinating the programmes of disparate government departments towards specific ends. So a major characteristic of British politics today is the functional fragmentation of government departments. Virtually the only co-ordinating function is performed by the Treasury, whose role is essentially the negative one of controlling expenditure. Given the sensitivity of the Treasury and the associated Bank of England to financial interests, Treasury control also operates to subordinate general economic concerns to financial ones. As a result, almost all the administrative experiments with planning and co-ordination, from Labour's post-war economic surveys to Neddy, to the DEA, to Policy Analysis and Review, to the 1975 Planning Agreements, have either failed or had limited success. Even the strong leadership of Margaret Thatcher, who has succeeded in enforcing her own preferences on the whole Government, was a purely personal phenomenon which did not enshrine itself in any institutional form, given the Prime Minister's antipathy to such innovations.

Fragmentation also characterises the relationship between government and the country's major industrial interests. Both the unions and employers' organisations play an important role in economic and industrial policy. However, neither are integrated into the policy-making process as in some countries. Indeed the tenor of Thatcherite policy-making is to exclude all such 'special interests' from decision processes. Instead the unions have come to perform the largely negative if powerful function of resisting incomes policies. The same is true for employers' organisations (the Confederation of British Industry, and trade associations). Of course, these are frequently consulted and when their interests have been threatened they have exerted powerful pressures on government (as with protectionism during the 1930s and nationalisation during the 1940s). But in the absence of an established corporatist tradition emphasising the values and interests shared between government, industry and unions, attempts to integrate the three have often looked contrived. Very often, new corporatist arrangements such as Neddy, or Labour's planning agreements, have been condemned in the press even before they have started, and have in any case never got to the level of detail necessary to put general agreements into practice.

Organisational inertia

A high level of public expenditure is not always synonymous with a co-ordinated economic policy, and in Britain the failure of planning has hardly reduced the size of the public sector. What explains the apparent antipathy to central co-ordination? Institutional fragmentation is part of the problem and this phenomenon itself requires explanation. Of course it occurs everywhere and organisational theorists would be quick to provide general explanations. But given Britain's economic problems and the myriad attempts to plan and co-ordinate policy, the failure to achieve anything more than *ad hoc* measures requires a more specific diagnosis. One factor stands out: a continuing failure to extend collectivist ideas about politics to institutional and organisational arrangements. The collectivist ideas (socialism, corporatism) of the twentieth century transformed British politics, but the impact of these ideas on organisations was minimal. More often than not, parties and politicians have attempted to superimpose organisational innovations on existing structures, with little thought of how the new arrangements will impact on the powers and values of existing bureaucracies. British civil servants are more resistant to planning and state intervention than are their European counterparts. They prefer an aloof style of government which intervenes indirectly through tax and monetary policy rather than by engaging itself in detailed social engineering. As a result, the reception given by Whitehall to Neddy, the DEA and other innovations has been cool. In France, planning and co-ordinating initiatives were actually led by civil servants. Further, within the political parties there has been remarkably little theorising on how and to what extent the state should intervene in economic and social life. Since 1950, the parties have tended to perceive a serious economic problem, to adopt a simple solution and then rather unthinkingly apply it. In a book on physical planning, Donald Foley interprets this tendency in British politics as an overriding sympathy with unitary solutions. His characterisation of the way in which post-war land use planning was formulated could equally be applied to economic policy:

It characteristically builds around seemingly self-evident truths and values and, in turn, bestows a self-justifying tone to its main propositions and chains of reasoning ... while it may contain highly rational arguments, it is characteristically superrational in its overall spirit (Foley 1963).

The failure to appreciate the importance of organisational values and interests has not affected those collectivist forces accounting for the growth of the public sector over the last fifty years. As a result, Britain, perhaps in a more acute form than many other countries, acquired a large and cumbersome public sector but little in the way of controlling or central co-ordinating structures. This has reduced the efficiency both of public services and of economic policy-making generally. When, after 1979, the Thatcher Governments attempted to impose more central control, they met with fierce resistance from societal interests and lower-level governments. This was all the more difficult to overcome because of the Government's own reluctance to establish the machinery and employ the extra civil servants necessary to impose itself effectively.

A final characteristic of economic policy and planning in British politics has been the very limited role played by Parliament. Chapter 3 will cover more specifically the problems of representation and accountability raised by the relegation of Parliament to the role of legitimiser. In some countries (notably the United States) there is often a trade-off between the 'efficiency' function of the central administration and the representative functions of the national legislature. Hence, in theory at least, what society may lose in the way of efficient government it gains in the way of increased accountability. In Britain, where Parliament plays a much less prominent role than does the US Congress, there is the possibility that the public have been denied both efficiency and accountability.

But this would be too simple a diagnosis. No discussion of political processes in Britain can be undertaken without reference to the secular economic decline which has affected the country over the last fifty years. Dealing with decline is much more difficult than dealing with growth, and many of Britain's political and administrative problems have been aggravated by the country's continuing economic sclerosis. Nor could economic policy or economic planning ever conform to some ideal mode. Planning is relative, and whatever its variety and in whatever country it has been tried, problems, anomalies and inefficiencies have occurred. Planning of the positive or even indicative type – the government making all major economic decisions or at least setting the main economic goals and specifying the ways to attain them – may, indeed, be incompatible both with the pluralism of modern democratic states, and with the unpredictability of an economically interdependent world. This accepted, the speed of economic decline in Britain and the urgency of our economic problems has called for a coherent and radical response on the part of governments and major economic interests. Policies have rarely been coherent and when radical have floundered badly. In the next chapter we examine the fragmented relationships between governments and central ministries which account in part for the absence of a cohesive and effective economic policy.

Chapter 2
Central decision-making

Who makes the major decisions in British government? A common assumption is that they are taken by the senior members of the political party which won the last election. Organised as Prime Minister and the Cabinet, they make the key decisions because they are supported by a disciplined majority in the House of Commons who ensure that the Government's programme will pass speedily into law. Unlike the US Congress, Parliament rarely refuses to co-operate with the executive, and the courts have limited powers to modify, let alone invalidate, legislation. A non-partisan, non-political civil service helps ministers formulate and implement their proposals effectively. There are some ambiguities in the traditional account. For example, no one is quite sure about the exact balance of power between the Prime Minister and the Cabinet; or between the Cabinet as a whole and the political party which supports it. Nonetheless, the assumption is that, to understand central decision-making, all we need to know is how top politicians organise themselves.

This apparent simplicity of decision-making has been seen as both a strength and weakness of the British system of government. Supporters of the system praise the clear accountability to the electorate which it provides through having the leaders of the government so clearly in control of decision-making. Critics fear that it gives too much unchecked power to government (which has often been termed 'an elected dictatorship') or produces unnecessarily sweeping policy changes when control changes after an election. Although both these views have some foundation in reality, they also conceal much complexity. Here we regard central decision-making as taking place at the intersection of several spheres of activity: Parliamentary and party politics, the government machine, and major societal and economic interests.

The political sphere

The structure of political decision-making in Britain is the most familiar, and therefore easiest to describe. Major decisions are made by the Cabinet, which is selected by the Prime Minister and comprises about twenty-three politicians, all but two or three in charge of major government departments – the Foreign Office,

Home Office, Department of Education and Science, Ministry of Defence, and so on. The Cabinet has a complex committee structure. Too many decisions need to be taken for the Cabinet as a whole to make them all, and it is in any case too large to debate many involved and detailed issues. Committees therefore make many decisions on behalf of the Cabinet and it is rare for an issue to reach the Cabinet itself without prior discussion in a Cabinet committee.

This is also partly due to the fact that few important decisions are the exclusive concern of any one minister or department. All government programmes cost money and therefore have both financial and economic implications. The Treasury, the main financial department, is naturally involved. Parliamentary time for debating legislation is a scarce resource, so collective decisions about the relative priority of government Bills must also be made. Decisions about defence must be taken with foreign policy in mind. Aid to industry has implications for Britain's trade policy and position within the European Community. It is a practical necessity, therefore, that there be interdepartmental consideration of all key legislation, and other policy initiatives. On the other hand, ministers are extremely busy people scarcely able to keep track of their own ministries, let alone other departments as well.

Hence, policy decisions are the product of inter-departmental consultations. These constitute one of the key political processes in Britain, and proceed on two levels. The first involves the civil servants. There are a large number of permanent inter-departmental committees which on a continuing basis consider the recurring issues in British government; for example, annual forecasts of public expenditure. A standing committee of civil servants considers the state of British agriculture, and what changes in farm subsidies are required each year. New legislation on, say, social security, is discussed by civil servants representing all the relevant departments, including Health and Social Security and the Treasury. In addition, new proposals are considered by specially formed inter-departmental committees of civil servants. In all cases the civil servants will be trying to identify crucial points at issue between departments. Arguing on the basis of some combination of long-standing departmental preferences and the attitudes of their ministers, the civil servants will then refer points which they are unable to resolve to committees of ministers. During the discussions between civil servants, representatives of each department will be alerting their ministers to points for which they will have to fight on ministerial committees. In view of the limited time ministers can devote to considering proposals from other ministries, this sifting by civil servants is essential.

For every committee of civil servants there exists an inter-departmental committee of ministers. These committees, committees of the Cabinet and reporting to the Cabinet, are amongst the most important institutions in British government. Yet their existence is supposedly secret, and their membership is never publicised. Their general composition is well known, however. The ministers from the most involved departments belong, and there are usually a small number of ministers (one of whom acts as chairman), who have no departmental interest in the issues at stake. Thus on farm subsidies, the committee will have representation from Agriculture, Fisheries and Food, the Home Office (responsible for agriculture in Ulster), the Scottish and Welsh Offices (responsible for

Scottish and Welsh agriculture), the Treasury (concerned about costs to the Exchequer), the Department of Trade (concerned with trading links with overseas suppliers of food) and the Foreign Office (also concerned with trading links with overseas suppliers and with the European Community).

The need to have a chairman with no departmental interest testifies to frequent fights between departments, which are best understood as conflicts between their enduring attitudes and interests. To continue our example, in any government, Conservative or Labour, the Ministry of Agriculture presses for more help for farmers, the Treasury resists increases in expenditure, and the Department of Trade opposes any proposal which increases protection and conflicts with trade liberalisation. Many of the major departments – Agriculture, Employment, Education, Trade and Industry – have links with approved interest groups, and the clashes between departments in Cabinet committees constitute one of the most important ways in which outside demands are voiced and combined into an overall policy. Of course this process takes place within rather strict and selective limits, so that outside interests constitute only one element in the 'departmental views' being advanced.

Even though many decisions are effectively taken by civil servants, and many others by Cabinet committees of which they are not members, it remains a powerful convention of Cabinet government that ministers (even members of the government not of Cabinet rank) are collectively responsible for major government decisions. A minister who cannot support or defend the important decisions of the Cabinet should resign. How strongly this convention survives is debatable. On the one hand, the lowest ranking of those holding a position in the government, such as parliamentary private secretaries, have been forced to resign if they made an overt show of defiance against a Cabinet decision, that is, abstaining rather than supporting the government in parliamentary votes. On the other hand, there have been several instances of Cabinet ministers disagreeing with collective policy. Thus James Callaghan was known to oppose the industrial relations policy of the 1964–70 Labour Government and indeed used his position as Treasurer of the Labour Party to encourage opposition to legislation based on the White Paper *In Place of Strife*. In spite of a strong feeling within the Cabinet that Callaghan should resign, he did not. Tony Benn returned the compliment during Callaghan's prime ministership, refusing to resign in spite of sharp differences with the economic policies of the Government. Benn used his position on the Labour Party's National Executive Committee openly to oppose the Cabinet's policy. Callaghan decided that it would be best not to ask for Benn's resignation, as he might have been a greater political problem if set free rather than remaining under some constraint as a member of the Cabinet. However, these instances remain interesting qualifications on the general principle of collective responsibility rather than proof of its demise. Certainly the Conservative ministers who have publicly opposed Mrs Thatcher, have done so only after or immediately prior to resigning. While in the Cabinet they have confined opposition to indirect references in speeches or unattributed press leaks.

As ministers ultimately have to support Cabinet policies, it is essential that government decision-making should provide for collective consideration of important policies. A key controversy about the way this is handled, and thus about the whole nature of central decision-making in Britain, turns on the relative power of the Prime Minister as opposed to the Cabinet collectively. An influential school of thought holds that the Prime Minister has such extensive control over the Cabinet that (s)he can in practice steer it in the direction (s)he favours. The Prime Minister's control over the Cabinet arises primarily from two major powers: the power to hire and fire – that is the power to decide who should be a member of the Cabinet, which post they should occupy, whether or not they should be removed from office – and the power over the Cabinet agenda – what is and what is not discussed.

These powers are considerable. Mrs Thatcher has used them vigorously to ensure that her views on economic policy prevail. Ministers appointed to key positions in economic policy-making such as Chancellor of the Exchequer have been uniformly 'dry', i.e. monetarist, in their views. Ministers thought to be insufficiently supportive of the Prime Minister such as Francis Pym (Foreign Secretary 1982–83) have been removed from office.

Yet the Prime Minister does not have unfettered freedom to appoint and remove Cabinet ministers. British political parties are coalitions of people of different views and beliefs. The range of views within a political party must find expression in the Cabinet. In a famous interview before she became Prime Minister, Mrs Thatcher claimed that she would not appoint people to her Cabinet who did not share her views because she could not afford to spend time arguing. The Prime Minister in practice appointed so many people to her first Cabinet who did not agree with her that she was actually in a *minority* in her own Cabinet. Only when her power was strengthened by victory in the Falklands War and the 1983 and especially the 1987 general election could she move decisively to weaken her opponents, the 'wets', within her Cabinet.

The power over agenda setting is exercised mainly by the Prime Minister's control over the composition of Cabinet committees. As noted, delegation of business to these committees is inevitable because of Cabinet size and pressures on Cabinet time. Yet they can be constituted in a way which favours the policy supported by the Prime Minister. Notable examples of this have involved committees handling defence policy during Labour governments. The decisions to build an atomic bomb during the Attlee Government and to re-equip Britain's nuclear missile submarines with multiple warheads (Chevaline) during the Wilson and Callaghan Governments were made by Cabinet sub-committees which did not fully reflect the range of views within the Cabinet itself. Many Cabinet members seem to have been unaware of the decision made by a committee supposedly in their name.

No doubt the secrecy inevitably associated with defence policy helped Atlee and Callaghan manipulate the decision-making process. The secrecy which generally surrounds the preparation of the Budget has also helped Prime Ministers to keep control of policy. Following normal practice, Mrs Thatcher's full Cabinet was not in control of the Government's economic policy in 1981; the Chancellor of the Exchequer, Sir Geoffrey Howe, in partnership with the Prime Minister, produced a budget which was distinctly unwelcome to the majority of ministers, who wanted a reflationary budget to stem the rise in unemployment. The Prime Minister did not.

The decisions we have discussed were intrinsically important. We should not assume, however, that they are representative of the normal workings of British government. Prime Ministers are unwise to push their Cabinet colleagues too far or to engage frequently in stratagems to push a policy past their Cabinets. Although no Prime Minister has been forced from office by his or her colleagues since Neville Chamberlain in 1940 (and that after near-defeat in wartime), the possibility always exists. The Prime Minister who disregards colleagues' views too blatantly runs the risk of encouraging a great degree of opposition in the immediate future. Mrs Thatcher's Cabinet colleagues since 1981 have insisted on being consulted more about the Budget, though Cabinet opposition to her economic strategy has certainly had little impact.

A final area of controversy concerns the degree to which both Prime Minister and Cabinet are constrained by the House of Commons in general and their backbench supporters in particular. The extreme rarity with which governments lose votes in the House of Commons has encouraged the belief that Parliament is a rubber stamp. Apart from the possibility that governments are persuaded by Parliament to change policy in anticipation of defeat, such a view is less true now than in the recent past. As we shall see in Chapter 3, both Labour and Conservative backbenches have been less willing of late to give unquestioning support to their governments. This increasing independence has produced some notable defeats on issues such as trade union reform during the second Wilson Government; nationalisation of the ports and aspects of the Budget during the Callaghan Government; and welfare benefits, student grants and Sunday opening during the Thatcher Governments. Callaghan's was the first government since the 1920s to fall as the result of losing a vote in the House of Commons. Finally, in some amorphous way, the government's standing in the House seems to filter out through lobby correspondents and the media to affect opinion in the country. Very few may listen to or read Parliamentary debates: the inability of a government to explain itself cogently in Parliament commands wider attention.

The Thatcher style

The long tenure of Mrs Thatcher (she has served for a longer continuous period than any predecessor since the beginning of the century) has raised important questions about her impact on the office and role of Prime Minister. This is not because of institutional changes that she has made. On the contrary, Mrs Thatcher has disdained institutional solutions to the problem of government. The Central Policy Review Staff was abolished after finding favour with one Conservative and two Labour Prime Ministers; although ministers have been allowed political advisers, little emphasis has been given to them. Instead, the Thatcher premiership has raised questions about the degree to which a radical leader can control the direction of British government. For Mrs Thatcher, to a degree unusual for a British Prime Minister, has clear and radical views on the sort of policy that government should follow.

In consequence her style has rested on forceful use of the prerogatives of her position, coupled with more compromise than has been noticed. 'Neo-liberal', 'monetarist' views on policy (nicknamed 'dry' as opposed to 'wet' by the press) were shared by only a minority of the Conservative Party and, at the start of her government, by only a minority of her Cabinet. The Prime Minister ensured, however, that supporters were appointed to the departments responsible for what, from her perspective, were the most important areas. All the Chancellors of the Exchequer appointed by Mrs Thatcher have been 'Thatcherite' in their economic thinking. In contrast, those 'wets' appointed have usually been given departments such as Northern Ireland or Agriculture, Fisheries and Food, which are not central to government policy. Moreover, prominent 'wets' have been removed gradually from the Cabinet when her political position was strong enough or her opponents' position weak enough for the move to be made. Norman St John Stevas, who had little following on the backbenches, was one of the first to go. Francis Pym, a 'wet' given the Foreign Secretaryship after the government was humiliated by the Argentine invasion of the Falkland Islands, was removed after the Conservative electoral triumph of 1983, as was the overly independent if 'dry' John Biffen after that of 1987. The gradual elimination of actual and potential opponents has made it more likely that Thatcherite views will prevail in the long run. Thus the Prime Minister has combined sensible political caution with a clear sense of the direction in which she will move if given the chance.

Mrs Thatcher also showed a clear sense of strategy in handling the Cabinet and its members. Cabinet meetings have been fewer than under her predecessors, fewer papers have been circulated within the Cabinet, and more important decisions – especially on economic policy – have been made not by the formal committees of the Cabinet but by informal groups chosen by the Prime Minister. One reason for the angry resignation of Michael Heseltine from the Ministry of Defence was his belief that he had been denied a reasonable opportunity to put his case to the Cabinet for continued British or at least European control of the sole remaining helicopter manufacturer in the UK.

None of these strategies has established total Prime Ministerial control however. The Prime Minister has lost many battles, sometimes by a show of hands against her proposal. Similarly, the Prime Minister has had to use every possible stratagem to try to influence the behaviour of ministers within their own departments. Ministers have been bullied or criticised in front of colleagues or civil servants as well as in private; friendly backbenchers have been encouraged to put ministers on the spot by asking parliamentary questions suggested by the Prime Minister; embarrassing material has been leaked to the press in order to put pressure on Cabinet critics. In spite of all this, and the constant fear that dissenters will be sacked, the Prime Minister has not prevailed totally within departments. This is one reason why domestic expenditure has been severely cut in relatively few areas (such as housing), so that overall government in Britain is larger (measured by the percentage of GNP it consumes) than when Mrs Thatcher took office.

Although the Thatcher Prime Ministership shows an unusual degree of vigorous policy leadership, it has not established presidential government in any form. Every available resource has been used to bend ministers to the Prime Minister's will, but she never totally succeeded. Paradoxically, her institutional conservatism has meant that no enhanced means were available to control policy directly and in detail. Lack of confidence in the permanent civil servants of the Treasury and Foreign Office led to the appointment within her office of special advisors on economic and foreign policy (Alan Walters and Anthony Parson); yet these were neither permanent nor effective. The abolition of the Central Policy Review Staff (CPRS) was not accompanied by any expansion of the Policy Unit, so that on balance the secreteriat and support staff were actually contracted by Mrs Thatcher. Perhaps ironically for someone disposed to distrust civil servants, Mrs Thatcher came to rely heavily on the man who was head of the Cabinet Office throughout her first two terms as Prime Minister, (Sir Robert Armstrong) for staff support. The Thatcher style may provde precedents for individual Prime Ministers seeking to influence their colleagues; it did not leave behind an institutionally expanded Prime Ministership.

The sphere of government

The attention paid to Parliament and elected politicians in the media can easily obscure the importance of other elements in decision-making. On taking office ministers become part of a government machine which has a timetable, proce-

Table 2.1 Major departments and ministries of the central government

Ministry or Department of	Ministry or Department of (cont)
Agriculture, Fisheries and Food	Home Office
Agriculture and Fisheries for Scotland	
Agriculture for Northern Ireland	
Attorney-General	Inland Revenue
	Lord Advocate
Cabinet Office	Lord Chancellor
Civil Service Department	
Civil Service for Northern Ireland	Northern Ireland Civil Service
Commerce for Northern Ireland	Northern Ireland Office
Crown Office (Scotland)	
Customs and Excise	Prime Minister's Office
	Scottish Development
Defence	Scottish Economic Planning
Director of Public Prosecutions	Scottish Education
	Scottish Home and Health
Education and Science	Scottish Office
Education for Northern Ireland	
Employment	Trade and Industry
Energy	Transport
Environment	Treasury
Environment for Northern Ireland	
	Welsh Office
Finance, Northern Ireland	
Foreign and Commonwealth Office	
Health and Social Security	
Health and Social Services for Northern Ireland	

Source: *Civil Service Yearbook* 1981, HMSO

dures and priorities of its own. The incompetent minister can easily be swallowed up by the part of the government machine he supposedly directs rather than shaping its priorities. Indeed, the first political relationship within the executive which confronts British politicians is that between individual ministers and their civil servants. British administrators have been traditionally organised into broad clerical, executive and administrative classes. Recent attempts at reform (notably the Fulton Commission in the late sixties) tried to break down these divisions and to nurture specialist skills, such as those possessed by the statisticians, economists and scientists – each a separate career grade within the Civil Service. In spite of these attempts, British civil servants continue in the main to conceive of themselves as general administrators rather than specialists, to promote circulation between departments and ministries rather than dedication to a particular speciality, and to maintain broad distinctions between the hierarchy of classes. The typical higher civil servant enters directly as an administrative trainee, and rises rapidly to an executive position with a fairly autonomous area of operation, whether it be supervision of mortuaries in the Home Office or collation of information on Southern Africa in the Foreign Office. If very successful, the principal will rise through assistant and deputy secretaryships to become permanent head of a ministry, whether as under-secretary or permanent secretary.

Civil servants are grouped into administrative sections with a startling range of functions. Outside the twenty to twenty-five large ministries, most headed by Cabinet ministers, there is no agreed list. Taking departments as those agencies voted on separately in the Parliamentary Supply Estimates, there are about seventy at the present time. Table 2.1 gives a summary listing of the most important.

In his early years, a higher-level civil servant may shift between two or three departments. For most of his career, however, he will be located in one of these in spite of the 'generalist' ideology of the Service.

Ministers and civil servants

The relationship between ministers and civil servants in Britain is a subject of humour (as in the BBC TV series 'Yes, Prime Minister') and also controversy. To what extent is the constitutional doctrine that civil servants are the obedient, non-partisan, politically-neutral servants of the ministers myth or reality?

Civil servants claim that they are willing to give loyal service to any duly elected government. It is their professional duty to make the government's priorities their own beliefs and attitudes. British civil servants are entrusted with much work, such as preparing answers to Parliamentary questions or speeches for ministers, which in other countries would be handled by political appointees. The vast majority of recent ministers – Conservative and Labour – have defended the loyalty of their civil servants vigorously.

At the same time, it is hard to believe that civil servants really are entirely without preferences of their own. Attacks on the neutrality of the senior Civil Service used to come from the left of the Labour Party which was concerned that civil servants because of their disproportionately middle-class, public school and Oxbridge backgrounds would be instinctively Conservative in their attitudes. In recent years the neutrality of the civil service has been attacked as vigorously by Conservatives who believe that the civil service constitutes a barrier to the Thatcherian revolution in attitudes and in the role of government. Sir John Hoskyns, who was one of the Prime Minister's advisers in her first term, has castigated civil servants for what he believes to be their role in bringing about Britain's economic decline. Thus both the right and the left have seen the Civil Service as a barrier to radical change in Britain.

What are the origins of this perception? Undoubtedly part of the situation is that British civil servants do see themselves as having a duty to alert ministers to the dangers of proposed policy changes. Such warnings can easily seem to be advocacy of no policy change at all. Indeed some civil servants have gone so far as to argue that they have the duty to lead ministers towards the 'common ground' of politics, thus restraining the extremist tendencies of politicians.

Other factors which influence civil servants include their own opinion about policies and the 'departmental view'. Civil servants cannot be seriously expected to have no views about policies even if they are expected to be non-partisan. People who have helped to devise and implement existing policy are likely, if they think that policy works well, to resist changes to it. Moreover, a continuing set of attitudes known as the 'departmental view' conditions the reaction of civil servants to policy proposals. The departmental view consists of general attitudes or beliefs about policy which have developed over the years in a department as a result of its experience, past crises or reactions to policies, and the constant dealings with interest groups in the department's field. For example, few senior civil servants within the Department of the Environment have wanted to challenge the prevailing interpretation of Britain's land use planning laws. At least until the mid-1980s the protection of Green Belts and agricultural land was given the highest priority – even though less restricted development has been favoured by some ministers. There is no doubt that ministers who propose a policy incompatible with the departmental view will have to fight very hard for it.

Ministers and civil servants thus may well disagree. What resources does each side dispose of in their dealings with each other?

Civil servants obviously command far more expertise than politicians. Although senior civil servants in Britain move from one department to another, they will have far more knowledge of policy issues than ministers, who move even more frequently and have even less prior experience. British politicians are uniquely dependent on permanent civil servants. Alternative sources of advice such as 'think tanks' on the American model are weak in this country; ministers are unable to make large numbers of political appointments (on the American model) or to bring in a large group of political advisers (the European *Cabinet* system). British ministers rarely bring into office with them more than a single political adviser. Their dependence on the assistance of permanent civil servants is therefore extreme.

Civil servants also enjoy a degree of autonomy because of their very numbers. Although constitutional doctrine used to state that ministers were responsible for every action of their civil servants, the doctrine has had to bow to the reality of large-scale government. Thus James Prior, the minister nominally responsible, refused to accept responsibility for a prison escape by IRA terrorists on the grounds that he could not have been familiar personally with the details of the situation. Mr Prior's decision not to resign – and the acceptance of his decision – reflected the widespread belief that ministers cannot be expected to know all that is being done in their name by civil servants.

Civil servants are also advantaged by the network of contacts which exist between them. As we have seen, every committee of government ministers has a corresponding committee of civil servants which is expected to resolve less important issues and prepare crucial issues for ministerial decision. In addition, civil servants in different departments are in constant contact with each other informally. Most issues arising in a department require that other departments be consulted or informed about what is happening. Higher-level civil servants in Britain know each other either from school or university, or through time together in the Treasury, from which many of the highest civil servants have 'graduated'. Life in Whitehall, at least at the most senior levels, has been compared to life in a village. Gossip as in many villages is extensive. Gossip can be used by civil servants opposed to their minister's plans to mobilise opposition from other departments as well. A minister may find himself opposed not only by his own civil servants but by other departments which his civil servants have mobilised against him.

What advantages do ministers have? In the first place, ministers enjoy unmatched constitutional legitimacy. There is no doubt that ministers are entitled to make the final decision in a way which civil servants are not. Ministers who know what they want, and who want something which is in fact attainable, can therefore insist on it being done. Civil servants in Britain are trained, to a greater extent than their counterparts in many other democracies, to obey political masters. The British civil servant has neither the French and Japanese bureaucrat's confidence in the superiority of his judgement to the politician's nor the American civil servant's belief in the legitimacy of using the legislature (Congress) against the political leadership of the department. This is not to say that the British minister will always be obeyed or that embarrassing facts will not be leaked to the press. It is to say that the British minister is more likely to find that his or her civil servants acknowledge in principle that the minister must be obeyed.

A second factor helping ministers is that their civil servants need them. Ministers perform certain functions which civil servants cannot. Ministers defend the department and its policies in public and in Parliament: civil servants do not (except before Select Committees – see Chapter 3). Ministers also fight each other to gain limited resources for their departments, such as money or Parliamentary time for legislation. Civil servants therefore need a strong minister, for without one their department will lose out. Civil servants have plans and priorities of their own, plans and priorities which require money or legislation. Ironically, these plans may best be advanced by the type of minister who is most likely to insist on his or her own agenda being implemented by the department.

Ministers and civil servants interact – sometimes co-operatively, sometimes conflictually – on dozens of different issues every day. There are times when ministers dominate, and there are times when civil servants dominate. Several factors determine who shall prevail. First is the personality of the minister. Ministers differ not only in their forcefulness or determination but also in the role they choose to play. Some are content to represent their department's views and interests, accepting their civil servants' proposals and agendas. Others are determined to make a mark on policy, insisting on their own or their party's proposals being implemented.

Second, a public commitment by a government increases the probability that the civil servants will accept that the commitment must be honoured. Manifesto commitments in particular are taken seriously by civil servants, (perhaps more seriously than by the politicians who make them).

Third, policies which are relatively simple or which have precedents are more likely to be implemented than policies which are technically complex or novel. This is not only because of the simplicity of the proposals but because ministers will be better placed to insist on their implementation and to monitor progress than if they are complex. The greater the complexity of an issue, the greater is the scope for bureaucratic manoeuvring to defeat it.

The relationship between ministers and civil servants is one of the most crucial aspects of British government. On that relationship depends the ability of voters through their elected government to influence public policy. It is interesting therefore that there is such widespread unease about this relationship. As we have noted, Conservative politicians have joined Labour politicians in arguing that the civil service can be a major barrier to policy implementation. All recent governments have experimented with the use of political advisers, policy units in 10 Downing Street, the Central Policy Review Staff (created by Mr Heath but abolished by Mrs Thatcher), and teams of advisers from business in order to strengthen the hands of ministers. The increased 'leaks' to the press by civil servants in order to defeat a policy they dislike has been symptomatic of the necessarily hidden discontent within the civil service that has risen sharply in recent years. The emergence of the Head of the Civil Service as a special adviser and executive for the government, or the role of Mrs Thatcher's Press Officer, Bernard Ingham, as manager of officially inspired press leaks, to take only two examples, has provoked a strong feeling in many quarters that civil servants are asked to play too overtly political a part. It would not be surprising if there were a major reform of the relationship between civil servants and ministers in the near future.

Government and outside interests

Both ministers and civil servants make decisions as a result of contacts with bodies outside government itself. Some of these bodies are other governments. A phone call from the President of the United States might cause the Prime Minister to make a major policy decision, as in the permission granted to the US Air Force in early 1986 to use British bases to bomb Libya. The United Kingdom is involved in a complex network of contacts with the other members and institutions of the European Community (these contacts and their implications are described in Chapter 7). Ministers, and even more civil servants, are also involved in regular though usually confidential and unpublicised meetings with the representatives of interest groups.

It is often not fully appreciated how deeply the norm of consultation bites into the practices of British government. The belief that major 'responsible' interests should be consulted before the government settles on a policy forms a part of unwritten British constitutional practice. At the same time, the nature and extent of that consultation varies from group to group, and is controlled to an important degree by government. Interest groups in Britain are obliged to try to influence government departments and ministers. The comparatively strict discipline of British political parties limits their ability to use Parliament. Leaders have their greatest chance to influence policy through persuading ministers and civil servants before a government is committed to the details of a policy, after which point any change looks like a confession of weakness or error.

Interest groups in turn have much to offer government. They can supply information, particularly scientific and technical information, to administrators relatively ill-equipped to evaluate policies themselves; the British civil service is at its highest levels composed primarily of generalists, not scientists or economists. Interest groups can also offer to help with the implementation of policy. British central government implements comparatively few policies directly. Much implementation is devolved to local government (see Chapter 6). Other policies are entrusted to interest groups. Thus the detailed implementation of policy on health and safety at work is controlled by a Commission dominated by the employers' group, the Confederation of British Industry, and the Trades Union Congress. If the government can secure the agreement of the relevant interest groups, it significantly reduces the chances of a damaging dispute over its policy.

The fact that interest groups in Britain are heavily dependent on early access to the thinking of ministers and civil servants gives the government a significant degree of control over them, however. Groups favoured by government can be given such access while policy is still easily changed. Groups not favoured by government will still be given the chance to state their views, but perhaps after the government's thinking has crystallised. Or the disfavoured group may be listened to politely, but without the government revealing its real intentions or displaying any willingness to change its opinions. In other words there are 'insider' groups with privileged access to government and 'outsider' groups which do not receive such treatment.

Perhaps the best example of an insider group is the National Farmers' Union. From the early years of the Second World War until Britain's accession to the European Community, agricultural policy was made after consultations which often had the air of negotiations between the government and the NFU. By 1987, however, the NFU was reduced to public protests and votes of no confidence as the European Community reduced subsidies and the Government complied. The Confederation of British Industry, which represents industrial employers, and the best organised trade associations representing employers in a single industry, have also had 'insider' status under most governments.

The relationship between government and financial institutions is a particularly interesting example of 'insider' status. One of the functions of the Bank of England, which is owned by the government and whose governor is responsible to the Chancellor of the Exchequer, is to report financial institutions' opinions to the government. In a sense, therefore, the governor is a lobbyist for the City within government. The relationship between the Bank and the City has been seen as one reason why successive governments have placed financial interests ahead of manufacturing interests. In reality, government concern to maintain the value of sterling against other currencies itself gave financial institutions considerable power, for the maintenance of confidence in its policies became a precondition for the successful defence of the exchange value of the pound. Several factors have recently reduced the close ties between Bank and the City. Greater reliance on monetary policy by recent governments has involved the Bank to a greater extent than before in implementation of government economic policy. The City itself has become more diverse in terms of numbers of firms (many foreign owned) and their functions. The comfortable 'old boy' network linking Bank and City works less smoothly, therefore, than in the past. Indeed, City financial institutions which had previously disdained conventional pressure group activity now feel the need for such representation.

Unions have had ambiguous status. It was the proud boast of one former general secretary of the Trade Union Congress (the overall federation of trade unions) that he had taken the movement out of Trafalgar Square and into Whitehall, i.e. that he had won insider status for unions. Unions were automatically and quite closely consulted by government on a wide range of important policies. The main period of union insider status came during the 'Social Contract' period in the 1970s when the Labour Government offered a general role in policy-making in exchange for wage restraints.

Several factors have inhibited the access of unions to government. First, powerful forces within the unions themselves have been opposed to what could be seen as too much compromise with government. Second, disputes with governments trying to impose changes on unions (e.g., Heath and Thatcher) have caused unions to withdraw from consultative bodies or meetings. Third, unions are generally underfunded and understaffed so that they have trouble taking advantage of the consultative opportunities they enjoy. Finally, many in British politics are fundamentally opposed to the practice of what has been called 'neo-corporatism', i.e. the making and implementing of major decisions in a partnership between government and major economic interest groups, especially those representing employers and unions.

Neo-corporatism has been a feature of politics in The Netherlands, Austria and Norway for several decades. Britain has at times also flirted with neo-corporatism. In the last years of the Macmillan Government the National Economic Development Council attempted to concert the policies of unions, government and employers. The first Wilson Government took the idea further in the creation of a National Plan, which was however soon abandoned. Heath sought a government-employer-union partnership in vain in the last years of his government, and the 1974–79 Labour Government advocated decision-making through a 'Social Contract' between government, employers, and especially unions.

All of these attempts failed although the Labour Government achieved some success for the two year period 1976–78. There are many reasons for this including the primacy British governments have given to financial as opposed to economic objectives, and the internal weaknesses of British interest groups, so that the leaders of the TUC and CBI cannot make agreements which are binding on their member unions or firms. The Thatcher Government has turned its back on neo-corporatist arrangements not only because it believes that they are ineffective but because it believes they are wrong in principle – government should not share power with interest groups. The unions have thus been totally excluded from any influence on the formative stages of important government policy. It is worthwhile noting, that not only the TUC but also the CBI finds itself consulted less. Indeed, a former director general of the CBI was reduced to threatening a 'bare knuckle fight' with the Thatcher Government, a most unusual stand for someone in his position *vis-à-vis* a Conservative government. Contacts between civil servants (and on a reduced basis ministers), and the CBI and TUC continue. So do contacts between ministers or civil servants and interest groups focussing on the problems of particular industries. A return to more neo-corporatist policies, in which policies are shaped in wide-ranging discussions between the government, the CBI and the TUC is unlikely without a change of administration. Interest groups will remain very important in the British system of government, but Britain has not yet come anywhere close to establishing a permanent neo-corporatist system.

Putting it all together

Central decision-making in Britain involves the interaction of political, administrative, and interest group structures. It would be useful to be able to indicate the relative importance of each. Unfortunately the balance shifts according to the importance of several factors. First, the nature of the issue helps to determine the way in which it is handled. Sanctions against South Africa involve political actors very heavily; safety and health at work is handled predominantly by the interest groups concerned. Second, the length of time that a government has been in power has a substantial impact. A newly-elected government has commitments from its manifesto to fulfil; a government which has been in power for some time is often short of ideas and is therefore grateful for proposals from civil servants who will have their own agenda of problems to be tidied up. Third, as we have noted above, the importance attached to negotiations with interest groups has varied from government to government. The Callaghan Government spent far more time and energy on interest groups than have the Thatcher Governments.

It is in part the variation – if not from year to year then from decade to decade – which makes it difficult to categorise central decision-making in Britain. A traditional interpretation of British politics has emphasised the centralisation and coherence of the system. The British Cabinet, united by party doctrine, supported by a disciplined majority in the House of Commons, and aided by a highly competent, obedient civil service is capable of making far more coherent policy than emerges from either the coalition governments of, say, Italy, or the

American division of powers between legislative, executive and judicial branches.

The traditional stress on the coherence of central decision-making in British government needs to be modified for a number of reasons. First political: British political parties, and so Cabinets, are coalitions of people of clearly differing views. Differences between 'wets' and 'dries' in the Thatcher Governments had their counterpart in divisions between left and right in the Labour governments of the 1960s and 1970s: such differences can be profound. Second, in attempting to win votes within occupational groups and regions, British governments have been prepared to make promises that are not always in the public interest or in line with the party's ideology. Promises as diverse as devolution for Scotland and Wales, continuing tax relief on mortgages, a bridge across the Humber, and subsidies for farmers and Austin Rover, have all been made by governments of different parties anxious to win the support of some supposedly strategic block of votes. British governments play the vote-catching game as well as most.

Another factor disrupting the supposed unity of British government is the divisions within the administrative sector. Departments, as we have seen, differ in their attitudes and concerns. The Ministry of Agriculture is much more supportive of farm subsidies, as is the Ministry of Defence of military spending, than is the Treasury. As a major part of the job of ministers is to represent the interests and attitudes of their departments, such differences create conflicts not only between civil servants but also between their ministers in the Cabinet. It is interesting to note that these centrifugal tendencies of government have created major problems in controlling expenditure. Numerous experimental techniques such as the Public Expenditure Survey and Programme Analysis and Review have broken down – in large part because of the determination of each minister to fight for his department's programmes. Indeed, any minister who gallantly offered to cut his department's budget in order to help the government reach its general objectives would be seen by Cabinet colleagues as showing such weakness or quixotic behaviour as to lose political strength permanently as was the case with Sir Keith Joseph when as Ministry of Industry he was obliged to accept continuing subsidies for British Steel in 1981.

It is also important to remember that British government has never become truly Prime Ministerial. The central agencies of the Cabinet or Prime Minister have shown no steady tendency to attain greater importance. The policy unit in 10 Downing Street established under Mr Callaghan has remained under Mrs Thatcher; the Central Policy Review Staff has disappeared. To some degree the Cabinet Office functions as a central agency of British government; in general, though, it remains true that there is a hole at the centre, with no individual other than the Prime Minister – supported by very limited resources – analysing or promoting policies from the viewpoint of the government collectively, as opposed to the balance of views between individual ministers and departments.

The administrative style of British government has always been to entrust the implementation of most policies to other people – local notables serving as Justices of the Peace until the late nineteenth century, local authorities, and, in a few policy areas, interest groups. Such devolution limits the degree of control that central government enjoys. It was traditionally said that a French Minister of

Education could tell you at any hour of the day what every child in France was studying: Labour governments were never able to eliminate all grammar schools from Britain even though it was a central part of their programme to do so. Administrative devolution saved central government the expenses and difficulty of running schools directly; it also limited the degree to which the Secretary of State for Education could make real decisions about what happens in schools. In belated recognition of this the Conservative, Kenneth Baker, tried in the mid 1980s to get control of limited but crucial sectors in his own hands, but even he could not enforce a wholly unified direction of education policy.

The coherence of central decision-making in Britain has also been limited by the weakness of 'umbrella' interest groups speaking for broad social groups – particularly unions and employers. The CBI and TUC have very little control over their members: they have not been able to make the same sort of commitment in bargaining with government as their counterparts in neo-corporatist countries. The TUC, for example, has never been able to take part in an incomes policy for long without individual unions – or elements within a single union – refusing to go along. British governments deal with interest groups which have not themselves achieved the same degree of unity as interest groups in, say, Austria or Sweden. In consequence, British governments themselves have to broker more conflicts than their counterparts in countries with more centralised interest group systems. At times central decision-makers are themselves disorientated by contending and conflicting claims from groups.

Central decision-making in Britain still offers the opportunity for politicians who know what they want to achieve it. The Atlee and Thatcher governments show that elections can indeed make a major difference in British politics. Yet behind the apparent simplicity lies the complexity of interactions between different spheres – political, administrative, and interest groups. Within each sphere, there is also less unity than might be expected. British government is formally and constitutionally highly unified. In reality it is substantially fragmented.

Current problems and possible reforms

Economic decline has raised questions about the extent to which the central decision-making process is appropriate to the needs of the late twentieth century. A whole series of questions were raised in the late 1980s about its nature and adequacy. Concern focused on a variety of issues, some of which we have encountered already.

The Civil Service and its relationship to ministers has, as we have noted, been under great strain. Both Conservative and Labour politicians have come to doubt that the Civil Service is sufficiently responsive to their needs. For their part, civil servants have found it more difficult to work with 'conviction politicians' who interpret any allusion to the practical difficulties of a proposal as disloyalty. Moreover, civil servants felt uncomfortably aware as a result of government manipulation of the press and vigorous use of the Official Secrets Act (see Chapters 3 and 5) that they were expected by at least some ministers to take part in political plots and stratagems incompatible with old ideas of civil service neutrality. Most people felt that the need had become clear for a fundamental review of ministerial-civil service relations.

A second area of controversy concerned what has been seen as the excessive secrecy with which British government is conducted. All governments like to keep some of their business secret. There are legitimate reasons for concealing military plans such as the movements of the Falklands Task Force or the exact location of the submarines that carry Britain's nuclear weapons. There are also occasions when governments try to conceal information because revealing it would supply political opponents with useful ammunition. Between these two extremes lies a grey area. Governments in most systems feel that they are entitled to confidential discussions of the options open to them without the public knowing either what options are under consideration or which politician is supporting which option. Such secrecy is justified on the grounds that effective consideration can take place only if discussion is shielded from public view. Thus in the United States the right of the President to gather information confidentially from his advisers has been recognised by the Supreme Court as part of what is known as 'executive privilege'.

It is generally agreed, however, that British government is one of the most secretive in the world – certainly among democracies. The Official Secrets Act, passed during a spy scare not long before the First World War (1911) makes unauthorised disclosure of official information a serious criminal offence. On taking office, ministers are given a code of practice which instructs them to remain silent on Cabinet business and discussions. Defenders argue that Cabinet government requires more secrecy than Presidential government. Honest debate can take place only if the discussions of the Cabinet and the views of its members do not appear in the newspapers the next day. Members of a multi-member executive can operate effectively only if assured of even more confidentiality than a single member (Presidential) executive enjoys. Second, it is said that, in practice, access to confidential information would primarily benefit not ordinary members of the public but interest groups trying to manipulate government policy.

Critics of our extreme secrecy remain unconvinced. They note that Cabinet government does without it in other Parliamentary systems, including those on the 'Westminster model' such as Australia and Canada. Such arrangements certainly allow British governments to cover up embarrassing events or decisions. Thus a civil servant, Clive Ponting, was placed on trial and could have been imprisoned for years for revealing (to a member of the relevant Parliamentary Select Committee!) that the government was covering up embarrassing information about the sinking of the Argentine cruiser, the General Belgrano. Only the refusal of the jury to convict (going against the directions of the judge) saved Ponting. Decisions about what sort of nuclear deterrent Britain should possess have been made with a degree of secrecy which precluded reasonable public debate. Almost as dangerous as the total concealment of information has been its partial concealment. The government's control of information has allowed it to steer public opinion by releasing information in support of its case while concealing damaging information. Dependence on 'official sources' for information makes journalists unwilling to offend politicians or civil servants without whose help they cannot function. The dependence of journalists on official sources and the willingness of British judges to ban the publication of official information whose publication was unathorised makes it highly unlikely that a British scandal could develop similar to the 'Watergate' or 'Irangate' scandals in the United States. To this date, the collusion between Britain, France and Israel during the Suez Crisis in 1956 has been kept secret in Britain while its details have been published in Israel and France. At present a civil servant who reveals information because he believes that Parliament or the public is being misled, has no legal defence. The British voter is denied information which in other political systems is commonplace. Journalists are dependent for information on sources – the Prime Minister and her staff, ministers or civil servants – who reveal information selectively and with particular purposes in mind. As for the argument that special interests would gain if secrecy was reduced, favoured interest groups already enjoy access to confidential information – at a price exacted by the government, however.

There are signs that official secrecy is beginning to crack. As the trial of Clive Ponting showed, it is harder to persuade jurors to convict people for revealing information to the public. Several scandals in early 1986 showed that ministers – including the Prime Minister or her staff – leak information extensively when it strengthens their political position to do so. Civil servants seem increasingly unwilling to accept that they should support ministers blindly by all means, including concealment of secret, disreputable or dishonest government action. Indeed, the Permanent Secretary of the Treasury, Sir Peter Middleton, was reported in 1986 to have ordered his officials to refuse to accept instructions which compromise their political neutrality and constitutional integrity. Such refusals may well in practice be revealed to journalists. With the general decline of deference in British society it is also unlikely that the general public will accept indefinitely that they should be less informed about government than their counterparts in other nations.

A third problem for British government has been the difficulty both Conservative and Labour governments have experienced in controlling expenditure. It is in their attempts to balance expenditure against taxes that governments come closest to being forced to set out their overall priorities. The willingness to cut expenditure in order to finance tax cuts, or to put extra money into one area (e.g. defence) rather than another (e.g. education) determine to an important degree the general policy. Of course, many expenditures are uncontrollable in the short term either because changeable only through legislation (e.g. on what the entitlements are to social security) or because a programme is so far advanced (e.g. a road is three-quarters finished) that abandoning it would be silly. A related constraint follows from the fact that many items of public expenditure are triggered automatically by changes in economy and demography. An economic downturn automatically increases unemployment and supplementary benefit expenditures. An ageing population increases spending on pensions and health care. Short of cutting benefits – never easy in a democracy – there is very little that government can do about such changes. Nonetheless, the way they use what control they have pulls together disparate policies into a general statement of priorities. One of the major tasks of the Treasury is to force ministers to consider whether a specific policy fits into their overall priorities. In general, however, attempts at control have not been as successful as had been hoped.

Several factors explain this. First, as we have noted, ministers are generally judged by each other, civil servants and the press more in terms of success in fighting for their departments' budget than in terms of their loyalty to the general policies of the government. Second, 'Treasury Control' depends usually on the willingness of the Cabinet – often through a special committee known as a Star Chamber – to reject departmental appeals for money. The Treasury has two ministers in the Cabinet – the Chancellor of the Exchequer and the Chief Secretary of the Treasury – but there is always the risk that the more numerous representatives of spending departments will combine to defend each other. Third, the political costs of offending vociferous interest groups which benefit from expenditure are likely to be greater than political benefits from modest total reductions. The headline 'Government Cuts Aid for Farmers' attracts far more attention than 'Government Cuts Expenditure by 0.01%' even though these possible headlines refer to the same event!

A number of attempts have been made in the last twenty years to improve the system. First, the PESC (Public Expenditure Survey Committee) tried to force ministers to consider overall trends by showing them each year what would be the costs of continuing *existing* policies. Second, a number of initiatives such as PAR (Programme Analysis and Review) tried to evaluate the *effectiveness* of current policies. Third, 'cash limits' were instituted by the 1974–79 Labour government in the hope of achieving more effective control of departmental expenditures. None of these initiatives have succeeded. The PESC system was undermined by procedures based on constant, or inflation-proof, prices. The building-in of inflation to PESC allowed expenditures to escape from control. The PAR system was defeated by the unwillingness of departments to expose major programmes to initial review by others. Cash limits, adopted as a desperate expedient to contain expenditure, can be made to look ridiculous if a department runs out of money before the end of the year, but has continuing, obviously necessary, obligations. In its attempts to control the huge aggregate figures for expenditure, the comparatively small Treasury certainly cannot revert to its pre-1960 practice of examining *individual* items of quite small expenditure. Controlling the broad aggregates will be a continuing struggle even though, possibly for the first time since 1945, the Thatcher Government did manage to hold spending steady in relation to Gross National Product in the mid-1980s. A left-wing government, no less than a right-wing government, will find, unless it is careful, that it has lost real control of the finances and with them its effective sense of priorities.

A final area of concern is the structure of Britain's legislature and its relationship to decision-making. The most obvious problem is the House of Lords, whose inappropriateness as non-elected partly hereditary institution has been clear since 1911, when the Parliament Act promised fundamental reform. In the late 1960s, only a strange alliance of the far Left and the far Right prevented this, as both preferred the *status quo* to a reformed Upper Chamber. Yet the pressure of legislation renders ever more necessary a 'revising' chamber to consider Bills more carefully than the Commons (which under 'guideline' procedures often passes Bills without ever debating large parts of them). The credibility of the

Lords, often criticised as an adjunct of the Conservative Party, has been strengthened by the frequency with which it has defeated the Thatcher Government on matters where members had a particular interest. Yet it has retained a conservative, if not a Conservative, bias; it is constituted in part on a hereditary basis inconsistent with modern values, and in part by appointment, which involves a dangerous degree of patronage, and even lacks a predictable membership as no one can be sure which peers, particularly which hereditary peers, will attend on any given day.

There are also worries about the degree to which members of the House of Commons retain sufficient influence over legislation and over government itself. Tam Dalyell, with his persistent probing of the Thatcher Government's policies during the Falklands War and its aftermath has shown that the individual backbencher can still have a significant impact. Select committees of the House of Commons investigate the problems and policies which are the responsibility of the different government departments. These have given backbenchers greater knowledge of problems and procedures than used to be the case. Yet they cannot strip away the secrecy which shields dealings amongst civil servants and ministers. Select committees usually end up tantalisingly close to, but short of, the full picture. Party discipline, though attenuated, remains strong enough to turn MPs in the short term into 'lobby fodder', voting for government Bills of whose content they are ignorant and which they even believe to be ill-advised. British MPs remain amongst the worst paid and worst equipped legislators in the democratic world.

Politicians in Britain are increasingly careerists. Men and women seek election to the Commons not merely to add interest to retirement from the army – or the unions – as was common in the past. They enter the Commons in pursuit of a political career. Yet the ordinary MP has few opportunities to exercise power. Its concentration in the hands of governments leaves many MPs frustrated, hoping for ministerial office if they are in the majority party, and hoping – more vaguely and more desperately – for their party to win the next general election if they are in opposition. The greater wish of the average MP to make a difference, in conflict with a structure providing few opportunities for him to exercise, may provide impetus for further Parliamentary reform. We shall take up these points in the next chapter.

Conclusion

Active MPs frustrated by the existing structure of government provide a metaphor for the entire process of central decision-making in Britain. British government has traditionally been centralised and secretive in its decision-making, and fragmented in its application. The old structures now have to serve a less deferential, more questioning, and politically volatile nation. The British pride themselves on the capacity of their institutions to adapt peacefully to change. There may be some question if recent changes are best adapted to the real problems (see Chapter 11). But there is no doubt that, for better or worse, they will noticeably alter the nature of central decision-making.

Chapter 3
The place of Parliament

The preceding discussion raises obvious questions about Parliament's role in decision-making. Is it simply a rubber stamp or can it in some respects function as an effective check on government actions?

Although we generally equate 'Parliament' with the elected House of Commons, it also comprises the nominated and hereditary House of Lords. Because this is removed from the centre of affairs it is, paradoxically, better able on occasions to achieve the collective and detailed assessment of government policy which reformers would like to see made by the Commons.

While the House of Lords is numerically dominated by hereditary peers, most of its more active members are those nominated by governments to a 'life peerage'. In addition, an active role is played on certain issues by judges and bishops who have achieved their position by merit. While hereditary peers still attend (some, of course, being distinguished in their own right), they do not dominate discussions although they may crucially influence voting.

This House has only delaying powers over legislation – which can, however, effectively kill it when a government is approaching the end of its term or would find difficulty reintroducing a Bill in the Commons. Being largely composed of elderly, well-established personages, its sympathies incline towards the Conservatives, and it grew increasingly out of sympathy with Labour during the 1970s. Delays and obstructive tactics are more likely to be directed at Labour than Conservative legislation. In this way much of the Labour Government's Trade Union and Labour Relations Act in 1974 was emasculated by amendments in the House of Lords. On technical Bills close to its members' interests the House takes an independent stand against any government: an example was the controversial Wildlife and Countryside Bill promoted by the Thatcher administration in 1981, which was amended on many points before it passed.

Nevertheless the major influence of the House of Lords is through persuasion and correction of details rather than direct defiance of the government. It is still worthwhile to get the support of its members because of their personal influence and weight, and the publicity this attracts for views promulgated in the House. In the last analysis, however, the role of the Lords is peripheral, and it is in the House of Commons that governments are formed and major debates take place.

The House of Commons meets for about 200–250 days of the year, on a reasonably continuous basis from late October to July or August. General debates, questions to and statements from ministers, and certain stages of legislation are debated in full meetings of the House from mid-afternoon to around midnight. Much work is done in specialised committees which meet both in the mornings and later, in tandem with meetings of the whole House.

Such committees are of two general kinds. Standing committees consider the technical details of legislation. Each government Bill put before Parliament receives a formal first reading and then a second reading on its general principles. This involves the whole House of Commons. By definition since a government normally has majority support in the Commons, Government Bills are almost always approved. After the second reading the Bill goes to a standing committee for a clause-by-clause review of its details. Occasionally the whole House of Commons may constitute itself as a committee for this purpose. Generally, however, standing committees consist of 40 to 90 members. A few of these are specialised (for example, the Scottish and Welsh Standing Committees, to which Scottish and Welsh legislation is referred) and have a relatively permanent membership. Generally, however, the question of which standing committee a Bill goes to is arbitrary, and membership shifts. Each is selected to reflect the balance of parties in the House of Commons so that a government party normally has a majority. After the technical parts are approved the Bill goes back to the full House of Commons for its report stage and subsequently its third reading. All Bills pass through the same stages in the House of Lords, normally after they have passed through the Commons. Bills can be introduced first in the Lords but this is not usual. If the Lords amend the Bill, then it returns to the Commons which considers those amendments.

Private Members Bills introduced by MPs without government backing, and Private Bills sponsored by an outside body (normally some local government) also go through these general stages. Without government backing, however, it is unlikely that they will survive all these stages to become law.

Since the Government in office so strongly dominates legislative proceedings, it is arguable whether the main function of Parliament is to pass legislation at all. In fact Parliament clearly has three functions. Firstly it scrutinises and, if appropriate, criticises government administration. Secondly, it legitimates, though rarely initiates, legislation. Finally it provides training and socialisation for potential recruits to the executive. It is perhaps the greatest indictment of the partisan Parliamentary system that the third function, in practice, though not in theory, is the most important.

The major instrument through which the legislature scrutinises the executive is the other main type of committee, the select committees. These are bodies whose membership is selected to serve for a Parliamentary session. They are often chaired by an opposition MP, and are expected to produce non-partisan reports on detailed aspects of government administration. They may concentrate on the financial side (as with the Public Accounts Committee), or on the work of a particular ministry (Agriculture, Social Services) or on a particular region (Scottish or Welsh Affairs). The committees examine documents and witnesses and issue reports on aspects of policy, which can attract widespread newspaper and television comment.

The role of committees in scrutinising administration is supplemented by the time allotted to questions which individual MPs can put to ministers, including the Prime Minister. Ministers are bound to reply, although their answers may be evasive. Verbal questions put in the House are supplemented by written questions and answers which are reported in *Hansard* (the transcript of parliamentary proceedings published each week). On certain days backbench MPs can also raise questions for a short adjournment debate at the end of the day's proceedings.

The opposition parties also debate broad aspects of government policy on the supply days allotted to them on the parliamentary timetable. These are used to criticise selected aspects of government policy, and to promote the opposition party's alternative policy, although at a very broad level. Given the secretiveness of both government and Civil Service and the influence of party rivalries, it is difficult for set debates to be really informed.

The House of Lords follows the same general procedures as the Commons. It has no power to delay financial bills and can only delay other legislation for a year, after which the Commons can ratify a Bill of its own. However, since the Commons will almost automatically support Bills backed by the majority party leadership, it is doubtful whether the Lords general debates are more of a formality than those of the Commons. What lends more excitement to the latter's proceedings is the presence there on major occasions of almost all members of the existing government and their rivals in opposition. The tensions which build up in this atmosphere are absent from Lords debates, which as a result are duller although often more considered and sometimes more informative. The main strength of the Lords is their ability to focus attention on areas neglected by the Commons and to improve the detail of Bills. An example of their technical work is the Select Committee on the European Community, which has functioned more successfully than its Commons equivalent (see Ch. 7).

Government and Parliament

The presence of both the actual Government and of the alternative Government (the Official Opposition) in the House of Commons has both advantages and disadvantages. It means that the chief policy-makers directly face elected representatives for most of the year, which makes for close and intimate communication. On the other hand, it means that proceedings are dominated by ritual quarrels between Government and Opposition which makes it difficult for the House of Commons to organise itself as a distinct entity, or to express an independent point of view.

All one hundred or so ministers in a British government have to be Members of Parliament or peers. In practice a large majority are MPs, and almost all the people who would replace them, were they to be defeated in an election, are also MPs. The government continues so long as it is supported by a majority of MPs, normally all members of the majority party. Indeed party cohesion is central to the functioning of parliamentary democracy as it exists at the present time in Britain. It is secured by various devices, such as the existence of a special office and officials (Whips) to maintain agreement and discipline, weekly party meeting to discuss policy, distribution of party and government patronage, etc. We consider these along with evidence of some weakening in cohesion below.

While single party majority government is the norm in Britain, there have been periods of coalition and minority government this century. There were coalition governments during the two wars, and between 1931 and 1935, the so-called 'National Government'. The first two brief Labour administrations in 1924 and 1929 were minority governments while between 1976 and 1979 the Labour Government, having lost its overall majority, relied upon a pact with the Liberals. These experiences are worth mentioning since the emergence of the Liberals and SDP as a significant third Parliamentary force may make formal, or informal, coalitions more likely in future.

Party unity and the need to keep 'their' government in office implies that even if a minority of MPs disagree with the majority in their party, they will still normally vote with them against the other party or parties. The presence of most ministers in the Commons means that out of the 350-odd members in a majority party, a proportion approaching a third actually form the government. The presence of so many ministers actually in the House of Commons clearly encourages party unity. Conversely, of course, it acts against the House developing views independent of the government in office. Although the leaders of the other party (recognised as the Official Opposition) are much more in the position of ordinary MPs, their constant desire to criticise their rivals along party lines with a view to winning the next election also inhibits the House from developing a 'Commons' view of most matters.

Within the government there is a whole hierarchy of ministers, from parliamentary private secretaries who act as factotums for the more important ministers, through ministers of state who are normally second in command in a large department, and non-Cabinet ministers heading their own departments, to Cabinet ministers who normally take responsibility for an important department or ministry and also participate in discussions of overall government policy. Usually this takes place in the weekly Cabinet meeting (chaired by the Prime Minister) and in the committees described above, which may include non-Cabinet ministers as well.

Whatever their status or role in the government, all its members are, as we have seen, formally bound by the doctrine of collective ministerial responsibility, even if practices have been changing to some extent.

Internal party disputes, with occasional spectacular exceptions, are generally fought out in Cabinet committees and spill over into the press, rather than provoking debates in Parliament. The last thing major parties want is to have internal clashes aired in general debate. Collective responsibility and party cohesion still operate to maintain the semblance, at least, of the united effective government so important to British political traditions; and in doing so reduce the accountability of British government to Parliament.

Parliamentary scrutiny of government

In one sense it is paradoxical to talk about Parliament supervising government as though the latter were quite a distinct entity. The government in office after all occupies its position only by virtue of majority support in the House of Commons, and all its members are normally MPs or peers.

As we have seen, however, departmental processes are too complicated to be controlled by one minister (or even a team of ministers in the more important departments). The government as a whole hardly exists as a decision-making entity. Only the twenty or so most senior ministers meet in Cabinet, and neither Cabinet nor Prime Minister has the administrative staff necessary for close supervision of what is done in their names.

Thus while members of the majority party or parties in the Commons may generally approve of their government's intentions, and hence vote on their side on crucial divisions, much that the executive does is unintended. Moreover, ministers, exposed to new information and Departmental views, may rapidly develop different ideas from those originally shared with their parliamentary supporters. In this sense governments do form a distinct body over and against other MPs; this distinction is even more evident when we consider that the government assumes responsibility for all that the Civil Service does.

Parliamentary scrutiny of government actions, in the sense of critically reviewing what ministers and civil servants do or intend to do, is important for two reasons. First the wider discussion, sometimes by experts, may improve the quality of the policies being pursued. And secondly, Parliament is in constitutional theory at least the main national institution representing the views of the population. In part the latter are expressed in support for parties in elections, which we shall discuss in the next chapter. The leader of the party with the largest number of elected members in the House of Commons is assumed to have had his policies approved and will therefore be asked by the monarch to form a government.

However, many problems unforeseen at the time of the election campaign emerge in the three to five years separating most elections. These will particularly affect certain individuals or groups. If sufficiently large and powerful, they will negotiate directly with civil servants and ministers. But they will probably also try, particularly if the government is not responsive, to get support in Parliament. For individuals or smaller groups ignored by the Civil Service, Parliament must often be a first recourse.

This is particularly true of groups organised to promote a particular object (such as changes in the law regulating abortion or divorce) rather than acting as representatives of a particular sector of society. These 'causes' are often too controversial for civil servants to wish to decide a policy. Since they are peripheral to the main issues dividing parties, governments too have usually no wish to act, at least until they have tested the degree of popular and parliamentary support which a change might attract. Promotional groups therefore concentrate on finding sympathetic individual MPs who will seek opportunities to publicise the proposed change or bring it forward as a Private Members Bill. The permissive legislation extending opportunities for divorce and abortion at the end of the 1960s was carried in this way. Promotional groups thus form an exception to the general tendency for interest groups to concentrate their prime lobbying on the Civil Service. To the extent that trade unions are excluded (particularly under non-Labour governments) from normal executive consultations, Parliament also becomes a focus for their lobbying attempts. The enquiries and hearings of the new select committees (discussed below) have also given a better opportunity for aggrieved groups to make known their views about current policy.

Group representations often involve cases of individual hardship. We shall discuss the very active response of most MPs to constituents' needs at the end of Chapter 4, along with the role played by local governments and courts, and éven the European Community institutions, all of which offer alternative means of redress to individuals affected by government actions. Parliament's representative role requires not only action in individual instances, however, but a collective response to aspects of general policy which may cause individual hardship. In other words, a concern with effective representation also implies attentiveness to the success and quality of government programmes, so the function of representation and the need for informed discussion of policy converge.

It is the contribution of Parliament to the general discussion of policy which we examine below. How effectively is Parliament organised for this task?

Strong government versus open government

We should start by noting two major obstacles to informed debate on policy alternatives. The first is the way in which parliamentary processes and procedures are designed to facilitate the party battle. The domination of business firstly by the government, and secondly by the official leadership of the next largest party, constitutes perhaps the major obstacle to independent collective initiatives by the House of Commons as such.

This institutional monopoly is, however, buttressed both by constitutional doctrine and the entrenched attitudes of many MPs. They consider that the government's ultimate responsibility to serve popular interests is guaranteed by exposure to a general election at the end of its term. In the interim, decision-making will only be disrupted by undue parliamentary interference. The task of the parties in Parliament is, therefore, to support their government, or if out of office to keep up morale by attacking the office-holders. As Parliament is simply an arena for partisan encounters it can have no collective and independent role *vis-à-vis* the government.

This belief is in turn linked to a broader, traditional emphasis, also embedded in constitutional theory, that government knows best what to do in the public interest, and should be left (at least between elections) to get on with it unhindered. This colours opinion on a wide range of practical questions besides the nature of parliamentary debate. It covers government secrecy (desirable, because it prevents too much outside intrusion into government business); reform of the relationship between party votes and seats in the House of Commons (undesirable, because the present system, though grossly unfair to third parties, generally allows one major party to take clear responsibility for forming the government); accountability of the leadership to members inside parties (undesirable because it renders leaders, who may become ministers, less able to act decisively on their own initiative).

We shall take up the last two points in Chapter 4. It is clear, however, that support of strong, unfettered government militates against effective outside scrutiny, inside Parliament or anywhere else. The justification is that 'the public interest' (a term often used to justify government action) can only be served this way. Governments must not be put under pressure to meet immediate demands, for to do so might result in an inability to plan for the future.

It is interesting that one theory (termed the theory of 'government overload' or 'pluralist stagnation') in fact attributes many of Britain's problems to the failure of government to fulfil this constitutional role; rather we have seen weak governments capitulating to popular demands. In this view the government has taken on too many responsibilities which it is not able to discharge properly and which get in the way of its primary functions. As against this, there is no evidence that popular demands are excessive (Ch. 4). Nor is it obvious that we do have a detached and impartial Civil Service unerringly determining what the nation will need in four or five years' time. Errors and biases too often creep in.

The case would be different if policy debates were simply about agreed goals. In a very broad sense there is of course agreement on the need to promote greater prosperity but little upon the appropriate allocation of that prosperity. Disagreements also arise on intermediate objectives: will nuclear development safeguard energy supplies or is it better to rely on self-renewing sources (sun, wind, tide) or on more efficient use of traditional fuels? There is no guaranteed answer to these often technical problems, and it is at least as likely that wider and more informed discussion would help government find better answers, as hamper it unduly. The growing belief that this is the case has spurred many MPs to develop new procedures for discovering and then discussing the justification, and likely outcomes, of government policy.

The obstacles to establishing even the simple facts can hardly be exaggerated, given the administrative secrecy already discussed. The selective management of information by government is best illustrated in the parliamentary context by the 'lobby system' of specialist journalists attached to Parliament. (Incidentally it is significant that British political reporters, almost without exception, are concentrated within Parliament rather than in the executive offices, where they have of course no official place assigned to them. This means that news about government comes secondhand rather than directly from within the system itself.)

The parliamentary lobby itself is a name given to specially privileged parliamentary correspondents of the main newspapers who spend most of their time in the 'lobbies' of Parliament. They are given confidential information and have ready access to ministers (rarely to civil servants). It is understood that in return they will reveal only what they are expressly authorised to publish, and use the rest solely as background material in preparing their reports. Failure to observe the understanding leads to exclusion from their privileges. A further consequence is that the information which gets published is that divulged at the initiative of the administration and therefore consisting of what it wants to reveal rather than what it wants to keep hidden. Two developments have undermined this way of managing news. One is the increasing practice of ministers and administrators briefing selected journalists, usually in order to have the story published as part of an attempt to resist or push policy proposals within the administration. This is an especially common tactic when resisting budget cuts, even on the part of such figures as the Joint Chiefs of Staff, the supreme military commanders. The briefing shades into the 'leak' of unauthorised news in the case of nominally subordinate administrators opposed to policies backed by their superiors.

Briefings still represent selective management of information in someone's own interest. The other process undermining the lobby system is the development of a more independent stance on the part of political journalists and their increasing practice of so-called 'investigative journalism' where stories are pursued at the initiative of the newspaper and followed through without buying information for silence. In line with this trend, journalists and newspapers have also been prepared to risk prosecution under the Official Secrets Act, the D notices circulated by governments to editors to prevent discussion of topics relating to national security, or the severe British libel laws, while refusing to reveal the sources of their information. The editors of some newspapers have recently withdrawn from the lobby and now explicitly quote their official sources.

In spite of these breaches, however, the ethos of the lobby system still predominates in British government. Information is for insiders rather than outsiders and government (or at least its constituent ministers and administrators) determines who shall be insiders. As peers and MPs depend heavily on published material for their own information, to supplement erratic personal contacts and the selective confidences of party leaders, government management of news deprives them of a major source of information just as much as it does the general public.

It is unlikely that live radio or television coverage of parliamentary proceedings will change this situation much, as what is broadcast tends to be set debates, covered by newspapers anyway. Only if Parliament itself develops procedures for uncovering and evaluating important information will broadcasts be more illuminating.

Scrutiny through select committees

One way to make information more widely available is to utilise parliamentary privileges to force investigation of important policy areas and publish the findings. Attempts to do this in the last twenty years have concentrated on extending the remit, and strengthening the organisation, of an old parliamentary institution – the select committees. As mentioned earlier, these are bodies with a relatively permanent all-party membership often chaired by an opposition MP and traditionally non-partisan, which are designed to investigate detailed policy areas and to produce agreed reports. In these, if anywhere, a parliamentary view can be expressed, and technical detail accumulated.

Moreover the experience of other legislative bodies operating in Britain seems to indicate that they are workable. In district and regional councils there is not the strict division between government and opposition which is made in Parliament. Instead all elected councillors are appointed to executive committees covering the main areas of policy and corresponding to ministries in the central administration. Party groups are represented on each committee according to their numbers, so the minority party in the single-chamber council is also in the minority on all committees, which are chaired by a majority member. Nevertheless the minority leader on each committee has special status. While practices vary according to the bitterness of party conflict within the locality, minority members tend to participate in all confidential business. Since the chief officer of each affected department sits with the committee and its conclusions are usually accepted by the full council, the minority has a good opportunity to influence policy. Often indeed the committee view overrides party lines. Where parties are strongly opposed, the majority party members will meet separately to decide on a line they will push through the committee. Nevertheless the system favours compromise and gives all elected representatives some say in administration. What becomes a great difficulty is coordination between committees.

Similarly the single-chamber European Parliament (see Ch. 6) handles much of its business in specialised subject committees, with debates generally being initiated by a statement of the committee's view through a *rapporteur*. It cannot be said that the European Parliament's views have carried much weight with the chief executive body of the Community, the Council of Ministers, nor with the European Commission of technocrats. But that is less the fault of its structure than of Parliament's late arrival on the scene and the effective national veto exercised by member countries over Community policy. Certainly the committees are successful in getting an agreed view and providing informative reports.

We can therefore set the development of the Commons' select committees against the practices of corresponding bodies. The most recent reform of the select committees in 1979 was the third major reform of the system in 13 years. The reform was approved in the House of Commons by 248 votes to 12. In this case, as in the case of the previous reform in 1971, the change resulted from a report of a parliamentary Committee on Procedure. This committee was set up in 1974 for the life of the Parliament and reported in August 1978. Its report was radical by most standards, asserting that 'the balance of advantage between Parliament and Government in the day-to-day working of the Constitution is now weighted in favour of the Government to a degree which arouses widespread anxiety . . . the Committee believes that a new balance should be struck.' The main proposal of the Procedure Committee was that the existing Expenditure Committee with its sub-committees, and the four specialist committees – the Nationalised Industries Committee, the Race Relations Committee, the Overseas Development Committee and the Science and Technology Committee – be wound up and replaced by twelve select committees divided on departmental lines. In addition the committee recommended that: committees should be empowered to order the attendance of ministers and the production by them of papers and records from whatever source; time should be set aside in the business of Parliament for debate of the committees' reports; committees should have more resources at their disposal; and perhaps most controversially, a new legislative committee be established to hold evidence-sessions to precede discussions in standing committee. The debate on 19 and 20 February 1979 on the Committee's Report was notable for its unanimity. All speakers, with the exception of Michael Foot, Leader of the House, and one other Labour MP, supported the main thrust of the Committee's Report. The government, however, showed little interest in the proposal and it was left to the new Conservative Government and Norman St John Stevas as Leader of the House to introduce the proposals based on the Procedure Committee's report; these were approved by Parliament in June 1979.

All the existing select committees were ended except for those dealing with Privilege, Election, House of Commons Services, Sound Broadcasting, Public Accounts, Statutory Instruments, European Legislation, and the Parliamentary Commissioner for Administration. The twelve new committees broadly paralleled the major spending departments: Agriculture; Defence; Education, Science, and Arts; Employment; Energy; Environment; Foreign Affairs; Home Affairs; Industry and Trade; Social Services; Transport; Treasury and Civil Service. In addition a Welsh Affairs Committee and a Scottish Affairs Committee were established.

In spite of the Procedure Committee's recommendations, these committees were not given powers to compel evidence from ministers, the chairmen were not to be paid, and they were not provided with any allotment of parliamentary time for the discussion of their reports. In addition, no changes were made to the existing legislative process.

The fact that three extensive changes occurred in just over a decade indicates that there is pressure in Parliament for closer scrutiny of the executive, but also offers strong *prima facie* evidence that previous changes have proved ineffective. Have the new select committees proved any more successful? It is certainly clear that they have resulted in more effective scrutiny of government policy and administration. However, the reform has left the basic power structure unchanged. In other words no matter how good a job the committees do, they are unable to hold the executive accountable because the government can ignore or reject the committee's findings. Occasionally a committee does change a government's mind if its criticism is backed by extensive and influential extra-parliamentary pressure. In this way the Home Affairs Committee played a significant role in the repeal of the 'sus' law (allowing arrest on mere suspicion) in certain cases, by publishing two reports, in the 1979–80 and 1980–81 sessions, advocating its removal, and by acting as a focus of both parliamentary and extra-parliamentary pressure. This, however, is unusual.

The problem is that select committees at present can hold government accountable only if government wishes to be held accountable. Of course if Parliament developed a 'legislative view' which transcended party discipline then it could change the nature of executive/legislative relations. However, such a development is very unlikely, for although the select committees usually produce unanimous reports, some of which are highly critical of government, even the members of the committee rarely vote for the committee against the party view. So, for example, none of the Conservative MPs on the Transport Committee voted against the government's decision to increase the maximum weight of heavy lorries in 1981 despite the committee's opposition to this change. Again, despite the Treasury and Civil Service Committee's objections to the government's economic strategy in both its 1980 and 1981 Reports, only *one* Conservative member of the committee, Richard Shepard, even *abstained* in the vote on the government's handling of the economy on December 13th, 1981. Likewise, even though the Transport Committee specifically objected to parts of the Transport Bill, including the government's plans for school transport, only *one* Conservative member of the committee, Peter Fry, dissented in the vote. Indeed in all the cases of dissent between 1979–83 the number of dissenting Conservatives on the committees was no greater than those not on committees. Needless to say, there was *no* occasion where all the members of a committee voted against the government on an issue, even where they had unanimously approved a report which opposed government policy.

The case of Clive Pontin provides perhaps the best evidence of why change is unlikely. As we have seen, Pontin, a civil servant, 'leaked' information to Tam Dalyell, a member of the Foreign Affairs Select Committee, about the sinking of the Argentine aircraft carrier, the *General Belgrano*, during the Falklands War. The most significant aspect of the affair was the reaction of the chairman of the committee, Sir Anthony Kershaw, when he received documents which showed that Parliament and the committee had been deceived by the Ministry of Defence on important aspects of the incident. There was no outraged determination to hold government to account, now that the means were available. Rather he took the documents immediately to his party colleague, Michael Heseltine – the Minister of Defence – so that a 'leak inquiry' could be initiated to find the 'culprit' who had provided the information. That the chairman of a select committee, a body supposedly probing government accountability, should react in this way well indicates the distorting effects on committee activity of both party allegiances and the Official Secrets Act. The scale of the problem was indicated by the lack of reaction by other committee members to the action of their chairman.

The root of the problem then, is that an elitist view of democracy legitimates executive dominance of the legislature in the eyes of most MPs as well as those of all ministers. As such the executive can determine, and therefore restrict, the power of the legislature. The most revealing evidence of this is the Civil Service memorandum containing instructions as to what the civil servants can, and more crucially cannot, discuss with select committees. Specifically proscribed are: advice given to ministers; interdepartmental exchanges; discussions in Cabinet committee; advice given by law officers; and questions involving public controversy. The memorandum extends for two pages and in effect proscribes most of the information the select committee would want, and need, to assess government policy. However, the memorandum has never been a matter of controversy. So while certain committees have questioned its consequences none have criticised its very existence. It is hard to conceive of anything which would more accurately reflect the dominance of the executive, and the passivity of the legislature, in Britain.

Party cohesion

Much of the preceding discussion has emphasised the key role of party cohesion and loyalty, both in maintaining the authority of the government and its mirror image, the relative impotence of Parliament. British parliamentary parties, particularly in the House of Commons, maintain a striking degree of unity – without parallel in most countries of the world. Party discipline stems in part from the government's close association with the Commons. Instead of legislature and executive being separated constitutionally to the extent that a legislator become minister has to resign his parliamentary seat, in Britain the situation is reversed to the extent that a minister has to have a parliamentary base. Government dependence on a Commons majority means that a critical and independent stand is a costly luxury for MPs in the majority party, who may thereby jeopardise 'their' government in a way which cannot occur where there is legislative-executive separation.

This situation came about as a result of two associated nineteenth-century developments: (1) the increase in the electorate, which reduced MPs' individual contacts with constituents and made them more dependent on their party for re-election; (2) the growth in business associated with increasingly policy-based parties and the administrative complexities of a developed society. This led governments to increase their control over parliamentary procedures and their own parties, in order to get legislation through.

At the present time cohesion is maintained through a variety of structures and influences. British electoral procedures (the single constituency simple plurality system, which we will be considering in Chapter 4) makes it difficult for third parties and independent MPs to get elected. It thus tends to produce majority governments and to encourage legislators and electors to think of Parliament in terms of two adversaries, alternating power between them. This makes MPs reluctant to dissent from their party because of the difficulty of being elected as an independent and because the defeat of one's own party may lead to its replacement by the opposing party. Although this system is under challenge from Liberals and Social Democrats (which, with 22.6 per cent of votes in 1984 got only 3.4 per cent of Commons seats) the self interest of Labour and Conservative is strongly bound up with keeping things as they are.

Where MPs were elected by small majorities they may feel particularly dependent on party support and fear constituency reprisals if they thwart the Government. Their party workers may not unreasonably feel that they campaigned for overall government policy, not the Member's personal views. In addition, if the MP belongs to a government party, his action may contribute to parliamentary defeat and thus bring the day of electoral reckoning closer.

This is a plausible argument but encounters mixed evidence. In the 1959–64 Parliament it was found that the Conservative backbenchers 'most likely to join [the major rebellions] were those who had lower career aspirations, weaker socialisation into Conservative identities and group orientations, and lower vulnerability to renomination challenges' (Schwartz and Lambert, 1972, Schwartz, 1981). However, from 1970 to 1974 these influences worked weakly if at all (Norton, 1978, 220). Indeed, a number of Conservative MPs who during the

1970–74 Parliament voted against European Community membership resisted strong constituency pressure in doing so, and successfully fought off attempts to deny them renomination. What is more, constituency pressure does not always push MPs in the direction of support for their front-bench. In the Labour Party there is certainly evidence that the pressure can work in the other direction, with constituency parties encouraging dissent. In 1981–82 great publicity was given to the number of staunch supporters of the previous Labour Government who were denied renomination in favour of a left-winger. Although the actual numbers involved are small this helped to promote the Social Democratic secession.

Parties themselves act to reinforce internal cohesion through a variety of strategies and mechanisms. Within the majority party the Party Leader is also Prime Minister and can therefore appoint MPs to government office as a reward for loyalty (and oust them for disloyalty). (S)he can also award honours and make other appointments. So, to a lesser extent, can the Leader of the Opposition. The Prime Minister has the power to dissolve Parliament and call a general election through a formal request to the Queen. The uncertainty of the result prevents this threat being made very often but it can promote cohesion on a particular issue. Edward Heath, Conservative Prime Minister from 1970–74 who was widely unpopular among back-benchers for his technocratic approach, lack of personal warmth and failure to distribute honours more widely, still secured a majority of 309 to 301 on the second reading of his much opposed Bill to join the European Community (February, 1972) by making the issue a vote of confidence, and thus indicating his willingness to hold an election if defeated.

Seconding the leadership in its efforts for unity are the party officials known as Whips, selected from MPs not in the Government (or alternative Government, in the case of the Opposition Party). The picturesque name comes from the analogy with the whipper-in of foxhounds, hardly a flattering analogy for backbench MPs! One of the Whips' powers is withdrawal of the whip from a dissident, with resulting loss of access to parliamentary order papers and backbench party committees. The ultimate sanction is expulsion from the parliamentary party, with an almost inevitable loss of party endorsement at the next election and, until recently, near-certain electoral defeat. On the side of positive inducements, while the Whips do not control access to office they do in effect allocate members to standing committees on government Bills, recommend members for standing committees on Private Members' Bills, and choose members for parliamentary and party delegations abroad. Once again, such incentives can be used to improve the atmosphere on the backbenches and thus encourage cohesion. In fact, as opposed to theory, Whips have three separate if related functions. They act as a channel of communication between the front and back benches; they organise and manage the business of the House; and they attempt to encourage cohesion. The first two functions are more important. Various Whips have publicly admitted their limited disciplinary powers and dissenters have boasted that they ignore them at will. Whips can and do encourage cohesion but cannot enforce it; similarly the Whips' patronage is limited and is employed to promote general good feeling rather than to influence Members directly.

Probably the most important influences encouraging cohesion are however, the psychological factors already discussed, based on party ideology. MPs after all join a party because they agree broadly, with its views. Entirely of their own volition and without external constraints they may be expected to support it most of the time. Even in cases of slight disagreement they will give it the benefit of the doubt.

'Ideology' (adherence to a particular doctrine or a programme) is often associated exclusively with the Labour Party. In considering the Conservative Party, the shared social and educational background of Conservative members is more usually given as the reason for unity. In fact this explanation is really ideological as it implies that this common background leads to a shared set of political values, which then predisposes most members to support the frontbench position. Not just support of party views but also dislike for those of the other side may play a powerful part. Although there may be ideological splits, particularly in the Labour Party, it can be argued that parties remain cohesive because no matter how much they dislike the other wing of their own party, they dislike the Opposition more. This is an explanation often given of the reluctance of the left wing to split away from Labour, and is frequently linked to the argument that the British electoral system would prevent a party formed from the left of the Labour party having any access to power.

While the argument may still work for the Labour left, it obviously no longer applies to the right, where the internal campaign for social democracy led to a secession of some of its leading members and the formation in 1981–82 of a separate Social Democratic Party. Yet in a negative sense ideology still seems to have exerted some effect on the Labour rebels, as they did not join the Conservatives but preferred to create a separate party which retained some aspects of Labour ideology. Again in seeking alliances they chose the Liberals rather than the Conservatives.

But ideology certainly did not prevent the Labour split, which may be seen as the end result of a long history of factionalism within the party, embodied in such groupings as Tribune and Militant Tendency, with their own organisations and even newspapers.

Factionalism of this kind has been much more evident in the Labour Party than among the Conservatives – one reason possibly why they have not experienced a secession similar to Labour's. There is, however, at least one area in which Labour, including its former members in the Social Democratic Party, is noticeably more cohesive than the Conservatives. That is the type of permissive legislation mentioned above. On major unwhipped issues (i.e. those where party leaderships do not take an official stand) such as abortion, capital punishment, divorce and homosexuality, there is still a very strong relationship between party and vote. Labour MPs tend to support the extension of abortion and divorce, and freedom for homosexuals, and to oppose the death penalty. Conservative MPs tend to take the opposite line. Labour is almost totally united on its point of view (with the exception of abortion on some occasions), but the Conservative Party is split, with roughly one-third agreeing with Labour and two-thirds opposing. This indicates that there are some shared values among Labour MPs which aid rather than hinder cohesion.

A last element of ideology which has united members inside both major parties, is belief in the necessity and desirability of strong, effective government. The general prevalence of this view has already been noted but it is particularly influential among Conservatives, because they see themselves as the 'natural party of government'. This implies that a Conservative government has a particular claim on the party in performing the task incumbent on it: to govern.

Dissent within parliamentary parties

Nevertheless governments cannot rely for ever on unquestioning support if things go too badly wrong. The British belief in strong government relies on it being successful, at least in the long run. The lacklustre economic record of the last twenty years has weakened its influence.

Along with a decline of deference towards government has gone a decay of the other forces making for party cohesion: for example, constituency parties will be less inclined to blame rebels when they themselves feel critical of the leadership. And if his own leaders are not achieving what an MP wants, the prospect of voting to weaken the government and allowing another party to gain power is less alarming than it used to be. Moreover, the successful rebellion of the Social Democrats sets a precedent for secession, makes the party leadership more sensitive and more responsive to individual views, and renders the party alternatives less stark than when governments were a straight choice between Labour and Conservative.

The secession of the Social Democrats was the culmination of increasing factional tensions among Labour MPs in the 1970s. This extended even to the traditional consensual and hierarchic Conservatives, though internal tensions there did not show themselves in quite so dramatic a form. Conservative factionalism is obviously on the increase, however. Under the aloof prime ministership of Edward Heath (1970–74) an identifiable body of Conservative MPs emerged with a hard line on monetary policy and social issues. When they took over the leadership with the victory and premiership of Mrs Thatcher, semi-public dissent from the prevailing monetarist orthodoxy became common, and increased in extent after 1980.

As Philip Norton (1978) has shown, the point at which dissent reached significant proportions in both major parties was in the 1970s – hardly surprising in view of the major economic difficulties which successive government policies simply seemed to worsen. Under Heath there were 69 divisions in which more than ten MPs dissented during the period 1970–74. At the same time, there were more persistent dissenters, with 41 MPs (12 per cent) casting six or more dissenting votes and 17 MPs dissenting on 20 or more occasions. In fact one Conservative MP (perhaps not surprisingly it was Enoch Powell) dissented 115 times.

Dissent has always been more widespread in the Labour Party, but it became almost epidemic in the 1974–79 Parliament. No less than 45 per cent of all whipped divisions in the 1978–79 session saw some Labour MPs voting against the government (whipped divisions being those where the leadership requires MPs to vote in a certain way). What is more, only 62 Labour MPs (19 per cent of the total) cast no dissenting votes, while 40 cast more than 50, and nine more than 100 dissenting votes.

All this continued when Margaret Thatcher was elected Prime Minister in 1979. Although dissent was not as widesprad as under Edward Heath, it was still common and on occasions spectacular. Under the first Thatcher Government at least one MP dissented on 10 per cent of the votes and there were 16 occasions on which more than 10 Conservative MPs defied the whip. On these 16 votes in fact a total of 393 dissenting votes were cast. The two most spectacular concerned the Immigration Rules. On the two occasions when there was a division, more than 50 backbench MPs took a less liberal line than the Conservative front bench. When the Conservatives were re-elected in 1983 dissent still persisted. There were rebellions in 1984 on the Trade Union Bill (40 dissenters) and the Local Government Bill (19 dissenters) and in 1985 on the Water Fluoridation Bill (48 rebels). In all these cases, however, the large government majority carried the day. They were not so fortunate in 1985 when there was a major rebellion over the siting of the third London airport, or more spectacularly in 1986 when the Shops Bill failed to obtain a second reading.

So many Conservatives objected to the Inspector's Report on the siting of the third London airport that the government Whips, certain that they were going to be defeated on an adjournment vote (a vote to end discussion on the topic) instructed Conservative MPs not to vote. In the end 70 backbench Conservatives defied these instructions and voted with the Opposition against the Inspector's Report which the government, of course, supported. As already indicated, however, the Government's biggest debacle was on the 1986 Shops Bill, where they were committed to extending hours for Sunday trading. 'Liberalisation' was opposed by a strong, if unusual alliance, between the Churches, the trade unions, the National Chamber of Trade and the Co-operative Society. Many Conservative backbenchers believed that the Bill would 'change the nature of Sundays' and many more were under considerable pressure in their constituencies. In the end no fewer than 72 Conservative MPs dissented and the government lost a bill which had been a significant element in the Queen's Speech.

There can be no doubt, therefore, that dissent within both major parliamentary parties has showed a major increase up to and beyond the secession of the Social Democrats, and that the 1970s were the crucial turning point in the process (which still continues). Can any reasons for dissent be identified beyond the pervasive threat of economic failure?

Certainly Heath's aloof style did nothing to avert tensions, but it is unlikely in the absence of other factors that it would have produced enduring effects – no more so at any rate than the sweeping Cabinet purges of Macmillan's last administration (1962–63). Dissent has continued under Margaret Thatcher's very different style of leadership.

A plausible explanation is found in the changing nature of MPs and the critical attitude of younger entrants towards the government. From 1967 younger MPs demonstrated stronger feelings of dissatisfaction about both their own role and the domination of the executive. In all 35 Labour backbench rebellions, both in the full House of Commons and in standing committee, which defeated the government over the three sessions from 1974–76, the background and date of entry of MPs into Parliament were related to rebellion. On the Labour side, newer middle-class MPs, less imbued with traditional notions of party solidarity and discipline, were more likely to dissent and subsequently influenced many older Members. New MPs, on both the Labour and Conservative sides, are more interested in their local position and hence see their role less as a parliamentary party voting machine and more as a representative of local party and constituency interests.

As we have noted, this change of mood is related to the conspicuous failure of governments to solve the economic and other problems of the last decade. It is difficult to believe in the infallibility of government when governments constantly prove fallible. While dissent has also had an ideological base in the internal disputes within parties, these themselves rest on opposing prescriptions for solving national problems. As the problems pile up internal disputes between adherents of a controlled or mixed economy, of social concern versus economic freedom, become increasingly widespread and bitter. What is common to the various protagonists is an increasingly critical attitude to the government of the day.

While dissent has not been confined to minor issues, governments can still expect to win the vast majority of votes if they have a clear majority, and can still rely on backbench support on votes of confidence. But MPs are not longer lobby fodder. Dissent, moreover, is a politicising experience; once MPs rebel they are more likely to do so again and their example will encourage others. In reaction ideological opponents then assert a similar right to oppose on questions on which they feel strongly. This means that governments with small majorities will have to consult their backbenchers or be more prepared to accept defeat on a variety of votes. While dissent has most dramatically manifested itself in the Labour Party, it is not confined to it. All this will make the future role of party leaders and Whips more difficult than in the past, even discounting the possibility of minority or coalition governments under a three-party or one and two halves party system.

The House of Commons in the 1990s

There is, therefore, no likelihood that dissent and cross-party alliances will abate. As MPs express their own views rather than those of their party's leaders, this reinforces their own propensity to take a more critical and independent stance, and encourages others to do so. Secondly, governments have increasingly come to accept dissent. At one time a defeat on the floor – certainly a defeat on a major Bill – would have been a resigning matter. Now a government is unlikely to resign except on an issue of confidence, and it will choose such issues carefully. For MPs this must in many cases legitimate dissent.

All this will produce more defeats for the government on the floor of the House and even more in standing committees, particularly if it has a small majority, or is in a minority. Experience with the minority Labour Governments of the mid-1970s indicates, however, that the government will still win most votes. Nevertheless increased opportunities to sway the balance means that party leaders and Whips will have to pay more attention to backbenchers (the ordinary MPs).

Does this mean that Parliament's role in policy-making will become greater, or only slightly less marginal? Simply having three sizeable parties could mean a greater making and unmaking of governments in the House of Commons. This might lead to greater interest in its proceedings, but whether it produces more informed debate and a greater influence on detailed policy-making depends very much on whether the scrutinising select committees are capable of shaking off their partisan constraints, breaking official secrecy, and formulating a 'Commons view' which overrides party loyalties. They have not, so far, but greater opportunities exist now than have done so for a very long time.

Chapter 4
Parties and electors

Earlier chapters have amply underlined the importance of political parties in government and Parliament. The Thatcher years, if nothing else, clearly demonstrate the difference made by changes in party control. The ideology of the party in power crucially influences economic management and even more crucially the distribution of benefits to the different sectors of society – what services will bear the burden of public expenditure cuts, and how far cuts themselves will be implemented or taxes raised.

Parties also have a key role in formulating political demands on behalf of the public, voicing them in Parliament and other representative bodies, and attempting to translate them into government policy. The responsiveness of government institutions to popular wishes, and thus the whole functioning of representative democracy in Britain, depends principally on them.

This has been recognised in constitutional doctrine with a move away from individually based ideas about representation, to the mandate theory. Originally representation was conceived as a relationship between individual MPs and their constituents: either the MP voted on policy according to his best judgement, and his conduct was assessed by constituents at the election through their support or rejection (the representative theory), or the MP consulted with constituents on each important vote, and acted according to their wishes (the delegate theory). These contrasting viewpoints are still very relevant to the question of internal party representation, as we shall see. But nationally, ideas about representation have had to be revised to fit the functioning of cohesive, strongly disciplined parliamentary parties for whom MPs as we have seen generally vote.

The theory of party representation is associated with the idea of the mandate. That is, that parties should at elections present a definite set of proposals which, if elected, they have a 'mandate' from electors to carry out. How well the theory fits actual practice we shall consider below, but it is obvious from what has been said that governments increasingly face emergencies not envisaged at the time of the election where they have to act in the absence of any specific indication of popular feelings.

There are of course many ways in which individuals can try to affect government policy e.g. through interest groups and contacts with bureaucrats and ministers. In subsequent chapters we shall explore others: through press and television, local authorities, European institutions, and the courts and legal processes. Many of these relationships are themselves influenced or mediated by the political parties. The single most important way in which ordinary people can affect the overall direction of the country, however, is by voting for a particular party at a general election. Parties are crucial, therefore, as an institutional link between the preferences and needs of individuals and the government policies which are meant to cater for them. They are the only organisation which directly associates sets of leaders with sets of political activists and electors under a common name and with shared political loyalties. The inclusion of such disparate elements often imposes severe strains on the party organisation. To understand these we shall need to consider the structure of existing parties and their relationships with each other. We begin, therefore, with a discussion of the parties themselves, before moving on to discuss their basis in changing social divisions and how this affects the relationship between electors' policy preferences and party support.

The changing party system

Until 1974 the parties themselves, and the type of party competition which existed in Britain, were regarded as stable and fixed. This is reflected in the voting percentages reported in Table 4.1. Two large parties, Labour and Conservative, had alternated in office over the post-war period, providing strong single-party governments based on sizeable majorities in the House of Commons. Apart from important but rare occasions (the invasion of the Suez area of Egypt in 1956, the abortive industrial relations legislation of the Wilson Government in 1969), these majorities remained firm in their support throughout each government's term of office. The Liberals had picked up in 1959 and

Table 4.1 British general election results, 1945–87

Year	Total percentages of votes received by:				% Turnout
	Conservative	Liberal*	Labour	Other	
1945	39.8	9.0	47.8	2.8	72.7
1950	43.5	9.1	46.1	1.3	84.0
1951	48.0	2.5	48.8	0.7	82.5
1955	49.7	2.7	46.4	1.2	76.7
1959	49.4	5.9	43.8	0.9	78.8
1964	43.4	11.2	44.1	1.3	77.1
1966	41.9	8.5	47.9	1.7	75.9
1970	46.4	7.5	43.1	3.0	72.0
1974 (Feb.)	37.8	19.4	37.1	5.7	78.7
1974 (Oct.)	35.8	18.3	39.2	6.7	72.8
1979	43.9	13.8	36.9	5.4	76.0
1983	42.4	25.4	27.6	4.6	72.7
1987	42.2	22.6	30.8	4.4	72.7

* Liberal/SDP alliance, 1983 and 1987

during the 1960s oscillated around 10 per cent, but never appeared very serious challengers of the Conservative–Labour hegemony. Despite one or two by-election and local successes, the Welsh and Scottish Nationalists had remained fringe parties. The Ulster Unionists, who had split from the Conservatives over their Northern Irish policy, could only hope to win some ten seats in that province out of the 635 in the House of Commons as a whole.

By 1974 the failure of both major parties to resolve the country's economic difficulties caught up with them. The Conservatives had presided over massive inflation and boxed themselves into a direct confrontation with the unions, while the memory of stagnation under Labour from 1966 to 1970 was too recent to render them a credible alternative. Economic decline had hit the peripheries harder than the still prosperous Midlands and South East of England. In Scotland the combination of a relatively worsening industrial situation with the prospects opened up by the discovery of oil in territorial waters, seemed to confirm Nationalist assertions about the benefits of greater political autonomy. The same (without the oil) could be said to a lesser degree for Wales. As a result, the Scottish National Party (SNP) took 22 per cent of the Scottish vote in February 1974, and won seven Commons seats: Plaid Cymru, the Welsh (Nationalist) Party, took 11 per cent of the Welsh vote and two seats.

Reactions against the major parties were not confined to the peripheries. In England the Liberals advanced their vote share to an unprecedented 19.4 per cent, though owing to the biased electoral system they obtained only twelve Commons seats. Conservatives and Labour received almost equal vote shares just below 38 per cent. Labour, having received a slightly greater number of seats, formed a Government without an absolute Commons majority till October 1974, when it called another election which more or less confirmed the results of the first; the Liberals received slightly less percentage votes but the Nationalists more, and the SNP beat the Conservatives into third place in Scotland with 30.4 per cent of the Scottish vote. For most of the succeeding period, Labour was able to govern only with support from minority parties for which they made concessions (e.g. by introducing Devolution Bills for Scotland and Wales).

In the general election of 1979 the Conservatives restored their vote to almost 44 per cent but Labour returned a post-war low of just under 37 per cent. The Nationalists slipped to their core support of around 18 per cent of the Scottish vote for the SNP and 10 per cent of the Welsh vote for Plaid Cymru. The Liberals retained almost 14 per cent of British voters.

The consistently bad returns for Labour indicated that it was failing to appeal to electors. Disputes about whether this stemmed from the fiscal and economic orthodoxy of the 1976–79 Callaghan Government, or from the activities and extreme policies of the left, racked the party from 1979 onwards .The strengthening of Conference control over the parliamentary leadership, which we describe below, together with the adoption of left-wing policies on withdrawal from the European Community, abolition of American bases in Britain, import controls and regulation of investment, provoked a secession of many leaders and MPs in 1981 to form the Social Democratic Party (SDP). In alliance with the Liberals, this won important by-election and local successes against a still divided Labour Party and a Conservative government discredited by the failure of cuts in public expenditure to regenerate the economy. The 1983 election confirmed electoral trends: while the Conservatives lost slightly (but won the election handsomely in terms of seats) the Labour vote slumped to near equality with the Alliance: 27.6 per cent compared to 25.6 per cent. The bias of the electoral system, however, ensured that Labour had 209 Commons seats to the Alliance's 23. Increasing disillusionment with all parties was reflected in the failure of more than a quarter of electors to vote at all. The 1987 general election also produced a low turnout and confirmed the parties' general standing, with the Alliance going down slightly and Labour up, but not significantly. The Conservatives' ability to retain a constant share of the vote over three terms of office was a considerable triumph which confirmed them as the electorally dominant party in face of a divided opposition.

Party factions and ideologies

The ability of party infighting to give birth to a new party demonstrates the importance of internal relationships within the parties. To understand why factions have emerged increasingly during the 1970s, we need to review the contrasting traditions incorporated within both Conservatives and Labour. Then we need to look at the structural and organisational changes which have been used by competing factions to increase their strength, and which in the case of Labour produced the secession of the SDP.

The origins of party factions go back to the creation of modern parties. The present Conservative Party emerged from a long series of amalgamations with groups splitting from its main nineteenth-century rival, the Liberal Party. These took place from the 1880s right up to the 1930s. Their consequence was to combine the paternalistic outlook of the old, landed ruling class, with its stress on an ordered hierarchical society where the poor were helped if they kept to their place, with the free-market philosophy of the nineteenth-century business classes. This supported opportunities for the aggressive individualist which often involved the removal of societal restraints and severe economic penalties for failure. The emergence of monetarist economic ideas which involved severe checks on government expenditure and controls, revitalised this line of thinking. In turn, this led to strong reassertions of the 'one nation' strain in traditional Conservative philosophy. Thus the two traditions of Conservative thought and their supporting factions often combine uneasily. Edward Heath and Margaret Thatcher, the most recent leaders of the Conservative Party, both represented the individualistic free enterprise side of Conservative ideology, in contrast to the previous leaders Home and Macmillan – scions of the hierarchical and paternalistic tradition. But since both sides wish to preserve the established structures of British society, they never diverge too far: the factional disputes of traditionalist 'wets' and monetarist 'drys' in the Thatcher Cabinets were about tactics rather than fundamental goals, and by 1987 it was difficult to distinguish the two.

Shorn of its business elements, the Liberal Party's preoccupation with individual freedom led it in the post-war period to oppose censorship and espouse such policies as abortion, while supporting welfare legislation on the ground that it enlarges freedom of action for the masses. It has been less cohesive in support of all these causes than Labour, however, as its few MPs come mainly from peripheral rural constituencies with a traditional outlook. The Liberals have always been firm on regional devolution, on extending ownership of industry to the workforce, with workers' councils sharing control with management (which they see as a distinct third course between state control and capitalism), and most consistent of all the parties, before the emergence of the Social Democrats, on European Community membership.

The ideological sources of Labour factionalism derive from the two groups who in 1900, founded a parliamentary committee and later, in 1906, founded the Labour Party. On the one hand, there were avowedly socialist groups who believed in class struggle, capture of the state by the workers and enforcement of their control. On the other hand, there were moderate reformers aiming at amelioration of social and industrial conditions in collaboration with the trade union leadership. This 'social democratic' tendency is identified in policy terms with comprehensive as opposed to selective state education and with the foundation and extension of the welfare state – the provision of free government health care and support for unemployment and old age. While this has involved heavier taxation of wealthy groups to pay for services to the poor, it has not led to the eradication of wealth or income differentials. Government takeover of industry has been supported on pragmatic grounds, either as providing needed investment for a particular sector or averting widespread unemployment. This is the ideology, along with support for the EC, which the Social Democratic Party has taken over.

In contrast, the socialists have advocated greater social equalisation through penal taxation of higher incomes, and confiscation of wealth; abolition of private schools; and complete government direction of the economy (including 'social ownership' of the greater part of industry). The difference between the two sides is deeper than exists between the Conservative factions and has given rise to much more bitter and prolonged struggles, culminating in the foundation of the separate SDP. It is seen in the continuing struggle between the centrist Labour leadership of Kinnock and Hattersley and the Militant Tendency – a semi-secret Marxist movement within the party which gained influence during the 1970s and early 1980s.

The Labour Party itself is only part of the wider Labour movement, embracing consumer co-operatives on the one hand and trade unions on the other. Since the latter control the block vote of their affiliated membership at the Annual Conference (amounting to some four million compared to about a quarter million for constituency delegates), they can effectively decide which ideological tradition will win Conference support. Until the late 1960s when their suspicion of government regulation drove a wedge between trade unions and the Labour moderates, trade unions regularly backed reformist MPs, helping to confine the choice of leader to the parliamentary party and to keep in his hands or those of his associates the writing of the manifesto, the authoritative statement of Party policy in an election. Since 1970 their support has been much less consistent. Socialists within the Labour Party have been disproportionately active in constituency associations. They have therefore sought to increase the control and influence of constituency committees and representatives. The organisational changes of recent years have been more connected with battles for control and influence within the party than with technical efficiency.

Party structure and organisation

Superficially, all British parties are organised the same way. The primary purpose of local parties is to fight elections, so their areas correspond to political boundaries. The lowest political and geographical unit is the ward – the local government constituency. Ward parties are grouped in a (parliamentary) constituency party. Both ward and constituency parties hold general meetings throughout the year, with social activities designed to raise funds and recruit members, and a flurry of campaigning activities at election times. Each has an executive committee, with chairman and secretary, who meet throughout the year to plan and organise activities. Unpaid officers of the constituency party may be supplemented by an agent, paid from central funds, who can provide more of an organisational impetus than unpaid part-timers.

The selection of local and parliamentary candidates is usually in the hands of the management committee of ward or constituency parties. Candidates have also to be accepted as eligible by the central party. Affiliated organisations may send their representative to a selection committee meeting (this gives affiliated trade unions through their local branches an important role even in local Labour parties).

Where several constituencies fall under one urban government, they may join together to form a city party. All constituency parties are grouped into regional organisations which do not have much importance except in Scotland and Wales. (Northern Ireland has its own Unionist, Nationalist and Labour Parties which are organised broadly on the lines described here but have no institutional link with all-British parties).

At the British level, constituencies are represented at the Annual Conference and through its executive or organising committee. Generally constituency associations send one or more delegates to the Annual Conference in proportion to their numbers. Along with representatives of affiliated organisations (women's and youth groups, trade unionists etc.), these propose and debate resolutions on policy, which are designed to influence the party programme.

Two other party organisations exist at national level. These are the central bureaucracy of the party (the central organiser who directs the local party agents, research departments, office staff) and the parliamentary party, consisting of the MPs and members of the House of Lords belonging to it. The leader of the party comes from the parliamentary party, invariably from the House of Commons, and will become Prime Minister if his party forms the government.

While the formal structure of all parties (even of the Nationalists in Scotland and Wales) conform to this general description, their internal relationships differ considerably. This is most clearly seen in the relative position of the central institutions: the Conference, representing the mass party, the leader and parliamentary party; and the central bureaucracy. In the Conservative Party, both Conference and bureaucracy are firmly subordinated to the leader. The leader, for example, appoints the chairman who manages both Conference and the central office. Resolutions sent by constituency parties to the Conference for debate are selected so that only those favourable to the official line are actually raised. Until very recently the leader turned up to speak only after Conference had officially terminated its business. Needless to say, Conference has no say in selecting the leader, who is elected by vote of the parliamentary party, and then accepted by the mass party organisation. Nor does Conference control the party bureaucracy, who are accountable solely to the leader or the leader's deputies.

The parliamentary leadership dominates the rest of the Conservative Party because, historically, the mass organisation was founded only after the parliamentary party had consolidated itself. It was, therefore, designed to function in a purely subordinate role, focusing mainly upon the generation of support for candidates and policies rather than upon discussion of them. There has always been a strong Conservative parliamentary party, so its dominance over Conference and the mass party organisation has been maintained.

A crucial change occurred inside the parliamentary party in 1965. Up to that point, the Conservative leader had 'emerged' by a process of consultation, which gave great scope to the previous leader and party notables to bias the selection, normally in favour of the hierarchical traditional side of Conservatism. From 1965, however, leaders have been elected by the Conservative parliamentary party, giving the more thrusting free enterprise group the advantage. An open election also gave opponents of the incumbent leader an opportunity which they never had before to canvass support as a group, and in 1975 Mrs Thatcher defeated Edward Heath as an outside candidate for the hard-line monetarists, following Heath's loss of the two 1974 elections. In this way the new, more democratic, Conservative procedure contributed to a sharp break in Conservative Party policy, away from the more consensual Keynesian intervention of the earlier period. By transforming the monetarists into a dominant minority, but still a minority, within the party, it also contributed to the factional quarrels of the 1980s.

The Liberal Party shows how a similar structure to the Conservatives evolved when its parliamentary representation declined. Reduced to half a dozen MPs in the 1950s, and a mere dozen even when its fortunes recovered, the parliamentary party could not claim to be more representative than the base organisations. This was particularly the case as Liberal policy put much stress on local autonomy and self-reliance. As a result the Conference has become a lively debating body shaping its own resolutions, the leader is elected by a wide postal ballot of most active Liberals, and constituency parties are self-regulating – they have to be since they generate most of their own finance. The national party has more need of the constituency parties than they have of the national party, so local enthusiasm and participation are at a premium. The same is even more true of the Welsh and Scottish Nationalist parties.

The Labour Party originated as a mass movement outside Parliament, which gained effective representation there only twenty years after its formation. One would expect, therefore, to find grass-roots participation more widespread than in the Liberal Party. Up to 1980, however, the Labour Party most closely resembled the Conservative Party. The leader was elected by the parliamentary party and simply accepted by the rest of the party. Although formally the National Conference was the ruling body of the party able to instruct the parliamentary party on policy, in practice the latter had asserted its complete autonomy under the pretext of deciding when and how agreed policy was to be put into effect. This meant that Conference proposals could often be effectively shelved. The party programme (the election manifesto) was written under the direction of the leader just as it was in the Conservative Party.

The Parliamentary Labour Party and its leadership could effectively dominate the mass organisation in the constituencies because of the structural peculiarity of the Labour Party already noted. The party is part of a larger body, the labour movement, also incorporating consumer co-operatives and trade unions. These are represented at the Annual Conference in proportion to their membership, or rather, the proportion of their membership who contribute money to the Labour Party. Contributing members of the trade union are those who pay, with their subscriptions to the union, a political levy – nonpayment of which is entirely the responsibility of the individual who must declare his desire not to pay (contract out). The number of paid-up contributors far outweighs the membership of the constituency parties. So long as the trade union leadership was dominated by fears of Communist and left-wing penetration, and had a fairly unstrained relationship with Labour Governments, they supported the parliamentary leadership. The union 'block vote' at the Conference was thus cast in support of policies the latter favoured and a National Executive Committee (NEC) elected who supported them. This was important because among other things the NEC controlled the central bureaucracy and constituency agents of the party.

Over the 1960s and 1970s Labour Governments along with Conservative Governments tried to exert more control over trade union activities, as part of a general effort to reform industrial relations and render British firms more competitive. This strained relationships with union leaders, who were also less worried about left-wing influence inside the unions as international tension slackened. The unions therefore ceased to exert their block vote automatically in favour of the parliamentary leadership, and hence the NEC and Conference became increasingly assertive and critical of the moderate leaders' policies.

This situation changed again under the common threat to both sets of leaders from Conservative legislation of the 1980s. This has passed from strengthening individuals within and outside the unions against the leadership (Employment Acts, 1980 and '82) to enforcing secret ballots in internal elections, on the question of whether or not to call a strike, and on the maintenance of political funds. Most of these go to the Labour party – providing more than four-fifths of its national finance, according to some estimates. The campaigns successfully co-ordinated in 1985–86 by the Labour and union leaderships, supporting maintenance of political funds in union ballots on the political levy, have brought them close together again. Faced by the need to defeat a uniquely hostile and determined government, union leaderships have increasingly thrown their weight behind the parliamentary leadership of Neil Kinnock, who is as a result starting to enjoy the same massive support from the unions as Attlee and Gaitskell had in the 1950s. From the viewpoint of the late '80s it is the opposition and reform movements of the '70s which seem the exception, rather than the dominance of party affairs by the parliamentary–union alliance.

The reformers of the late '70s and early '80s focused on three demands. The first was for parliamentary and local candidates to be initially chosen by constituency selection committees, and to be fairly frequently reviewed and if necessary dismissed by them. The introduction of mandatory reselection in 1981 was obviously a move towards making MPs and councillors delegates who reflect the views of their supporters, rather than representatives exerting their autonomous judgement. The second demand was that the National Executive Committee should control the writing of the party programme and manifesto. The third was that the leader and deputy leader should be elected by a wider electoral college in which active constituency members would have an influence, equal or greater than that of MPs. In the electoral college as it finally emerged, trade unions have 40 per cent of the vote and MPs and constituency parties 30 per cent each.

The re-emergence of a pragmatic parliamentary leadership supported by the unions has nullified the hoped-for impact of these reforms. A centrist leadership was elected by the college, few MPs have been de-selected by their constituencies, and election programmes continue to be designed by the leader and his associates. Apart from their practical impact however, acceptance was also seen as victory in a battle for power between socialist sympathisers, who dominated the constituencies, and the social democrats entrenched in the parliamentary party.

To fight the socialist drive for domination of the constituencies, various social democratic organisations had been founded within the Labour Party. Despairing of the Labour Party both as a likely election winner and as a vehicle for their policies, several prominent members of these left Labour to form, in 1981, an independent Social Democratic Party. This offered a compromise between the public expenditure cuts of the Thatcher administration and the sweeping controls then advocated by Labour. Thus, it won, with the Liberals, a string of impressive by-election successes. Concurrently its membership grew to 60,000 during the year, although its MPs were reduced to only four after the 1983 election.

The SDP from the outset aimed at building a strong constituency organisation on the general British model. It also encouraged full internal participation of its membership through extensive working parties and circulation of discussion documents. Like the other parties, it established a National Conference to debate resolutions and hear reports. However, the emergence of the strong and rather authoritarian leadership of David Owen de-emphasised many of the formal arrangements for wide consultation; attention centred on the figure and pronouncements of the leader to a considerable extent – at least until his effective removal in 1987 following his opposition to merge with the Liberal Party.

All British parties have chairmen but they are normally much less important than the leader, if not subordinated to him. An exception occurs in the case of the Welsh and Scottish Nationalists, where their limited parliamentary representation has usually made the chairman, selected by the mass party, more dominating than any of the MPs. The Nationalist MPs have been forced by the nature of their position into a more gradualist position than that of enthusiastic activists outside Parliament, and this has made for tensions in periods of electoral success.

Election arrangements

Just as internal organisation may favour one faction at the expense of another, so the rules for translating party votes into Commons seats are far from neutral or purely technical. In Britain not only do the biases of the electoral system determine the relative political success of the parties (since it is Commons seats rather than popular votes which decide which is to form the government), they also affect the choice of party representatives and leaders, so materially influencing the course of internal struggles.

Popular votes are translated into Commons seats through the 'first-past-the-post' or 'single-constituency simple plurality system'. The UK is divided into 650 constituencies, each represented in Parliament by a single MP. The seat goes to the candidate who attracts more votes in the constituency than any rival – a plurality – regardless of whether or not this proportion is over 50 per cent – a majority. Indeed, in a four-candidate contest the proportion voting for the winner could be as little as a third.

The results of such contests throughout the country then determine the overall balance of seats in the House of Commons, and hence the government. Almost all candidates elected attract support as the nominee of a party. Votes given on the individual attractiveness and personal appeal of the candidates in the normal urban or suburban constituency are less than a thousand out of an average party vote of thirty to forty thousand. Consequently they will all vote in the House of Commons to support the government chosen by the party leader and will continue this support on all issues that do not create acute internal divisions within the party.

Constituency outcomes thus determine the party composition of the government but such results are as much affected by the method of counting and the division of constituencies as by the popular vote for parties. Where the electorate vote strongly in favour of one party or another, the result is reasonably reflected in the distribution of seats. Where there is a relatively even split, the distortions created by the existing system can push the result arbitrarily in favour of one side.

The most spectacular examples of bias on a national level have been where a major party with slightly less of the popular vote than its rival actually gained more Commons seats and formed the government (the election of February 1974 is the most recent example). This has not had much practical significance since in such cases popular support was clearly moving towards the party which took power and the outcome was accepted even by the ousted party. Such results tend to emerge because Labour, for example, wins a disproportionate number of small, depopulated central city constituencies and of Scottish and Welsh seats, which are more numerous in relation to population than English. The Conservatives win more country seats which in the peripheries have a limited population over a large geographical area. Despite periodic adjustments by Boundary Commissioners, such anomalies are probably inevitable in any constituency-based system which takes other criteria into account than simple equalisation of population.

Since these anomalies tend to balance out they are not too serious in terms of the national result. What does introduce systematic bias is winning by pluralities inside a large number of constituencies. This means that parties with a minority of supporters scattered over a lot of constituencies pick up no Commons seats at all. This is true for Labour in the South of England and for the Conservatives in the North of England, Wales and Scotland. It is not that the other party lacks substantial support in these areas, but simply that the system of apportioning seats does not reflect it. The result is that the parliamentary leadership of both Labour and Conservatives is now regionally biased in a way their voters are not. Labour MPs almost exclusively represent the big cities of Wales, Scotland, the North of England and also Inner London. Conservative seats are disproportionately located in the Midlands, South West and South East of England and usually form semi-rural or suburban constituencies. The regional and urban–rural division between the parliamentary leadership of the two parties is very marked, and was even more exaggerated by the 1983 and 1987 elections, in which the Conservatives, for example won no seats at all in Glasgow and Liverpool. In 1983 (outside Inner London), Labour elected only three MPs in southern England. A marked difference emerges in Parliament, which is just not apparent in the voting bases.

Through the mechanics of the system the major parties gain in areas of relative strength what they lose elsewhere. But smaller parties lose out entirely. If they have concentrated support in one region they may gain a block of Commons seats in rough proportion to their strength, as did the Scottish and Welsh Nationalists in 1974. If they attract wide support which is not particularly concentrated they may gain next to no seats although they receive a large percentage of the national vote. The prime victim of this bias are the Liberals and Social Democrats which, with over a quarter of the votes in 1983, received less than a twentieth (3.6%) of Commons seats, a result repeated in 1987.

There are, of course, many alternative systems of counting votes employed in other countries. These are generally referred to as proportional representation systems, since their aim is to bring the party proportions of legislative seats into line with their overall proportions of national vote. Most of the proposed systems would require larger constituencies represented by several MPs; this is to allow large minorities to be able to elect at least one MP. Instead of solely determining the choice of MP, the largest proportion of party supporters would then elect say two MPs, and the two minorities perhaps one each. Various technical ways of apportioning constituency votes exist, but all would have roughly similar effects.

Depending on which scheme of proportional representation was adopted and the particular level of their vote, the Liberals and SDP might place anything from 50 to 150 MPs in the House of Commons with Labour and Conservatives getting proportionately less. Not unnaturally these parties plan to press for some kind of proportional representation if they ever get a share in government. Given the present distribution of political support in Britain, this would make it likely that no party had an absolute majority of seats in the House of Commons, so that any wishing to form a government would require the support or collaboration of other parties. Instead of the single-party governments we have had up to date (even when they did not have a complete legislative majority, as in 1976–79), we should always have coalition governments grouping a number of parties. This would produce great changes in the way governments behave, but the situation would reflect more closely the distribution of preferences among the electorate.

In Britain, though without much justification from the history of other countries, peacetime coalition governments have generally been regarded as weak and indecisive. Proportional representation has been discussed in stark terms of greater representativeness at the cost of weaker government, if the electoral system is changed; or stronger government at the cost of less representativeness, if it is retained. Given the general bias towards strong government discussed in Chapter 3, it is not surprising that the majority of politicians have opposed moves towards proportional representation. Even on the left wing of the Labour Party, it has been felt that if Labour were not in power, it would be better to have a Conservative government with clear-cut policies than an amorphous group in the middle. Proponents of electoral reform argue against adversary politics of this type on the grounds that the simple plurality system and single-party government lead to crushing party discipline, opposition for its own sake and constantly changing policies with changes of government. Greater representativeness should not only be supported for itself but because it improves opportunities for individual representatives to respond flexibly to popular preferences.

Now that a significant political group is pushing for change, some proportional election system may emerge in the foreseeable future. Not only would it alter the shape of the party system and government formation by providing permanent niches for smaller parties, it would also – owing to a more representative selection of MPs – affect the nature of internal party leadership. No longer, if their national support holds up, would Labour MPs be predominantly urban and northern, and Conservative MPs suburban and southern.

For most of the post-war period, however, this contrast has obtained, and has been partly responsible for pushing the parties into opposing lines of policy which can also be seen as regional: the Conservatives favouring a free-enterprise economy tailored to the more prosperous regions, whereas Labour endorse subsidies and protection from foreign competition in order to reduce unemployment in the peripheries – the 'North–South divide' so much discussed in the run-up to the last general election.

Parties and social cleavages

These policy differences also stem from the fact that parties (like the government ministries examined in Chapter 2) tend to defend the interests of associated groups – particularly those they see as voting for them. We have already identified regional divisions between parties. Another obvious division is class, the Conservatives attracting more of the middle-class vote and Labour more of the working-class vote. Region and class are not, of course, independent of each other, nor of other social factors such as race and religion. They all exert complicated and interwoven effects which we consider below.

Region, religion and race

Regional differences used to be considered irrelevant to British politics. The rise of nationalism in Wales and Scotland highlighted differences previously masked by a common language, the facade of unitary government, the economic preponderance of the South East and Midlands of England and the national coverage of the London press and other media. None of these factors works unambiguously to eliminate regional differences. Welsh nationalism has as a major goal the preservation of the Welsh language (now, with about 500,000 speakers, shared by a fifth of the population of Wales). Scottish nationalism also finds support in indigenous literary and linguistic traditions.

As Chapter 6 demonstrates, unitary government in Britain is largely a myth: under its forms lurk a variety of governmental arrangements with much scope for local resistance to centralising tendencies. Economic disparities between a relatively prosperous core and declining peripheries provoke nationalist feeling as much as they damp it, especially when discoveries such as North Sea oil seem to indicate that the region might be more prosperous on its own (e.g. in Scotland, 1972–76).

The case of the press is even more striking. Britain is unusual for the countrywide circulation of newspapers produced in the capital, as also for their sharp division between 'quality' newspapers with serious analysis and discussion of news, aimed at the wealthier and more educated groups, and 'popular' newspapers with limited news coverage conveyed in screaming headlines and simple, direct presentation of sport, sex and gossip. The papers which carry these techniques to their extremes, with a corresponding reduction of print compared to pictures, may attain a national circulation of up to $5\frac{1}{2}$ million. The best-selling quality newspaper attains over one million, again on a national basis (see Table 5.1 below).

These facts, however, have obscured the equally striking point that some local and regional newspapers have not only survived but have flourished more vigorously in recent years than the London papers. Most of these papers are evening or weekly, but the further one gets from London the more well-established dailies are found in the main cities. These have a different character from the London press: since their basis is regional rather than class, they bridge the gap between quality and popular coverage. For such papers almost anything that happens in their locality is prime news. In Scotland, for example, with a distinctive press, regional issues are bound to get extensive coverage, so there is inbuilt encouragement for nationalist feeling of some sort.

Television and radio have in the past been centralised, although they have always had a regional structure. Under the impact of political events and the consequent rise in regional consciousness, this has been strengthened. Only 44 per cent of directly produced television programmes on the more popular television channel of the British Broadcasting Corporation (BBC 1) now emanate from London, compared to 36 per cent from the regions. Whereas the regional companies' contribution to national independent programmes used to be nominal, more emphasis both in guidelines and in practice is now devoted to directly produced regional programmes. Local radio stations based in each large city are attracting larger audiences. All these developments mean that within a nominally centralised structure, regional voices are increasingly heard. In turn, regular expenditure by the media in each region builds up a core of professionals in journalism and the arts which is available to repertory theatres and other local ventures. Arts Council spending in the regions grew from 50 per cent of its total to 70 per cent in the 1970s, financing a network of local theatres and arts centres which operate fairly independently of London and temper its cultural monopoly.

Government recognition of the social distinctiveness of Wales and Scotland, and attempts to stave off nationalism with some political concessions, have resulted in the areas having separate legal and institutional arrangements. The extreme case is Northern Ireland, which not only had a devolved government and parliament for fifty years (1922–72) but also its own savage religious conflict between Catholics and Protestants, a near civil war, and an even more precarious economic base than the rest of Britain.

The English regions are less distinctive, partly because they lack traditions and institutions to focus their grievances against the centre. The striking decline of the North and Midlands in recent years has made it impossible for any government to ignore totally their distinctive problems of poverty and unemployment (Ch. 1). Such problems are economic rather than nationalistic. But even Scottish and Welsh feeling results from a complex interplay of social and economic factors rather than from pure cultural nationalism.

One of the historic differences between the North of Britain and the rest of the country is the impact of massive Irish immigration there during the nineteenth and early twentieth century. This was compounded by the settlement after the Second World War, predominantly in the same areas, of a quarter of a million Poles and Ukrainians. The primary legacy of Irish and East European immigration (as well as of lesser foreign influxes such as the Italian) has been to augment the strength of the Catholic Church in the northern areas. One quarter of the population of Glasgow is Catholic and the same balance obtains in Liverpool. Education in religious schools as opposed to the largely non-denominational state system perpetuates social differences, which have been sharpened by the close ties of both religious communities with the opposed factions in Northern Ireland. Labour support in the West of Scotland and in Lancashire has centred on a Catholic working-class vote rather than a purely working-class one. This contrasts with the insignificance of religion as a social and political division in southern England.

The increasing settlement of West Indians, Pakistanis and Indians (3.6 per cent of the British population) has also produced disproportionate local effects owing to their concentration in particular areas. Generally deprived, their position is worse when they are settled in poorer inner city areas or in cities and regions whose economic base has declined since they arrived – the West Midlands and the textile towns of the North. The urban protests of the 1980s have increasingly evolved from being a protest of both black and white in declining areas against neglect, to an explicitly black, largely West Indian, reaction against what is seen as a biased and prejudiced authority structure. Disturbances of this type, on a scale and destructiveness not seen in Britain since before the First World War, may well continue while the perception of bias and the conditions underpinning it remain. This is a new factor in British politics which gives enormous relevance to control of the coercive forces (police and – ultimately – military) which we consider in Chapter 9.

All these developments combine with pre-existing differences to heighten regional distinctiveness, which in turn is preserved by the low level of geographical mobility among the British. Regional differences do not simply or even mainly contribute to nationalist party support of course. Given the Liberals' long-standing support for regional home rule, their new effectiveness with the SDP may well prove attractive in the regions. Labour's policies of active help and subsidy for the peripheries also render them natural regional spokesmen except for periods when they are in power in Westminster, or discredited by recent failure as a government to cope with regional problems. Labour's overwhelming electoral victory in Scotland in 1987 fuelled renewed demands for devolution given the total divergence of the Scottish mandate from the English.

The fact that Labour is at one and the same time the representative of the peripheries and the spokesman of the working class testifies to a certain overlap of class and regional loyalties. A major regional difference is precisely the distinctive working-class ambience of the North compared to the middle-class ethos of the South of England. These differences arise in the first place from the different class proportions living in each region: more working-class in the North and middle-class in the South. Each dominant class group tends to shape the outlook and aspirations even of the other classes living there to a disproportionate extent, a tendency which is reflected to some extent in voting behaviour.

Class changes

At the present time, therefore, class influences are also regional influences and vice versa. The effects of class itself, independent of region, have been much affected by the social developments of the past two decades. Like the political developments reviewed earlier, these are intimately bound up with the functioning of the British economy in the post-war period.

As noted in Chapter 1, Britain has been in the paradoxical position, during most of those years, of achieving greater prosperity in absolute terms (i.e. in comparison with its own past) while declining relatively, through experiencing a lower rate of growth than other countries. Internally, absolute growth, combined with a certain redistribution of income from clerical to skilled manual workers, and the increasing employment of women who contribute a second family wage, provided the bulk of the population with more money than in the past, indeed produced an 'affluent' society spending large amounts on both the basics and the comforts of life. These tendencies have continued during the 1980s against the gloomy background of industrial closures and increasing unemployment. The world-wide fall in inflation, and hence the growing real value of salaries and wage increases, have meant that those who have a job are better off, on the whole, than they were before. Of course there are many exceptions: public sector workers for example, have fared relatively badly under a government committed to restraining expenditure. Changes in tax and welfare legislation to favour the better-off have meant though that other groups have done spectacularly well. The major costs have been borne by the unprecedented numbers of unemployed (around 13 per cent of the workforce in the mid-1980s) whose income has been drastically cut by the fact of losing their job. The majority in work are, on average, still better off than before.

The decline of British exports and manufacturing industry over this period has on the other hand meant that the British population increasingly spent more money than the country as a whole has earned, leading to a recurrent imbalance between what is earned by exports and paid for imports. Increasingly effective foreign competition has destroyed many British enterprises, particularly in textiles, steel and shipbuilding, and produced long-term unemployment, particularly in outlying parts of the country (again accentuating regional discrepancies). These trends were aggravated by the slackening in world trade and economic activity over the early 1980s. Though world recovery and North Sea oil ensured a temporary respite for the rest of the decade, simultaneously, therefore, most individuals have experienced greater prosperity, combined with greater insecurity as prices rise and jobs are threatened.

Effects on class differences

The most obvious is the increasing affluence of the population as a whole, including most manual workers. As the nature of their jobs changes, and they acquire better housing and consumer durables and patronise the same supermarkets and multiple stores as the middle class, they become less distinctive in terms of overall lifestyle.

The elimination of the more glaring class differences is also speeded by attendance at the same type of (comprehensive) school and similar housing in large modern estates on the fringes of cities. However, more of the working class still live in rented and council houses while the middle classes generally purchase theirs through a long-term mortgage. Thus the standards of amenity vary. The contrasts are still much less than between the slum and sub-standard properties near city centres, in which most workers lived 60 years ago, and the substantial villas and semi-detached houses with gardens, where the bulk of the middle class lived at that time. Increasingly many manual workers have also become owner-occupiers, aided by the Conservative policy of selling council housing cheaply to the tenants.

Writers of the 1960s saw such trends as contributing to the 'embourgeoisement' of the working class – their assimilation to a middle class outlook, leading in politics to a weakening of the Labour Party and strengthening of the Conservatives. With hindsight we can see that tendencies to assimilation have worked both ways. As differences in income decline, members of the middle class have in many respects become more like manual workers. They too are provided for by supermarkets, comprehensive schools and a National Health

Service. With the application of computer technology to clerical and higher level tasks, their traditional job security is undermined and they are threatened with immediate redundancies and structural unemployment. Cuts in public expenditure designed to stimulate private enterprise or to bring imports into line with exports, even threaten the permanency of government employment, a long-standing bastion of middle-class professionals and managers. This opens up the possibility of a new politico-economic cleavage between those workers supported by public taxes and those who gain no direct benefit from them, although there is no evidence from the last two elections to show that this is happening at the moment.

In such circumstances it is perhaps not surprising that the last decade has seen a major increase in the strength of white-collar unions (which now have a membership of around half of clerical and related workers, with a heavy concentration in government employment). White-collar unionism may undermine the cloth-capped image of earlier periods, but it subverts the bowler-hatted image as well. For example, the traditional association between trade union membership and Labour voting has been weakened – at least partly as a result of so many more professionals and clericals becoming trade unionists. At the same time a union-ised worker has been more prone to vote Labour than a non-unionised worker, whatever his occupational level. Assimilation proceeds from both sides of the earlier divide.

In the midst of these changes the proportion of electors who are class-conscious, in the sense of spontaneously identifying themselves with a particular class in response to a survey question, has remained fairly constant at around one half of the population, between the mid-1960s and the mid-1980s. A significant decline appears however in manual workers' willingness to identify with the working class, which has declined from 46 per cent in the 1960s to 39 per cent today. Non-manual workers are more inclined than previously to identify with the middle class (Robertson 1984). This seems to show that occupational and social changes have had a more negative impact on working-class solidarity than on middle-class cohesiveness.

It is probably more relevant in assessing the impact of class divisions to note the emergence of a large intermediate grouping of the population, standing between the solid middle class and the traditional working class. Unlike the latter they have non-manual, relatively 'clean' occupations, heavily concentrated in the services and administrative sectors. A large proportion in this sector are women, of working-class origins, working as secretaries, sales personnel and clerks. These characteristics serve to distinguish them sharply from the old middle class of male professionals and managers, who enjoyed a considerable degree of authority and autonomy in their work, or even from the 'petty bourgeosie' of small shopkeepers and artisans responsible for their own fate. Whether or not one adds to the grouping the manual workers who act in a supervisory role as foremen or floor managers, or schoolteachers and nurses whose deteriorating salary and conditions have reduced their old security and status, it is obvious that there are increasing numbers, a third or more of the population, who have lost their old class roots and the certainties this gave them.

The effects of class change: partisan de-alignment and electoral volatility

The political effects can be seen in the process of 'partisan de-alignment' which – already apparent in the 1970s (Sarlvik and Crewe, 1983) – has gathered momentum in the current decade. What has happened is that decreasing numbers of electors have their party choice made for them, in terms of solid class position or trade union membership or other social characteristics which combine to push them in a predetermined political direction. Their exposure to new associates and new experiences, as they change from one social or regional location to another, and their concurrent development of new needs and interests, all encourage them to reassess old party commitments and votes – not on a once-and-for-all but on a continuing basis. For the process of social change, once started, is a continuous one, responsive to the dynamics of technological and economic development. This means that electors, once displaced, have little opportunity to settle into a new social location which would bind them once again to a party and a particular point of view. Rather, they are likely to move on both socially and psychologically, and re-assess their party support from election to election.

Such attitudes are reflected amongst the electorate as a whole in the phenomenon of 'electoral volatility' – major changes in party votes from election to election. Labour has been most affected recently by this, dropping nine per cent between the elections of 1979 and 1983. The Conservative vote on the other hand has remained stable. However, such stability is only relative, in the light of long-term decline in the older parties' vote. The Labour and Conservative near-monopoly of the vote in 1951 (when between them they received nearly 97 per cent of the votes cast, with a high turnout of 82.5 per cent) was 73 per cent in 1987, on one of the lowest turnouts of the post-war era (72.7 per cent).

Such a massive withdrawal of confidence from the major parties cannot be exclusively explained through change and social dislocation among electors. That might prompt switches *between* the major parties but not *away* from them. 'Partisan de-alignment', in this sense also stems from the failure of both major parties to halt long-term economic decline, or to ameliorate its consequences in terms of deteriorating public services and acute social and regional disparities – reflected above all in growing unemployment. This has generated disillusion and mistrust among voters which has prompted growing numbers to abstain altogether. Others have begun to look beyond the traditional parties of government to new and untried (but for that reason as yet credible) alternatives.

All this provides opportunities for parties capable of breaking out of the economic impasse, shedding old class images and transcending the old divides along the way. The traditional parties have tried to do this. Mrs Thatcher's policies can be seen as an attempt to swell the numbers of small property-holders and entrepreneurs and to reward their enterprise and willingness to take economic risks. Unfortunately, such initiatives have failed to resolve the fundamental economic problems, while helping to exacerbate class divisions. Neil Kinnock's acceptance of the return of much nationalised industry to private ownership while continuing to stress the need for selective economic intervention and for welfare is a response to the same electoral demands. His pragmatic policies lifted

Labour out of the electoral trough of 1983; it remains to be seen if they offer a better solution to the long-term problems.

The fact that the major parties cannot count on unquestioning support to the extent they formerly did also gives new parties an unrivalled opportunity to profit from government mistakes and any lack of credibility on the part of the official opposition. This advantage was dramatically demonstrated by the Liberal–Social Democratic Alliance's staggering electoral gains in 1983, in face of the muted popularity of the Conservative government and the total lack of credibility of Labour under Michael Foot. At such a conjuncture, the older parties' lack of appeal stems not only from their perceived economic failure but from their association with vanishing social divisions.

Class continuities

Of course, the tendencies towards a breakdown of class barriers are less where society and economy have continued on traditional lines. Within such areas, ways of life are still distinctive as between the different classes, mobility is lower and the intermediate sector has not expanded to the same extent as elsewhere. Hence class consciousness is higher: in Glasgow over three-quarters of electors spontaneously identify with a class compared to slightly over half in London. Here again we find regional and class differences entwined: Scottish images of the English for example, assimilate national and class differences, endowing Scots with all the working-class virtues and vices and seeing the English as inherently middle and upper class.

All this suggests that the changes we have discussed are not spread evenly throughout the population. Class consciousness and class feeling continue in certain 'purer' areas and groups. This is particularly the case as those at the extremes of the class structure have experienced less mobility than others. Britain has managers and administrators drawn heavily from exclusive backgrounds and a lower working class descended from generations in the same position.

A worker in a traditional manual occupation, living in established working-class housing, belonging to an old craft or labouring union, tends to divide up the world in terms of traditional distinctions between 'them', the bosses, and 'us', the working people. Similarly a top manager or professional, living in a middle-class enclave, will blame a unionised workforce for the lamentable state of productivity and industrial discipline, while absolving himself and his fellows from responsibility. This has been the philosophy behind Conservative industrial relations legislation, aimed at restricting the unions legally, on the one hand, and enforcing their responsibility to individual members (through secret ballots) on the other.

Class conflict or class de-alignment in the 1980s?

What is not clear, however, is whether individual union members will act as a restraint on union action when economic conditions improve and firms are again eager to buy off industrial trouble to take advantage of expanding markets. In other words, is the seeming muting of class-based industrial and political action under the Thatcher Governments a permanent change or only a temporary lull induced by the threat of unemployment?

The evidence on this point is conflicting. On the one hand there is no doubt that hostility to the unions and impatience with old class hostilities contributed to the replacement of Labour by the Conservatives in 1979. These widespread feelings were harnessed by the government in their successful confrontations with the steelworkers (1980), railwaymen (1982–83) and miners (1984–85), and were used to justify their restrictive legislation on union picketing and internal balloting – in part a weapon in these struggles and in part a consolidation of the government's victory. The total defeat of the National Union of Mineworkers (NUM) after a year-long strike in 1984–85 was all the more impressive in that the union's left-wing president, Arthur Scargill, couched his rhetoric in terms of the old-style class struggle, while the Nottinghamshire coalfield not only continued working but formed a breakaway 'business' union dedicated to getting a better deal for individual members. This attitude characterises many of the new expanding unions such as EETPU (Electricians, Electronic, Telecommunications and Plumbers' Trade Union). It also seems characteristic of those strategically placed groups, such as the Police Federation and the water workers, which the government has sought to placate because of their stranglehold on vital public services.

Can it be said then that the nature of class divisions, most sharply expressed in trade union militancy, has fundamentally changed, with obvious implications for the wider labour movement and the conduct of party competition? Before answering we have to consider certain pieces of counter-evidence which render the picture more complex than government rhetoric would have us believe. Certainly unions have been restrained by new legislation but even more by declining membership (from just above 12 million in 1980 to just below 10 million in 1985) and their weakened bargaining position. These are above all due to unemployment – people who lose their jobs cease to belong to a union while unions cannot bargain very effectively with employers willing to close down if they are pushed too far.

Nevertheless, as noted above, unions have been quite effective in raising the wages of those in work, that is, of their existing membership, substantially above the rate of inflation. Secondly, the very attempt of government to confront the unions has resulted in an intensification of industrial disputes. The miners' strike of 1984–85 was the longest and most bitter in post-war Britain, with the government openly using courts and police to deter working-class groups mobilised in defence of communities and jobs. In the end public opinion turned against the government, reversing any attempt to capitalise on the victory in electoral terms. Such a bruising confrontation cannot help but raise class consciousness, at least among certain groups, and convince many, not necessarily only miners, that the class struggle is intensifying.

Other unions have learned from the failures of direct confrontation not to refrain from industrial action but to stage a mixture of short disruptive strikes and working to rule, which is much harder to defeat. The long-drawn-out action by schoolteachers (1985–86) forced the government to improve its initial salary offer and helped radicalise this traditionally quiescent profession. The print union,

Sogat, in dispute with the newspaper proprietor Rupert Murdoch, who had sacked all their members, tried a whole series of unconventional tactics, including appeals for public sympathy and support, which have involved many more participants in public demonstrations than before. The dispute was punctuated by a savage riot in Wapping, outside the works, in early 1987, and also gave rise to prolonged legal actions against the union.

Governments' assertiveness in industrial relations thus carries a considerable potential for rebounding on themselves and creating greater problems of public order than ever existed before. Equally threatening from a Conservative point of view is the renewed support of the unions for the Labour Party, as the surest way of reversing their defeats and avoiding even further restrictive measures. We have seen how unions and party have already drawn together in order to retain political funds, which go mainly to Labour. Labour in power would probably retain certain Conservative legislation – it is difficult to argue against secret ballots and greater union democracy for example – but undoubtedly seek to co-operate with unions rather than confront them. As part of a package they would be willing to modify restrictive legislation, particularly on picketing and on union liability for damages arising from disputes.

Restored and re-assertive unions do not necessarily imply more industrial action and greater class militancy. The first stages of union recovery, in the mid-1980s, have been associated with support for a markedly moderate Labour leadership. One cannot, however, ignore the record of major strikes and confrontations with employers and governments (of all political complexions) which have punctuated the last 25 years of British politics and which in various ways provoked the demise of the Labour Governments of Wilson (1964–70) and Callaghan (1976–79), as well as of the Conservative Heath (1970–74). The balance of power has shifted, at least temporarily, to the government under Mrs Thatcher, but the level of confrontation has escalated rather than fallen.

How can one reconcile extensive industrial hostilities with the evidence for a weakening of the class structure and its associated partisan alignments, reviewed above? To understand this we have to appreciate that a developed industrial society like the British is a complex of many different groups and individuals, enmeshed in diverse socio-economic situations. While many of these involve a relaxation of rigid class divisions, working-class groups which continue to perform traditional manual jobs in a relatively isolated social environment will continue to be as class conscious as before. They will react to declining economic circumstances with increasing militancy, as they suspect employers of trying to maintain their profits by reducing the real value of wages.

Although the members of this group constitute a minority (perhaps about a fifth of the electorate), they are of course just the kind of worker to be found in big, large-scale industrial locations. The very nature of their employment helps to define their outlook. They will tend to be miners, car workers, factory workers of all kinds – exactly the location where a strike disrupts the rest of industry. It is significant that the 'set-piece' confrontations of the last two decades involved the miners (1972, 1974, 1984–85), the Ford car workers (1978), the engineering workers (1979) and steel workers (1980). Only the transport strike in the early months of 1979 involved a somewhat different group, centring on the lorry drivers, whose 'service' status renders them less 'traditional' than the others.

Such industrial confrontations are exacerbated by the concentration of another relatively stable class group, the employers and managers, in positions of authority in large enterprises. These are exactly the people whose political attitudes are diametrically opposed to those of class-conscious workers. The very institutions – employers' federations and manual trade unions – which are responsible for industrial relations are dominated by representatives of these groups and tend as a result to adopt quite inflexible tactics against each other. This confrontation then becomes a recipe for industrial unease and unrest.

In the juxtaposition and conflict of these polarised class groups we find an explanation for the likely continuance of industrial trouble in Britain. Though important in their effects, the class attitudes underlying such strife are confined to a minority, but they are nonetheless quite capable of continuing as class barriers break down elsewhere.

It is true that the habit of industrial action spread over the '70s and '80s to sections which had previously avoided it: white-collar workers and professionals in the Civil Service, ancillary workers in the National Health Service, teachers. Here, however, outright withdrawal of labour has been rare, and a variety of forms of non-co-operation practised which have not had the massively disruptive effects of the industrial strikes. If class assimilation involves other groups taking over some of the traditional outlook and behaviour of the working class, increased white-collar militancy paradoxically becomes an indication of the breakdown of class divisions rather than its enhancement.

The growth of white-collar militancy demonstrates that class de-alignment does not necessarily eliminate strikes – it simply changes their nature. Street picketing is replaced by publicity campaigns, total closedown of the establishment is averted as selected groups of members absent themselves from work, while others carry on at a reduced level and continue to draw their pay. Modes of future industrial action may lie away from the public confrontations of the Thatcher era, with their threat of escalating violence, but be no less disruptive because of this. Ultimately, the solution to industrial conflict depends on managers as well as, and perhaps even more than, unions. To the extent that these begin to be drawn from intermediate, less stable class groups like increasing numbers of their workforce, we might expect some increase in understanding and mutual tolerance between the two sides.

This does not automatically happen however, as we can see from the parliamentary parties. In terms of social origins and background, never have the groups been more similar, even as they have increasingly diverged in policy terms. Aristocrats and large industrialists in the ranks of the Conservative Party and its leadership are increasingly balanced by new professions. Gone increasingly, are the Labour MPs of solid working-class origins sponsored by the trade unions – their place taken by professionals and semi-professionals indistinguishable from other parliamentarians.

All MPs, in fact, share a similar middle-class background. Conservative MPs are only slightly more distinguishable in terms of higher income, private education, political connections, more exclusive religious affiliation and private wealth.

Labour MPs come predominantly from intermediate levels, practising the talking professions of teaching and journalism. Conservatives are more likely to originate in the business classes and traditional professions, like medicine and law. Of the present leaders, Neil Kinnock's background is working-class but his career has been (typically) upwardly mobile. As the daughter of a small shopkeeper and university graduate in chemistry, Margaret Thatcher's background is similar to that of many Labour MPs. In one respect, however, her sex, she is of course untypical of the vast majority of MPs of any party.

Electors' preferences and values

The social similarity between parliamentary leaderships leaves us with the task of explaining why more working-class individuals have generally voted Labour and most of the middle-class Conservative (even if this is now declining and some of it is attributable to regional influences). Voting is linked not to what the parties are in terms of social background but to what voters feel they can do for them. Before looking at voting directly, we should explore the preferences electors have and see how they come into being.

Individual preferences are often described as though they were naturally public and political, rather than personal and private. Thus assessment normally begins with attitudes towards the regime and leading national institutions, such as Parliament and monarchy, democratic processes, and the rule of law. All these receive widespread endorsement from the British population. It is worthwhile noting, however, that while the British are proud of their political institutions they are also capable of appraising the performance of governments coolly and realistically: 29 per cent of schoolchildren in one sample felt the government can on occasion do more harm than good, and even at the height of wartime success in 1944, 57 per cent of adults felt that politicians were either out for themselves or for their party (Dennis, Lindberg, McCrone 1971).

General attitudes of this kind obviously have importance for the climate in which politics is conducted, but do not directly affect party support. To relate this to electors' concerns we have to examine demands more closely linked to immediate political action.

On these, recent studies have identified two sets of considerations underlying reactions to the immediate issues of party politics, in so far as the latter can be identified through survey questions. The first relates to a more equal distribution of wealth and opportunity. This is associated with support for the Welfare State. It can thus be seen as an assertion of socialist, egalitarian ideals against more hierarchical, Conservative ones. A majority supports redistribution and more extended welfare, even at the cost of higher taxes.

The other general considerations used in judging specific political proposals are support for traditional moral and cultural values against permissiveness and alternative life styles. This involves opposition to abortion and sexual licence and by extension, disapproval of immigration and its unknown effects on British society. Here a majority of electors are for tradition and against change. (Robertson 1984: 133–39). The distribution of support on egalitarianism and welfare obviously favours Labour but on the second dimension of traditionalism it favours the Conservatives, thus leaving open the question of which will have the advantage in a particular election. In a broader sense, we can see majority attitudes in both areas as involving a suspicion of change except where it is immediately beneficial. We will see below how this works in detail to determine the casting of votes and the electoral victory of one major party over the other (Tables 4.3 and 4.4 below). So far the Alliance is not seen by most electors as having a particularly clear position on either egalitarianism or traditionalism, and political judgements still tend to be made in terms of the two established parties. The Alliance only gains in where both of these are for some reason unappealing.

Generally, one gets the impression that electors think in terms of goals to be achieved rather than specific policies to be adopted. The latter are the concern of governments, and electors evaluate their success in terms of reaching the 'obvious' agreed objectives of egalitarianism or traditional morality than by how they have sought to attain them. To gain some inkling of what electors think the most important goals of public policy should be, we can look at replies to general survey questions on important problems facing the country and the individual.

Overwhelmingly (to a level of 70 per cent) answers to general queries stress economic concerns – cost of living, prices and employment – as the ones which are central. Housing, rising crime and the problems associated with immigration are also emphasised, but less heavily (an average level of 20 per cent or below). All replies are concrete and immediate-relating to prices for the week's shopping, the adequacy of incomes to meet them, and the comfort and safety of the home environment. They are the factors which most closely affect the day-to-day existence of individuals and families within their local community. General national concerns such as defence, or abstract causes such as aid to the under-developed countries to the Third World, scarcely figure at all (rarely attracting endorsements of more than 10 per cent).

Participation

The impression that people's central concerns are their own and their families' well-being receives further support from a study of political participation carried out with a nationwide sample of electors in 1984–85 (Parry, Moyser and Day unpublished papers, 1986). Three-quarters of the respondents saw their political activity affecting themselves or their family 'very much' or 'quite a lot', compared to 56 per cent who thought that it affected the country as a whole. Eighty-five per cent reported themselves as voting in the general election and 68.8 per cent as voting in most local elections (much higher incidentally than the proportions of electors who actually turned out on these occasions). Apart from voting, the highest levels of participation were reported for contacting MPs (9.7 per cent), local councillors (20.7 per cent) or local bureaucrats (17.7 per cent). These encounters were highly likely to cover personal or family problems, with housing taking pride of place. Protest activities such as signing a petition (63.3 per cent) or attending a meeting (14.6 per cent) were also likely to centre on local and environmental problems, as were the group activities involving 11–14 per cent of the respondents.

These examples show that political participation is more widespread than has been thought, but also that it is heavily focused on alleviating personal or local problems, probably highly specific in nature. More general interest and concern is limited. Places on public bodies are restricted in number so it is not particularly surprising that elective councillors and MPs constitute less than half of one per cent of the adult population. Voluntary participation in party and other political work is also limited. Individual membership in a political party (often nominal to the extent of being in arrears with subscriptions) extends at most to five per cent of the population; the proportion engaged in active political work, whether within or outside the established parties, is certainly lower. While almost three-quarters of registered electors turned out to vote in the general election of 1987, it is an exceptional local election which attracts as much as 40 per cent. The first direct election for the European Parliament in June 1979, an occasion of considerable political significance, attracted only 32 per cent of electors, which was hardly bettered in the second election of June 1984.

If politics do not predominate, what does concern British electors? Evidence on the primacy of personal and family goals comes from surveys on 'the quality of British life' carried out in the mid-1970s. Asked what the quality of life meant to them personally, the largest single number (23 per cent) referred to family and the home, with another 10 per cent mentioning friends and neighbours. Sixteen per cent stressed traditional values and priorities, among which bringing up children held pride of place. Half the sample therefore spontaneously mentioned traditional family-centred concerns.

These were not challenged by any of the qualities mentioned by the other half of the sample. Eighteen per cent mentioned money and the cost of living, and 17 per cent their basic standard of living (in the sense of obtaining adequate necessities). While clearly worried about their material circumstances, such electors could be equally concerned for their families as for themselves. Certainly very few wanted to improve their personal standard of living (only 3.5 per cent wanted more consumer durables, luxuries or more extravagant ways of enjoying themselves). Support for these conclusions comes also from a survey of London electors interviewed in the early 1960s, at a high point of post-war prosperity, which tried to establish the complete range of their overall values and aspirations. Out of eight possible concerns into which answers were classified (public-political, social status, moral, family-centred, basic health, monetary, technical and educational), personal goals came overwhelmingly first. Eighty-six per cent put basic health among their leading three concerns, while 80 per cent put family and friends. Public or political interests were mentioned first by only 6 per cent and money was rated as a leading objective by just 19 per cent. Technical expertise was valued highly by a third, and social status by only slightly less, while morality was a leading preoccupation for a quarter. Education similarly concerned one-fifth.

These rankings are perhaps not surprising, but they are of great interest in showing which personal concerns predominate. The well-being of family and friends is paramount. While basic health attracted slightly more attention, it was clear from the context of the replies that this was directed more to nature than to the National Health Service. Most people worried about the consequences of a fatal or crippling illness rather than about the quality of the medical care they would get if it occurred. This is confirmed by replies on basic aspirations from a national survey carried out in 1980: people's strongest motivation was to provide a better life for their family, while there was an equally strong desire for the children to do better in life (*The Times*, 26 June 1980). The solidarity of families is also attested by the enormous extent to which children continue to model themselves on their parents. Friends and media influence their leisure and clothes, but basic beliefs and values are derived from parents.

On this evidence, government will most clearly meet the wishes of electors when they serve the needs of the family, and of kinship and friendship networks. How can they best do so? The concern with health gives one pointer: towards adequate medical services. The earlier evidence we have cited also shows electors to be strongly (though not exclusively) concerned with the economic well-being of the family unit, with the effects of prices and inflation and unemployment. They say so repeatedly when asked about important problems. It is just possible that in their aspirations for their family, they could be equally greedy and unrealistic as if they simply pursued individual advantage. That their economic expectations are inflated is asserted by commentators who see Britain's current problems as aggravated by the 'overloading' of governments with far too many problems and concerns. According to them, post-war electors in Britain as in other developed countries have demanded ever-expanding help and financial aid from governments. Since they will not be re-elected if they do not comply, policy-makers have expanded the range of government services far beyond practicable limits, with a consequent decline in administrative efficiency (as most of the problems they face are insoluble anyway). The remedy of the 'new right' to some extent followed by the Thatcher governments has been to 'unload' government by selling off nationalised industries, and encouraging private health and welfare services, and using the savings to reduce taxes. The rather homely nature of British electors' concerns does not however fit this picture of vaulting aspirations for ever-increasing government provision. Nor does their mild scepticism about government competence. The most relevant evidence comes from studies of the relationship between government economic performance and voting intentions (as recorded by the polling agencies). These give the reactions of electors in aggregate to upsurges in prosperity and downturns in recession. Possibly the most striking finding is that electors punish governments for economic downturns by changing their intention to vote for them (or at least many electors do). But greater prosperity does not attract votes to anything like the same extent. Governments are not, in other words, rewarded for giving the population more, but get sharp adverse reactions when they give them much less.

Such behaviour is obviously not a product of rising popular expectations. It is simply aimed at retaining the present standard of living rather than constantly expanding it. Further evidence for this is found in the tendency of electors to downgrade their expectations in the face of bad economic performance, to accept in the face of rising inflation that their standard of living will get slightly worse, and to recognise that governments can do little to affect it. All they ask under these conditions is that the situation does not deteriorate markedly – in which case, understandably, the government experiences widespread losses in voting support.

Electors' private preferences therefore relate primarily to the stability and well-being of the family and of its relatives and friends. They are much more anxious to preserve it from disruption (whether through financial troubles, bad housing or neighbourhood changes) than to raise its standards and ambitions to any very marked degree, though they have hopes in the long term for their children. Obviously immediate benefits and improvements will not be spurned – in some cases they may be essential to prevent family disruption, where living conditions are very bad. Nonetheless, a prevailing impression is of electors struggling to preserve what they have, and initially suspicious of change because they expect things to get worse rather than better. They have certainly been encouraged to believe so by most of the social and economic forecasts of the last decade.

Social influences on electors' preferences

What shapes these private concerns of electors, and what consequences do they have for political processes? The first question is easily answered. In spite of an escalating divorce rate and the publicity given to marital breakdown, the family is still the main agency through which individuals orientate themselves to the world. Not surprisingly, a major value inculcated by this experience is of the importance of the mutual bonds binding its members and of the necessity of preserving them from undue strain. These are lessons which prevail regardless of class, milieu, or region of origin. Even single individuals continue to be oriented to the parental family, and most of those divorced start a new one or at least retain their children within a truncated family unit.

Class, region and other social influences enter at a later stage, that of defining the family's needs in light of its social conditions. Low-income families have as their most obvious need some improvement in their material standards. Families in better circumstances may be more concerned with crime and social problems in the neighbourhood, which particularly affect their children's upbringing. Where both financial and environmental problems are less immediate, declining moral standards and a lessening respect for authority may seem to constitute the major threat to family well-being.

There is no evidence of any manipulation or distortion of individual's natural preferences by outside bodies. Indeed, all the evidence points to the inability of the press or television to affect individuals' basic outlook and values, which are directly derived from parents within the family. Anti-social attitudes and behaviour stem primarily from broken or deprived families rather than from media influences, though where the break-up has already occurred television may give pointers to anti-social action.

Different social locations point the common concern with family security in different directions – towards diverse perceived needs and preferences. Translating family needs into policy terms is not straightforward. If the prime need is for greater material support, how does this facilitate a voting choice between incomes policy and free collective bargaining, especially when both are advocated as the quickest way to greater prosperity and economic specialists disagree about their effects? If an elector wants to avert the decline of an inner-city neighbourhood, does he choose more immigration plus money for inner-city renewal, or less of both? Are declining moral standards to be redressed by greater censorship, and restrictions on divorce and abortion, or is political action counter-productive within this area?

In assuming that electors can make an easy jump from their private preferences to the public policy options available, most discussions of voting and party competition (not to mention other forms of political action) make a great mistake. It has proved difficult even for highly trained specialists to weigh up the costs and benefits of such relatively simple choices as the site for a third London airport. Lacking their skills and resources, electors cannot even hope to translate their need to increase family income, for example, into the economic alternatives being urged. If British democracy works in the sense of citizens being able to select party policy alternatives on the basis of their own needs, it must be through some kind of simplification which relates the party programme they choose at elections to their personal situation, at least in the long term.

Party competition

The way the parties present their policies is crucial to simplifying public choices in a relevant way. At least in the period since the 1920s, major British parties have avoided direct arguments about the merits of their own policies or demerits of their rivals'. Instead their election manifestos, detailing the party record in government and future programmes, talk about policies and problems almost as if the other parties did not exist. Reading the manifestos put out by different sides for a campaign leads to a delusion that several quite different elections are taking place, so radically do their definitions of the situation differ!

The reason for the contrast is the different emphasis placed by rival politicians on different policy areas. Table 4.2 shows these in terms of the average percentage of sentences in the Conservative and Labour election manifestos devoted to each of 26 broad topics. Apart from references to social services (where, however, Labour supports their expansion and Conservatives advocate economy and more efficient administration), the parties clearly differ in the attention they pay to various areas. The Conservatives stress the importance of the Commonwealth, regional priorities, individual enterprise and efficient administration much more than Labour. Conversely Labour emphasises a controlled economy, social justice (i.e. equality) and support for international co-operation.

These differences closely reflect the divergent ideologies of the parties. Labour focuses on central government planning, basic services and equality. Conservatives stress government economy, decentralisation and individual

Table 4.2 Mean percentage of sentences devoted to each broad area of policy by Conservative and Labour manifestos, 1924–87

Areas of policy	Labour (%)	Conservative (%)
Empire, special foreign relationships	1.5	4.3
Decolonisation	2.0	1.0
Regionalism	1.1	3.2
Freedom	0.3	3.0
Enterprise	1.4	9.3
Democracy, constitutionalism	3.4	3.1
Controlled economy	11.5	1.0
Economic planning	7.6	1.7
Regulation	2.0	3.2
Labour groups	3.8	1.9
Agriculture, farmers	4.0	5.3
Other minority groups	1.5	2.2
Culture	1.8	1.8
Economic stability	8.5	6.1
Protectionism	1.2	3.8
Productivity	4.0	3.7
National effort	0.4	0.5
Social justice	4.3	0.9
Technology	2.2	3.2
Conservation	1.3	1.3
Military	1.6	3.2
Government performance	1.5	7.1
Incentives	0.5	4.5
Peace	4.3	2.6
Social services	17.5	15.3
Internationalism	9.2	6.0

enterprise. Clearly, therefore, the contrasting emphases of the rival manifestos are deliberate. British parties compete for votes by highlighting those issues which they think will appeal to electors and on which they are more likely to be associated with a generally approved course of action. Conversely they ignore issues on which they think their competitors might have the advantage. Selective emphasis, rather than direct confrontation, is the essence of party competition in Britain – a tendency exaggerated by the mass media both for simplicity of presentation and more dramatic impact. Selective emphases are also the tactics employed by Liberals and the SDP – not that the positions of these parties will have much direct effect so long as they appear moderate. Before they develop a stronger image of their own through actual association with government, third parties will gain more from the lack of attractiveness of Labour and Conservatives than from the positive inducements they themselves can offer.

Electors' voting decisions

How do parties' selective emphases ease the translation electors make between their personal and family need for more money or a better environment, and the public alternatives available to them? Or do the parties' selective emphases distort individual preferences and make them appear other than they actually are?

The parties' presentation certainly simplifies electoral choice. For the parties discuss issues as if they fitted neatly into a number of sharply separated areas, in each of which there exists an obvious policy of 'betterment' which one party is more qualified to tackle than the other (taking the choice as lying between Conservative and Labour). Because electors are at the receiving end of the whole simplifying process as relayed through the media, they divide current issues into 'areas' or 'problems' which are even broader and more basic than the ones used in the manifestos. Table 4.3 lists the fourteen problem areas into which British electors generally classify the specific issues which confront them in national elections. Issues regarded as falling within one area are judged as though they had no implications for others.

These broad policy areas do not interest electors equally. More are affected by welfare and redistribution of wealth than by government regulation of monopolies; crime in the streets has also a more general impact than foreign affairs. Whether an issue, once it comes up in an election, causes large, medium or small numbers of electors to shift their vote is indicated in the third column of Table 4.3.

Table 4.3 Areas into which electors classify issues

Broad policy area	Specific issues corresponding to each area	Extent of impact	Favoured party
1 Civil order	Law and order; measures against crime; death penalty; rioting; strikes and demonstrations; anti-system parties and problems caused by their strength	Large	Conservative
2 Constitutional	Questions involving established institutions (e.g. monarchy, Parliament and relations between them); democracy; civil rights	Medium	Conservative
3 Foreign relationships	Membership of NATO and other foreign alliances; détente; attitude to Communist powers; membership of EC; national prestige abroad; colonies and decolonisation; overseas aid; attitudes to war and peace	Small	Conservative or Labour depending on circumstances
4 Defence	Military spending increases or reductions; importance vis-à-vis other policy areas; nuclear arms	Small	Conservative
5 Candidate	Likes and dislikes about candidates; leading candidates performance	Variable	Labour or Conservative depending on circumstances

6 Government record and prospects	Current financial situation and prospects; expectations; economic prosperity, depression, inflation; government corruption, inefficiency; satisfaction with government in general	Variable	Labour or Conservative depending on circumstances
7 Traditional	Support of traditional/Christian morals and Church; abortion and birth control; temperance; religious schools and education	Large	Conservative
8 Ethnic	Immigration and foreign workers; attitudes to minority groups and their advancement; discrimination; school and housing integration; language questions	Large	Conservative
9 Regional	National unity; devolution and regional autonomy; regional equalisation of resources	Large	Conservative
10 Urban/rural	Farmers and rural interests; agricultural subsidies	Small	Conservative
11 Socio-economic redistribution	Social service spending; importance of social welfare; housing as a problem; housing subsidies; rent control; health and medical services; social reform; pensions; aid to other services such as education; action in regard to unemployment; full employment, employment guarantee	Large	Labour
12 Government control and planning	Nationalisation; state control of the economy; general government power and control; management and regulation of environment	Small	Conservative
13 Government intervention in favour of small businessmen	Action against monopolies; big business power, trade union power; protectionism and free trade	Small	Conservative
14 Individual initiative and freedom	Closed shop and action in relation to it; incentives; level of taxation; support for free enterprise economics	Small	Conservative

Not all of these areas will be relevant in any one election, of course (see Table 4.4 below). Typically, electors are confronted with four or five important issues, each of which fits into one of the broad policy areas.

How does the emergence of an issue affect party fortunes? This depends on which party is seen as 'best' in the area to which the issue belongs. To decide this we must return to the question of personal needs. The evidence points to electors' overwhelming concern with personal and family security. This renders them cautious on the whole and rather pessimistic in their expectations about social

Table 4.4 Issues in British general elections, 1950–87

Election date	Specific issues important in campaign	Broad policy area*	Extent of impact	Party favoured	Estimated net gains from issues Conservative (% vote)	Labour (% vote)
1950	Military threat from USSR	4 Defence	Small	+ Con.		
	Attlee as successful PM	5 Candidate	Medium	+ Lab.		
	Churchill as inspiring alternative leader	5 Candidate	Medium	+ Con.		
	Cost of living, unemployment	6 Govt. record	Medium	– Lab.		
	Achievement of welfare state	11 Redistribution	Large	+ Lab.		
	Nationalisation of steel	12 Control	Small	+ Con.	+ 3.6	+ 2.7
1951	Fear of 'cold war', desire for peace	3 Foreign	Small	+ Lab.		
	Attlee as successful PM	5 Candidate	Medium	+ Lab.		
	Churchill as inspiring alternative leader	5 Candidate	Large	+ Con.		
	Cost of living, unemployment	6 Govt. record	Large	– Lab.		
	Housing shortages	11 Redistribution	Large	+ Lab.		
	Nationalisation	12 Control	Small	+ Con.	+ 3.6	+ 2.7
1955	Eden as successful government minister	5 Candidate	Medium	+ Con.		
	Attlee as successful former PM	5 Candidate	Small	+ Lab.		
	Economic prosperity	6 Govt. record	Large	+ Con.	+ 4.5	+ 0.9
1959	Post Imperial defence. Unilateral disarmament	4 Defence	Small	+ Con.		
	Macmillan's confidence and performance since became PM	5 Candidate	Medium	+ Con.		
	Economic growth and prosperity	6 Govt. record	Large	+ Con.		
	Pensions increases	11 Redistribution	Large	+ Lab.		
	Nationalisation	12 Control	Small	– Lab.		
	Tax reductions	14 Initiative	Small	+ Con.	+ 6.3	+ 1.8

Year	Issue description	Issue	Size	Direction		
1964	Deployment East of Suez	4 Defence	Small	+ Con.		
	Wilson as inspiring alternative PM	5 Candidate	Medium	+ Lab.		
	Balance of Payments	6 Govt. record	Medium	− Con.		
	Legislation on immigration	3 Ethnic	Large	+ Con.	+ 1.8	+ 2.7
	Housing shortages, pension extensions, health, education	11 Redistribution	Large	+ Lab.		
	Nationalisation	12 Control	Small	− Lab.		
	Trade union powers	13 Intervention	Small	− Lab.		
1966	Entry to the EC	3 Foreign	Small	+ Lab.		
	Wilson as sound PM	5 Candidate	Medium	+ Lab.		
	Aversion of immediate balance of payments crisis	6 Govt. record	Large	+ Lab.	0	+ 7.2
	Social service improvements	11 Redistribution	Large	+ Lab.		
	Trade union powers	13 Intervention	Small	− Lab.		
1970	Opposition to the EC	3 Foreign	Small	+ Lab.		
	Wilson as best PM available	5 Candidate	Small	+ Lab.		
	Price rises, wage freeze	6 Govt. record	Large	− Lab.		
	Control of immigration	8 Ethnic	Large	+ Con.	+ 3.6	+ 1.8
	Housing shortages, shortfalls in social services	11 Redistribution	Large	+ Lab.		
	High level of taxation	14 Initiative	Small	+ Con.		
1974 (Feb)	'Who governs Britain?'	2 Constitutional	Medium	+ Con.		
	Entry to the EC	3 Foreign	Small	− Con.		
	Heath as confrontationist maladroit PM	5 Candidate	Medium	− Con.		
	Industrial relations, rising prices, wage freeze	6 Govt. record	Large	− Con.	− 3.6	− 3.6
	Disunity of Labour Party	6 Govt. record	Small	− Lab.		
	Nationalisation	12 Control	Small	− Lab.		
	Miners' strike	13 Intervention	Small	− Lab.		

Table 4.4 (Cont.)

Election date	Specific issues important in campaign	Broad policy area*	Extent of impact	Party favoured	Estimated net gains from issues Conservative (% vote)	Labour (% vote)
1974 (Oct)	Entry to the EC	3 Foreign	Small	– Con.		
	Heath as unsuccessful PM	5 Candidate	Medium	– Lab.		
	Settlement of industrial troubles, prices: higher wages	6 Govt. record	Small	– Con.		
	Housing shortages and promised remedies: social legislation	11 Redistribution	Large	+ Lab.		
	Nationalisation	12 Control	Small	– Lab.	– 2.7	+ 1.8
1979	Reform in law on picketing: fighting increased crime	1 Civil order	Large	+ Con.		
	Fair deal for UK from EC	3 Foreign	Small	+ Lab.		
	Competence and moderation of Callaghan (Lab. PM)	5 Candidate	Small	+ Lab.		
	Firmness of Mrs Thatcher (Conservative leader)	5 Candidate	Small	+ Con.		
	Breakdown of incomes policy; government vacillation: unemployment and inflation	6 Govt. record	Medium	– Lab.		
	Extension of government bureaucracy and regulation	12 Govt. control	Small	+ Con.		
	Power of trade unions, need for reform	13 Intervention	Small	+ Con.		
	High level of taxation, increase in individual initiative	14 Initiative	Small	+ Con.	+ 6.3	0

1983					
Assertion of British interests abroad, in particular success in regaining Falklands	3 Foreign	Small	+ Con.		
Divisions over defence policy, unilateralism	4 Defence	Small	– Lab.		
Firmness and sincerity of Mrs Thatcher as Prime Minister	5 Candidate	Large	+ Con.	+6.3	
Lack of credibility of Michael Foot (Labour Leader) as alternative PM Government competence	5 Candidate	Large	– Lab.		
Reduction of inflation	6 Govt. record	Large	+ Con.		
Labour divisions between left and right	6 Govt. prospects	Large	– Lab.		
Trade union unpopularity	13 Govt. intervention	Small	– Lab.	–7.2	
1987					
Unilateralism, retention of American nuclear bases and British deterrent.	4 Defence	Small	+ Con.	+4.5	
Prosperity, good management, reduced social services, privatisation	6 Govt. record	Large	+ Con.		
	1 Redistribution	Large	+ Lab.	+2.7	
	14 Initiative	Small	Con.		

* The numbers attached to each broad policy area are those given in table 4.3.

and political change. The large-scale upheavals of the post-war period (urban renewal and resettlement, unemployment and industrial uncertainty, immigration, technological change) have all disrupted settled patterns of behaviour, including traditional family relationships. These have been further undermined by political enactments which have made divorce easier and removed children more from parental control.

Electors are being reasonable, therefore, in expecting proposals for change, except where they produce immediate material benefits, to carry adverse consequences for their security. Their fear of change points out an obviously desirable goal within each area. Law and order should be maintained, the constitution respected, Britain should continue to be strong abroad, living standards guaranteed, traditional moral values upheld, government interference resisted, personal freedom defended, and so on. With its emphasis on maintaining traditional morality and the established structure of society, the Conservative Party has generally been associated with these 'obvious' policies in most areas and has gained the electoral advantage when they become important.

This is not true of all issue areas, however – otherwise Britain would not have a competitive party system. In the field of welfare and redistributive legislation (i.e. policies which take money and resources from the more wealthy to spend for the benefit of those less well off), the electors who stand to gain constitute a large majority of the population. Since the material benefits are concrete and immediate, electors as we have seen tend to favour more redistribution and more welfare. When these issues have become important, they have pushed electors towards the Labour Party, which is clearly associated with such policies.

No one party has a record of consistent success in foreign affairs or in smooth running of government, nor do they have a monopoly of attractive candidates who might become the Prime Minister. Hence these issues are not permanently associated with either major party but are credited to one or the other depending on the particular circumstances of each election. The fourth column of Table 4.3 shows which parties are credited with the best policies in which area and the possibility both have of gaining credit on foreign affairs, candidates and government record. Of course, such assignments are changing with the growth of other political alternatives. Nevertheless since the SDP and Liberals are not yet associated with a clear record, electors in the late 1980s still make their main decisions on the basis of Labour and Conservative appeals, voting Liberal or SDP if they find the major parties equally unattractive.

Since Labour and Conservatives have been evenly balanced electorally, the crucial winning votes have gone to the one most favoured by the important issues of the campaign. As Table 4.4 shows, the balance of issue advantages has swung between parties over the post-war period. Although the majority of issues which might potentially emerge favour the Conservative Party, the record shows that redistributive and welfare questions are so centrally important that they appear in most elections, thus redressing the situation in favour of Labour.

What contribution to change is made by electors' reactions to important issues? Overall, a large-impact issue such as civil order, or welfare and redistribution, when it emerges in an election, produces a net change of about 2.7 per cent in favour of the party to which it 'belongs'. This is a net change, concealing reciprocal movements of votes between the major parties themselves, and between each major party and the non-voters and third parties. A medium-impact issue (for example one affecting the constitution) produces a net change of about 1.8 per cent, and a small-impact issue a net change of about 0.9 per cent.

Using these figures we can actually state what overall changes in voting will be produced by a given set of campaign issues, by adding up the net changes which each issue salient in the election will produce. These overall gains and losses are shown in Table 4.4. In 1987 for example, the Conservatives gained 4.5 per cent of their vote of 42.2 per cent from the issues prominent in the campaign.

In spite of the crucial importance of the 'floating voter', it remains true that only a minority of electors are sensitive to campaign issues. Personal and social circumstances render one policy area of paramount and enduring importance to most of them. For example, an unskilled labourer in the North of England, hovering on the fringe of the poverty line, is likely to be concerned with welfare benefits to the exclusion of all else. Unswayed by any issues coming up in a particular election, such a person votes Labour consistently, since in all conceivable circumstances Labour will extend welfare more than the Conservatives, and this is crucial to the well-being both of himself and his family. For equally understandable reasons, a high-status professional in the South of England tends to vote Conservative all the time.

Social circumstances may in this way give such a clear indication of the type of policy beneficial to the family that choice between public alternatives becomes relatively simple. The enduring concern of most electors with a particular policy area explains two notable features of British elections. One is the relationship between voting choice and class: in 1983 a plurality of manual workers voted Labour and a majority of non-manual workers voted Conservative. These proportions were higher in earlier elections. As we have noted, some of this is a regional rather than a pure class effect. The importance of both factors, however, stems from their influence in 'fixating' most electors on certain policy areas by rendering these of prime importance for the individual and his family.

Such electors then cast a consistent vote for a particular party, thus explaining a second feature of elections: the great stability of voting choice revealed by all election surveys. In May 1979 86 per cent of Labour voters recalled voting Labour in October 1974 and 67 per cent of Conservative voters recalled voting Conservative at that time. Such electors were choosing in terms of a consistent policy preference which endured regardless of the particular circumstances of each of these years. In this way they contribute to a stable basic vote which each major party can expect to receive even in the absence of favourable issues in a particular campaign. This was at the level of 42 per cent of the total national vote for Labour and 41 per cent for the Conservatives up to the beginning of the 1970s. In the course of the next two decades it declined to 28 per cent for Labour and between 37 and 38 per cent for Conservatives – a radical 'de-alignment' of major party support. This reflects the influence discussed above of greater affluence, the break-up of old class divisions, and the greater importance of regional location. These changes have altered personal and family circumstances to the extent that enduring policy interests are no longer apparent to so many electors, whose sensitivity to the effects of issues in each campaign is thus greatly enhanced. Obviously these have weakened the Labour Party more than the Conservatives. The fall-off in these basic votes also means that many more electors are volatile in the sense of being willing to contemplate support for the Liberals, SDP or the various nationalist alternatives, which in turn makes it possible that third parties will in the future hold the decisive Commons votes, as in the Parliament of 1974–79.

Other British elections

So far we have confined our discussion to general, i.e. national British elections, ignoring the two other types of regular election held in Britain. These are local elections (held every three years to elect district and regional councillors respectively) and elections to the Parliament of the EC. In both, voters react in essentially the same way as in general elections. The British government is more visible and familiar to the majority of electors than either the local or European bodies, about whose exact powers they are unclear. This is partly due to the prominence given in the British press and television to the doings of the national government, which is true even for local newspapers and programmes. It is also due to the fact that practically all the candidates in the other elections are associated with the parties represented in the British Parliament.

As a result electors react to candidates in local and European elections very much in terms of how their party is performing in the national government (or in opposition to it). Since most British governments are buffeted by economic circumstances and have to impose restrictive measures, elections at the local and European level tend to go against the governing party. Increasingly during the lifetime of a British government, control in the localities passes into the hands of opposition parties, adding to its difficulties in getting compliance with its policies. We shall discuss this phenomenon in Chapter 6.

National issues thus push electors sensitive to campaign circumstances into changing their previous vote. Many electors, as in general elections, always vote for the party pointed out by their social circumstances as best on the issue most imortant to them. The salient issues at local elections – in spite of the efforts of Liberals and nationalists to inject other concerns – centre round increases in rates (the local property tax) and extensions to welfare by providing more subsidised housing for those less well-off. The basic vote for the Conservatives thus consists predominantly of taxpayers who own their homes, and the basic vote for Labour of the tenants of council-owned and subsidised housing. In the major cities this has given Labour an advantage, while in rural and suburban areas with a predominance of owner-occupiers, the Conservatives have been permanently in power. Recent Conservative successes in forcing local authorities to sell council-owned houses to sitting tenants can be seen as a bold attempt to redress the electoral balance in their own favour even in traditional areas of Labour strength.

The directly elected European Parliament established in 1979 is relatively unknown to most electors. This is particularly so as its relationship to the executive bodies of the EC is unclear. Reactions to candidates tend to be shaped by reactions to national parties and governments. This widespead confusion about what the parliament is and what it does led to most electors not bothering to vote in the two elections of 1979 and 1984. Local elections also have a low turnout. This compares with the approximately three-quarters of electors who vote in general elections when the issues are well publicised and the outcome seems important.

The different reactions at the various levels may disappoint the local patriot and the fervent European. They are perfectly understandable given the information electors have and the varying importance of the outcomes. Local and European elections are less likely to lead to significant change than the general election.

It does seem, therefore, that the British make sensible and understandable decisions when presented with the opportunity of choosing between political parties in elections. Admittedly this involves some simplification of the complex realities. Specific policies are overlooked, long-term linkages are made between particular parties and broad issue areas, and interconnections between the latter are ignored. Choices are made in terms of the importance of the issue area, either its enduring importance to the individual or (for a minority where the importance of an issue is not obviously determined by their personal situation) its centrality in the campaign itself. Nevertheless such simplifications are not distortions, and they are closely related to the way the parties choose to present themselves.

Elite manipulation or electoral autonomy?

This very fact has produced criticism that the parties mislead electors to their own advantage, by persuading them to oversimplify politics and ignore radical solutions to the real problems facing the country. To see how far such criticism is justified, we have to consider several interrelated points. The first is that electors' concern with personal and family security itself causes them to distrust radical solutions which bring the possibility of disruption and change. Their reaction to Conservative and Labour extremism in the early 1980s was not to support it but to desert these parties. Distrust of radicalism is, moreover, based on a family-centred outlook which seems perfectly natural and not imposed on electors by media advertising or party propaganda.

Are the real political problems (in the Marxist interpretation, questions of the unequal distribution of power and wealth) hidden from electors by the fact that the parties never raise them? We have noted that socio-economic redistribution is one of the basic principles on which electors base their judgements and constitutes one of the commonest issues in British national elections (see Table 4.4). And the Labour and Conservative parties do differentiate themselves noticeably on this and other issues (see Table 4.2). It is understandable and not 'false consciousness' on their part, that many electors concern themselves with general prosperity, rising crime rates or immigration – issues which can have an immediate concrete impact on family circumstances – rather than with remote and problematic questions of the distribution of power.

The issues which have been important in elections of the post-war period are, moreover, closely related to central problems or achievements of the time. The restrictions and controls of the immediate post-war period, along with the threat from the cold war, were replaced by reactions to the growing prosperity of the 1950s, and then by concern with Britain's faltering economic progress and the social problems of the affluent society over the last twenty years. Major decisions, such as restrictions of union power and entry to the EC, are fully emphasised (see again Table 4.4). Thus real questions of pressing importance do seem to be raised by the parties and voted on by electors.

Given all this, does party propaganda nevertheless lead electors to oversimplify and miss the connections between different areas of politics, such as a link between the present power set-up, economic sluggishness, and bad social conditions? The problem is that the existence or non-existence of such a link and its exact form is hotly disputed by theorists and specialists. No obvious connections between policy areas exist, even for sophisticated decision-makers. So action on one area has to be planned without regard to its effects on another, since it is not known what the effects will be. Electors who simplify by dividing policies into broad areas which they assume to be sharply separated, are not stupid nor are they necessarily misled. It is difficult to see what other basis they could use for evaluating public policies comprehensively and easily, or for holding decision-makers accountable.

The election victory of one British party over the others does, on this evidence, genuinely mirror electoral reactions to issues of central importance. It is not decided on the basis of a 'politicians' ramp' which leaves all major questions to be decided elsewhere. Whether such reactions then get translated into effective government policy is another matter, related to the institutional arrangements discussed in the two preceding chapters.

Chapter 5
The mass media

The conclusion of the last chapter, that genuine issues are presented to electors and voted on in elections, is so central to an assessment of British democracy and so important in discussing what should be done about current problems (see Chapter 11) that it requires further examination. This must focus on the mass media – the press, radio and television – because it is through these that issues are presented to the public, and electoral reactions reported to politicians and parties. The media thus channel the major flow of political information between electors and parties, particularly through their news reports and comments – not only on overtly political matters but also on the major social, economic and international issues of the day.

How far in fact do these become issues *because* the media choose to emphasise them – rather than having an objective impact of their own? Electors may well evaluate the issues presented to them quite sensibly and intelligently on the basis of the information that they have. But is that the most relevant and best information – and would they decide differently if the issues were presented another way, or if different issues were emphasised?

In the past, analysts and commentators tended to regard the British media (with the notable exception of mass-circulation newspapers) as a fairly impartial means of transmission for diverse opinions and views – a concrete embodiment of the 'free marketplace of ideas' so valued by theorists of democracy. Indeed, great efforts to demonstrate total neutrality were made – particularly by the BBC in the '50s and '60s – by enforcing a strict rationing of time for the expression of opposing views. This particularly applied to coverage of the two major parties during election campaigns.

As party competition, particularly in the '80s, has become more combative and abrasive, so increasing criticism has focused on the means by which it is transmitted, since coverage is increasingly interpreted as favouring one side or another. The critiques of the media take various forms, but most opprobrium is directed at their alleged lack of objectivity. Television, radio and the press are accused by the left of being biased against the Labour Party in particular and socialists in general, as well as women, and ethnic and sexual minorities. On the right, the criticism is as vocal, the main targets being media 'permissiveness', i.e. a bias in favour of centrist, consensus politics. Such an alleged bias extends beyond party politics and political issues to media ownership, control and management, and to the official and unofficial links between incumbent governments and media managers. Much of this chapter will be devoted to an analysis of these, especially of ways in which the interests of particular governments are reflected in actual media performance. Before proceeding however we need to look in more detail at the actual structure and position of the British mass media in the late 1980s.

Organisation, ownership and control

Perhaps their most striking feature, already noted in Chapter 4, is the relatively high degree of centralisation. Most people who read newspapers read national dailies with London editorial bases. The readership of these papers is shown in Table 5.1.

Sunday papers also have a national mass readership. With the exception of the peripheries which have genuinely regional newspapers, most local papers in Britain are just that – local. Unlike some equivalents in the United States, Germany or Italy, they have no readership beyond their immediate area. Despite the qualifications made in Chapter 4, therefore, it is true to say that most people in Britain read papers which are firmly rooted in a London-centred political, social and economic world.

The same is true of exposure to radio and television. In 1982 independent (commercial) local radio accounted for 33 per cent of all radio listeners, BBC local radio for 6.3 per cent and BBC 1, 2, 3 and 4 for virtually all the remaining 60 per cent. While the BBC radio networks have regional studios and programmes whose output increased in the '60s and '70s, they are still heavily London-based, as are the two BBC Television channels. Independent Television has a more federal structure, consisting of ten regional and five network companies. Even so, only 16 per cent of programmes put out in 1979–80, for example, were specifically local in origin, the remainder being designed for national transmission. ITV's Channel Four is also managed from London.

It comes as no surprise that in such a centralised system ownership is also highly concentrated. Indeed in the newspaper world, the tendency has been towards ever greater concentration, with large conglomerates taking an increasing share. In addition, a new style of press baron, typified by Rupert Murdoch and Robert Maxwell, has emerged. Unlike the long-established families, such as the Rothermeres, Harmsworths and Beaverbrooks, typically associated with newspapers in the 1960s, these are self-made men with extensive national and international interests in publishing, television, and other areas, determined to stamp their personal authority on the editorial policies of their papers. Local papers too are often owned by large conglomerates – about 50 per cent of regional evening sales are accounted for by five companies. However, most local papers do pursue independent editorial lines (Tunstall 1983: 174). Compared with continental Europe – although not the United States – television ownership is relatively dispersed, thanks largely to independent television's federal structure. The BBC is, of course, state owned.

Ownership is one thing, control another. Most commentators distinguish between mechanisms of *public* accountability and control, and the essentially

Table 5.1 The major national Daily and Sunday newspapers, September 1986

Newspaper	Sales (millions) Jan–Dec '83	Jan–June '86	Political allegiance	Ownership
Qualities				
Daily Telegraph	1.25	1.15	Conservative	Private company controlling interest held by Lord Hartwell
Financial Times	.211	.251	independent (right of centre)	Pearson
Guardian	.445	.524	independent (left of centre)	Non-profit making Scott Trust
Independent*		.320	independent	Employee/private company
Times	.370	.471	independent (right of centre)	News International owned by Rupert Murdoch
Sunday Times	1.28	1.14	independent (right of centre)	News International
Observer	.754	.778	independent	Lonrho
Sunday Telegraph	.734	.678	Conservative	Private company controlling interest held by Lord Hartwell
Mass				
Daily Express	2.0	1.85	Conservative	Fleet Holdings Chaired by Lord Matthews
Daily Mail	1.85	1.80	Conservative	Associated Newspapers Rothermere and Harmsworth families as major shareholders
Daily Mirror	3.3	3.04	Labour	Private company owned by Robert Maxwell
Daily Star	1.4	1.4	Conservative	Fleet Holdings
Sun	4.1	4.06	Conservative	News International
Today	–	.300	independent	News International
News of the World	4.03	4.84	Conservative	News International
Sunday Mirror	3.57	3.05	Labour	Robert Maxwell
Sunday Express	2.6	2.3	Conservative	Fleet Holdings
Mail on Sunday	1.5	1.6	Conservative	Associated Newspapers

Source: Various, including ARC Advertising
* First published Oct 1986 – Circulation as of that month

private control exercised by owners, employees and trade unions. Devices for public press accountability are minimal in Britain (with the exception of government censorship which we will address later). The Monopolies Commission can, in theory at least, prevent mergers or takeovers which increase concentration to a level not considered in the public interest. But the Monopolies Commission has been seriously circumscribed by the simple economic fact that most mergers and takeovers are effectively rescues of ailing papers. Faced with such prospects as a *Times* owned by Rupert Murdoch or the possibility of no *Times* at all, the Commission's hands have been tied. Until the 1970s, the Press Council, a voluntary self-regulating body, was generally admired as a responsible check on the abuse of press power. But the Council of the 1960s was dominated by a strong chairman, Lord Devlin, and the newspaper industry was dominated by two press magnates, Cecil King of IPC (which owned the Mirror Group) and Lord Thompson who owned the *Times* and *Sunday Times*. Both men believed in consensus politics and journalistic self-restraint. All changed with the appearance of Rupert Murdoch in 1969 who, having bought the *Sun*, clashed continually with the Council during the 1970s and 1980s. Since then, most of the popular newspapers have challenged Press Council decisions over such issues as reporting the details of the private lives of public figures, publicising sensitive facts in criminal cases and publishing prurient materials. With the breakdown of consensus in the industry, the Press Council has ceased to exert an effective control over irresponsible journalism.

More important than either the Press Council or the Monopolies Commission are the controls exercised by owners, employees (mainly journalists) and the trade unions. Newspaper owners have always been reluctant to grant total editorial discretion to editors. If anything the editors of the 1980s have less freedom than ever before. Of established national dailies, only the editors of the *Guardian* and the *Financial Times* have true freedom over their papers' political and economic editorial line. The newly-founded *Independent* has as its *raison d'être* the assertion of responsible journalistic freedom, but these exceptions constitute a small minority. Criticism that wealthy and determined entrepreneurs try to shape public opinion by stamping their personal political preferences on particular newspapers is therefore quite justified.

Trade union control over the national (and to a lesser extent the local) press has attracted considerable attention over the last 20 years. Most of the debate centres on the introduction of new technology and the exercise of restrictive practices by old-style craft unions. Until the mid-1980s these unions (notably the National Graphical Association (NGA) and the Society of Graphical and Allied Trades (SOGAT)) managed to maintain very high manning levels on Fleet Street and successfully prevented the introduction of new technology. By 1986, however, both SOGAT and the NGA were concluding deals with almost every newspaper owner which involved reduced manning levels, transfers to new high-technology plants and other productivity improvements. Rupert Murdoch's News International's move to a new plant in Wapping, accompanied by an effective lock-out of non-co-operating SOGAT and NGA members, was the catalyst for these new deals. While violence at Wapping, where police and pickets clashed over a period of many months, undoubtedly raised the political salience of the new technology, only on very rare occasions have the unions interfered with the *editorial* policy of papers. When they have, it has usually been over the reporting of union activity.

The broadcasting media are under much stricter public controls than the press. Independent Television is supervised by a powerful quango, the Independent Broadcasting Authority (IBA). Its major responsibility is the periodic granting of regional and network, as well as local radio franchises. Should a company be badly managed or not produce the right mix of programmes then a franchise may not be renewed. This has happened quite often, the last major shake-up occurring in 1982. The IBA is often criticised, but it has certainly helped maintain reasonably high standards of quality. As with the press, there is an increasing tendency for ITV companies to be owned or partly owned by large international conglomerates with diverse media interests. How and to what extent this affects programme content it is impossible to say, certainly much less than in the case of most of the press.

Unlike ITV, the BBC is a highly centralised, unitary organisation effectively controlled by a board of governors appointed by the government. Board members are established figures and the chairman (no woman has ever held the post) is particularly well placed to determine policy. Beneath the board, a director general is responsible for the day-to-day running of all BBC services. The first chairman of the BBC, Lord Reith, established the principle that the public interest was best served by limiting public access to popular culture. Although much modified since, this basically elitist, paternalistic ethos continues to prevail, as anyone familiar with Japanese or American television would confirm. The BBC's programme mix continues to arouse controversy but it is the question of political control that has inspired the most heated debate. We will return to this issue in the next section.

Unions have an extensive membership in television and radio but their activity has not been a subject of great public dispute. The same cannot be said for reporters and commentators, however, who are widely acknowledged to have significant discretion over programme content. Depending on the network involved, this almost certainly reflects a preference for 'middle-brow', middle-class values – which is not surprising given that most key BBC and ITV editorial staff are themselves university-educated, middle- or upper-middle-class men and women. Put another way, broadcasts in Britain are as much determined by what a small group of programme makers and managers believe is good for the people to see or hear, as by what the people actually want. Ratings (surveys of viewers and listeners by programme audience) can be important in affecting the standing and content of programmes, but these do not, as in the USA, dictate policy. Quality (what the managers themselves believe to be worthy) is just as important. This is an important cause of protests by moral campaigners who want the content of programmes more strictly vetted so as not to cause offence to traditional sexual and moral standards. Such protests can themselves become politically important.

Bias and political control: the enduring debate

Political control

In no country are the media completely free from government control. Even in the United States – which probably has the freest media of any nation on earth – matters of defence and national security can lead to censorship. And in all democratic countries, libel and slander laws circumscribe press and broadcasting freedom. In Britain political control of the media takes direct and indirect forms. Directly, the Official Secrets Act applies as much to the media as anyone else and the press can be served with 'D' notices, requesting editors not to mention certain topics on grounds of security, which constitute a form of self-censorship. Indirectly, the government can subject the media to a variety of pressures including public and private criticism, changes in taxation and licencing policy and, in the case of the BBC, the appointment of sympathetic chairmen and members of the board of governors, and the application of official 'pressure'. The director general of the BBC (Alasdair Milne) seemed to have been led to resign in 1987 through a combination of such factors.

Direct controls are used infrequently. 'D' notices were introduced during the Second World War and continue to apply during hostilities or on matters affecting national security. They are voluntary, however, the idea being that the press, even if it is aware of military secrets, will withhold them in the national interest. During actual hostilities the system has worked very well – indeed the issuing of a 'D' notice is often unnecessary because editors are aware of the need for secrecy. During the Falklands War, for example, Peter Preston, editor of the *Guardian* noted:

'If your country is at war, your readers won't thank you, your country won't thank you and your paper won't thank you for a dramatic exclusive which manages to get 2000 British soldiers killed; that was clear, we all knew that and we all operated on that basis. But it didn't actually stop us trying to find out what the strategy was, what the likely stages of events were and so forth; but we were trying to behave as responsibly as we could.' (Hetherington, 1985 p. 282)

It is the use of the Official Secrets Act and the government's invoking the need to protect 'national security' during peacetime that has aroused much greater criticism. As earlier chapters have indicated, the main victims of the Official Secrets Act are government officials and politicians rather than the press or broadcasting companies. Even so, the media are often indirectly affected. When in 1983 Sarah Tisdale, a junior Foreign Office clerk, sent details of the arrival of Cruise missiles in Britain to the *Guardian*, the paper found itself also possibly in breach of the Official Secrets Act. In the event, the paper felt obliged not to publish the documents and, after protest, to hand over the photocopies for official identification. Governments may use the courts more explicitly. In 1986, the intelligence agency, MI5, successfully took out an injunction against the *Guardian* and the *Observer* to stop them publishing allegations about inefficiency in MI5 by a former employee, Peter Wright. Wright's book *Spycatcher* was published in several countries in 1987. As it was banned in Britain, the government felt obliged to take legal action against British newspapers publishing even extracts of the book, which was widely available outside Britain.

The whole lobby system, whereby journalists are given unattributable information by government spokesmen, stems from a combination of the Official Secrets Act and the general obsession with secrecy in British government. Clearly the system gives the government great control over what aspect of policy and decision-making should be allowed to reach the public and what not. It has almost certainly diverted the media from reporting on and investigating what goes on in Whitehall and particularly in the Cabinet. It is much easier to report Parliament or political party activity than to penetrate the essentially secret world of Whitehall. This said the system does depend on a degree of consensus within the Cabinet and within the media. The number of leaks from within government reached flood proportions in the 1980s, with, in the most celebrated case, the Prime Minister's associates using leaks in the most cynical fashion to discredit another minister (over the Westland Affair, see Ch. 2). As a result the lobby system has come close to breaking down. At least three papers, the *Sun*, the *Guardian* and the *Independent*, have decided to no longer abide by lobby rules.

Indirect political controls mainly affect the BBC. In some respects the BBC is in a very delicate position. Since 1964 it has accepted the need to show 'balance' in its reporting. In this sense it is in a similar position to ITV which is required by statute (The Broadcasting Act 1981) to maintain a 'proper balance' and to ensure that 'all news is presented with due accuracy and impartiality'. At the same time the BBC is state-owned and its finances (the licence fees) are determined by government. Finally, the BBC broadcasts the World Service, which is effectively the propaganda voice of British national interests abroad. Unlike the Voice of America and other propaganda networks, however, the World Service is *not* directly controlled by the government. For many years, these problems barely surfaced. The BBC was an establishment organisation which assumed the mantle of the 'voice of Britain' at home and abroad. From the 1950s on, however, the face of broadcasting changed dramatically. Both television and radio were subject to commercial competition; broadcasting output increased greatly; a larger and more varied staff were employed; the pace of technological change quickened and last, but not least, British society and British politics became more conflictual and abrasive.

Both Labour and Conservative governments have directed their ire at the BBC. Harold Wilson, Labour Prime Minister 1964–70 and 1974–76, was convinced that the Corporation was biased against the Labour Party and himself personally. Even more vitriolic have been the comments made by Margaret Thatcher and her chief party officials, notably Norman Tebbit, all of whom believe that the BBC (and particularly television news and Radio 4's *Today* programme) are biased towards the left of centre. What can governments do to control the BBC? In theory, quite a lot. In 1986 the appointment of 'Duke' Hussey as chairman was widely perceived as a political appointment designed to redress alleged left-wing bias. Governments can also threaten to withhold licence fee increases, or as in the mid-1980s they can threaten to change the whole funding system. The Conservative Government was disappointed by the findings of the Peacock Commission, however, which was established by the government to investigate the BBC's finances. Margaret Thatcher supported the introduction of revenue from advertising; but Peacock refused to accept this, and instead opted for small modifications in the existing system.

Governments can also apply behind the scenes pressure on the board of governors. For example, in 1985 the Corporation decided not to broadcast a production of *Real Lives*, which involved interviews with convicted Northern Ireland terrorists. Leon Brittan, the Home Secretary, had asked the board of governors to advise against showing it, as it was not in the national interest. The director general complied, although it was eventually shown at a later, politically less sensitive, date. Brittan insisted that this did not constitute censorship, although given the delicate position of the BBC it was very close to being censorship. Perhaps the most celebrated case of government disquiet with the BBC was the Tory chairman, Norman Tebbit's, virulent attack on the Corporation's coverage of the American air strike on Libya in 1986. In the event, the BBC refused to accept the allegations of anti-American bias. Also in 1986, the BBC decided not to screen a controversial play about government decision-making at the time of the Falklands War. One scene apparently depicted the Cabinet making decisions on the War with one eye on the forthcoming general election. No evidence of government pressure on the BBC exists in this case. It was, apparently, more a matter of the Corporation anticipating problems. If this is so, it constitutes a particularly insidious form of censorship – prior restraint – and demonstrates just how nervous the BBC had become by the mid-1980s. Indeed, the Corporation has drawn up a complex monitoring system whereby all politically sensitive programmes have to be referred to the director general for approval.

Clearly the BBC does not enjoy total political freedom, but its position should be viewed in proper perspective. It remains essentially independent of government. Compared with most state-owned broadcasting networks, even those in Western Europe, it is remarkably independent. Overt political control remains out of the question. Even if a government managed to fill the board with its own men and women – a highly unlikely possibility – they would have great difficulty persuading programme makers to toe the government line. It may well be, of course, that the BBC and other media are in fact biased against particular governments, politicians or interests. What is the evidence in support of this charge?

Bias

No one disputes that most of the British press is biased. Most papers (Table 5.1) promote a particular political party with the Conservatives having a substantial (and increasing) advantage. This is reflected not only in editorials, but in the reporting of political news. In democratic countries overt bias in reporting is relatively unusual. In American journalism, for example, there is a clear distinction between reporting and editorial/opinion writing. As a result, the reading of front page political news reveals little about the paper's editorial line. While this could be said to some extent of the British quality press, even here front page opinion is common, and among the tabloids it is almost impossible to distinguish between facts and opinions. Given the potential influence it could exert on elector's voting decisions the pro-Conservative bias in the press must be a cause of concern. It almost certainly derives from the simple fact that newspapers are privately owned and therefore attract investors and owners who support free enterprise. Papers also increasingly rely on advertising revenue, which is unlikely to be great if a paper takes a strong left-wing line and is staffed by committed socialists. Unfortunately, little research has been conducted on the effects of newspaper bias on electors. Most readers are aware of the political line of the papers they read (Kellner & Worcester in Worcester & Harrop 1982). But we simply do not know to what extent, if at all, values and prejudices are changed or reinforced as a result of reading a highly partisan paper.

At least press bias is explicit. The major charge against television and radio is that, while most members of the public believe it to be objective and impartial, it is in fact biased in favour of certain social, economic and political values in a peculiarly indirect way. As noted earlier, such criticisms are made both on the left and the right, although the major academic critique has come from the left. In four major publications, *Bad News, More Bad News, Really Bad News*, and *War and Peace News*, the Glasgow University Media Group has launched a major onslaught on the objectivity of both the BBC and Independent Television News (ITN). On the basis of a systematic analysis of programme content the studies found a pervasive and consistent bias against the unions in particular, and the working class in general, in British television news reporting. *Bad News* summed up its findings as follows:

[Television lays the] blame for society's industrial and economic problems at the door of the workforce. This is done in the face of contradictory evidence which, when it appears, is either ignored, smothered, or at worst is treated as if it supports the 'inferential frameworks' utilised by the producers of news (*Bad News* 1976: 267–8).

Broadcasters were shocked and outraged by these, and similar later, findings. Many simply could not believe them and suspected some political motive behind the studies. Press articles and television programmes attempted to challenge them, but the authors were unconvinced. Eventually, another academic, Martin Harrison, challenged the findings in an important book published in 1985. Harrison looked carefully at the evidence and concluded that the Media Group's studies were all badly flawed: counter-evidence was ignored, statistics misinterpreted, conclusions exaggerated (Harrison 1985: Conclusions).

None of this is to suggest that television news is unbiased, or even that the reporting of industrial conflict is objective. Harrison set himself the task of exposing the flaws of an existing study. Much research remains to be done before definitive conclusions can be drawn. What can be said now with some confidence, is that television and radio news show no bias in favour of the two extremes of the political spectrum. In a sense this is inevitable, given their brief to achieve balance. During a period when the two main political parties have been polarising to left and right, 'balance' can very easily be interpreted as favouring the centre. At the same time, neither the Conservatives nor the Labour Party can complain that they receive insufficient coverage. An Oxford Polytechnic study has shown that the BBC makes more mention of the Conservatives than Labour, ITN favours Labour slightly, while both networks refer substantially less to the Liberals and Social Democrats. Such an overall bias is natural given that the Conservatives were in government – and the networks have to report government activity. But some bias continued to apply even when the references examined related only to the *political parties* as such. If the 'bias towards the centre' critique is valid, it cannot therefore be based on the extent of coverage given by the media.

It must be based on the assumption that the networks make persistently *unfavourable* comments about the two older parties and the government of the day. This they may do when referring to (say) Militant's activities with the Labour Party, or to the extreme (right wing) Monday Club's role in the Conservative Party, but we have no hard evidence to support this claim.

On the moral (or cultural) rather than political dimension, the right-wing critique may be on stronger ground. Television employees are generally middle-class, culturally liberal men and women. Programme content, especially documentaries and drama, reflect these values. Rarely do such programmes promote the virtues of a more Draconian penal system, protecting the foetus, censorship of pornography or more restrictions on homosexual relationships. While this is true, liberal sentiments on these issues also tend to outweigh conservative views among most Members of Parliament and senior civil servants; and it is they who make and implement the laws on such questions – often with little regard for public opinion. It is hard to see, therefore, that this constitutes a unique media, rather than a general societal, bias.

There is one area of slanted coverage which undoubtedly exists, but which has received very little scholarly attention – the media's treatment of foreign news. Here, much independent specification of the agenda for political discussion is undoubtedly evident. A natural disaster in Asia can be given top news priority or very low priority depending on the competing domestic and international stories. Coverage of the internal politics of nearby European countries often takes second place to coverage of American politics – perhaps reflecting official (Foreign Office and government) concern with preserving the 'special relationship' between the UK and the US. Vietnam became an important issue both within and outside the United States, partly because of graphic television coverage. Famine in Ethiopia was reported in newspapers some months before it became a matter of national concern. It was, of course, the painful BBC television pictures of starving Ethiopians which elevated it to the status of top news story.

What about the effect of television on elections? Is bias evident here, and irrespective of bias, can television change people's voting intentions? Little overt bias exists for the very good reason that each party is allocated a limited amount of air-time proportional to their electoral strength. Although this discriminates against new and minor parties with a potentially greater appeal it is probably the only reasonable agreed rule that could be applied. Television producers and commentators go out of their way to be seen to be fair in their treatment of election-related material. Some research on the effects of television on elections has been conducted. In their analysis of the 1983 General Election, Gunter, Sverrevig and Wober found that floating voters and new voters were twice as likely to say that television helped them how to decide to vote – and that potential Alliance voters were especially likely to be influenced. However, the same study reports that four out of five voters said that television did *not* help them make up their minds (Gunter, Sverrevig and Wober 1986). Of course, these are measures of voter's *perceptions* which may not always be accurate. But it does seem that television has some effect.

Finally, how do television and the press handle public opinion polls? Careful research on this topic reveals a tendency which is, perhaps, true of TV and press reporting generally. No matter how trivial a poll result is, or how unlikely its findings, wide coverage is given. Put another way, polls are treated as hard news. Even when public opinion is static, editors will be quick to infer shifts in opinion from poll results, or they will pick up unreliable polls and project their findings as evidence of fundamental change (Crewe in Crewe and Harrop 1986). In the vital weeks before an election this must have some effect on voting intentions, and the case for controls over the publication of opinion polls is strong.

Conclusions: the media and British politics

No one disputes that the media – and especially television – are an important influence on politics. With the relative decline of grass-roots political activity, associated with closely knit class-homogeneous communities, most people now receive information about politics via television, radio and newspapers. Bias undoubtedly exists. In one sense it always will, for there can never be any such thing as completely objective media coverage. Most newspapers do not even pretend to be objective and network television will always tend to reflect the dominant and consensual values in society. Given this, criticism will no doubt continue. Moreover, as competition between channels and broadcasting formats (cable, satellite) intensifies, and the Conservatives deregulate television and radio further, the networks may, as in the USA, be tempted to commercialise the presentation of news and opinion, thus opening them up to charges of trivialisation and oversimplification. Again, the simpler the message, the less likely that it will challenge a sort of lowest common denominator values which most people can accept.

What we have shown, however, is that politics affect the media, just as much as the media affects politics. If British politics continue in their present confrontational style this will be reflected in newspapers and in television and radio – however hard the networks strive to achieve 'balance'. No matter how party politics develop, however, one thing is certain; no government will find it easy to control the media. Whatever their political complexion, British newspapers and broadcasting companies are highly independent and government interference is strongly resented. Governments have found it just as difficult to control the BBC – even though it is nominally owned and, indirectly, financed by them. The media may be biased and otherwise imperfect, but they are far from being the instruments of politicians and civil servants.

Chapter 6
Sub-central decision-making

Britain – a differentiated polity

Parties and elections are not the only way in which individuals can make their views felt or get government to solve their problems. We have already examined the activities of interest groups. Besides relying on the representations of such groups to ministers and civil servants, individuals can also seek redress for their grievances through the courts or administrative tribunals (Ch. 8).

An immense variety of personal problems are raised by, or involved in, the administrative process. Many of them are too idiosyncratic to impinge on parties or pressure groups and are not suitable for court rulings (e.g. whether a lamp post could be situated outside a dark entrance for the convenience of the elderly and infirm). Such matters are commonly taken up with political representatives, usually the MP or local councillor, but sometimes a member of the European Parliament or of the House of Lords. Since these problems impinge directly on the individual – to a greater degree than the great affairs of state – the importance of the political response to them cannot be exaggerated, both for making British democracy work and for rendering it better liked.

In this context it is scarcely possible to overestimate the importance of local government. Both elected local councillors and local officials are a key source of help to individuals with problems. At its simplest, local government is closer to the people and more aware of their needs than central government whether in the guise of Parliament or the executive, though constituency MPs often stimulate local action. The often neglected role of local authorities in tailoring administration to personal needs must be underlined – it is an important facet of representative democracy and crucial in maintaining its popular support.

In addition to this representative role, local authorities also carry out the bulk of the country's administrative business. They implement the great bulk of central decisions and their attitude is crucial in determining whether or not the policies will be effective. They are not mere agents of the centre; they also negotiate with it in many areas on a basis of near equality. Local government has thus to be examined as a major actor in national policy-making.

This conflicts with the conventional presumption, strongly endorsed by national politicians of Thatcherite leanings, which regards Britain as a unitary state where Parliament, the executive and the Civil Service decide policy throughout the land and apply it uniformly. In this view, elected local councils are seen as a necessary adjunct – confined, however, to essentially mundane and supplementary functions (e.g. street lighting and cleaning). This picture is misleading. As Chapter 2 has already demonstrated, central government is not particularly unified. On closer inspection it dissolves into a collection of departments and ministries, with diverse views and considerable autonomy in their areas of operation, which bargain with each other, posing considerable problems of co-ordination for the Cabinet and the Treasury. If changes are to be effectively implemented, they have to be negotiated rather than imposed. At another level, the European Community is only one out of a range of international bodies to which Britain belongs. Central government is in many ways constrained by the ability of EC institutions to take decisions without reference to it. Indeed membership of the EC has fostered direct links between the Commission and local authorities which often bypass the national government (see Chapter 7). It is misleading, therefore, to view Britain as clearly directed by a decisive central government whose leaders know best. That image needs to be replaced by the picture of Britain as 'a differentiated polity'.

This is a useful label for four characteristics of British government. First, there is the non-executant character of the centre – that is, the fact that central departments, with the obvious exceptions of Defence, Inland Revenue and Social Security, do not deliver services. The Department of Education and Science does not build schools, hire and fire teachers or to date, decide directly upon the school curriculum. Second, following from this, the centre is dependent upon a range of other agencies – including, but not restricted to, local authorities – for the delivery of services. A minister's reputation lies in the hands, not of his civil servants, but of local officials. Third, government provides a vast range of services and each has its own organisational arrangements. There is a high degree of fragmentation in the means for delivering services. Finally, these disparate means are not effectively drawn together to form a coherent whole; the system is disaggregated. It is not simply a case of the left hand not knowing what the right is doing. To compound the situation, left and right are often blissfully unaware of each other to the extent that their independent initiatives create mutual problems. It is very well to increase council house rents to save money but the policy will fail if another department pays for the increase through its benefits – as indeed happened to the Department of Health and Social Security in the mid-1980s.

The 'differentiated polity' is characterised, therefore, by fragmentation, disaggregation and interdependence. Britain can be described, without too much exaggeration, as a 'centreless society'; there is not, as the media would have us believe, a single omni-competent centre but a series of centres, often acting independently of each other and sometimes confounding each others' actions.

Varieties of sub-central government

A first step towards documenting these points is to describe the sheer variety of governmental organisations in Britain. Table 6.1 provides an illustrative listing.

Table 6.1 Types of public sector organisations in Britain

1 The centre
Functional departments (e.g. DES, DHSS, DoE)
2 Sub-central governments
   (i)   Territorial ministries (e.g. Scottish Office)
   (ii) Intermediate institutions (e.g. regional offices of the DoE)
   (iii) Non-departmental public bodies
       (a) Public corporations
       (b) National Health Services
       (c) Fringe bodies:
          (1) Executive (e.g. MSC)
          (2) Advisory (e.g. CFBAC)
          (3) Tribunals (e.g. Industrial Tribunals)
          (4) *quangos (e.g. National House Building Council)
   (iv) Local government (including +quelgos)
   (v) Sub-central political organisations
       (a) Political parties
       (b) Interest groups
       (c) Professions
3 International bodies with authority in Britain (European Commission, European Court, etc.)

Source: Rhodes, 1988

Notes
* The term 'quango' is used here in its original meaning to refer to semi-private bodies or quasi non-governmental organisations.
+ quelgo, or quasi-elected local government organisation, refers to consortia and joint boards/committees of local authorities.

In this table, the 'centre' has been given a restrictive although common-sense meaning: it refers to Westminster and Whitehall or, to put it more formally, to central political institutions in the capital city. This chapter focuses upon the relations between these institutions and sub-central political organisations and governmental bodies within the accepted boundaries of the state. (The next chapter deals with the European Community and its impact in Britain). The consequences of our definition of the 'centre' should be obvious from a cursory inspection of the table. Thus, territorial ministries and intermediate institutions are regarded as species of sub-central government although conventionally viewed as part of the 'centre'. They are treated as sub-central government because of their location outside the capital city and, most important, to pose the question of whether or not they exercise discretion in policy making.

If this approach violates conventions, it also has an immediate advantage. It draws attention to the multiplicity of organisational forms through which services are delivered. There is no satisfactory classification for all the many manifestations of British government at central and other levels, but even a simplified scheme poses questions about the degree to which it is both fragmented and disaggregated. Equally these organisations are embedded in complex and differing sets of relationships, which Figure 6.1 summarises.

Territorial representation refers to the representation of ethnic-territorial units (i.e. Scotland, Wales and Northern Ireland) at the centre and the activities of

Figure 6.1 The scope of sub-central government

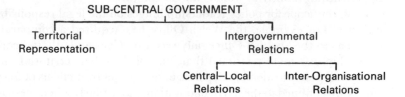

territorially based political organisations. *Intergovernmental relations* (IGR) refers to the relations between the centre and all forms of governmental organisations outside the centre. It is sub-divided into *central-local relations* or the links between central departments and local authorities and *inter-organisational relations* which encompass all other types of sub-central government – hereafter referred to as SCG – including the nationalised industries, the national health services, the regional organisations of central departments or intermediate institutions and non-departmental public bodies. Quite obviously, sub-central government is complex and *not restricted to local government*.

There is a lot of it out there, especially from the standpoint of the centre, but numbers are not necessarily a good indicator of importance. A brief glance at levels of expenditure and manpower demonstrates its crucial role in policy-making and introduces the various forms it can take. The *territorial ministries* have a number of distinctive features which differentiate them from the run of central departments. First, they are organised on a territorial not a functional basis, located in the periphery, not Whitehall; and they are responsible for a wide range of functions – they articulate *both* territorial and functional interests. Consequently for all other types of government in their respective peripheries they are not just one of many central departments but the prime port of call; they are 'their centre'.

Second, the territorial ministries have a wider range of roles compared to the normal Whitehall department. Their additional roles include adapting UK policies for implementation in the periphery, promoting policies which reflect national differences and needs, and lobbying for resources not just for a single service but for the minority nation as a whole.

Finally, the territorial ministries operate in a dual political environment; the shared environment of UK politics and the individual environment of its nation with its distinct ethnic identity, sub-central political organisations, legal, educational and religious institutions. Northern Ireland provides the clearest example of this distinctiveness.

The key feature of the territorial ministries is their dual character; they are simultaneously in the centre and for a territory. The key question concerns their degree of discretion and the conditions under which it is exercised. At first sight, it would seem that any policy leadership by the territorial ministries will be severely constrained by the functional politics of Whitehall. In other words, the territorial ministries could simply be second-division departments which follow the policies decided by the first division functional department in Whitehall. In this case their discretion would be confined to log-rolling or supporting the functional ministries in the expectation that they will benefit from any additional resources made

117

available. However, it is possible to identify a number of conditions under which the territorial ministries' role is not so confined.

First, the scope for policy leadership hinges on the legal responsibilities of the ministry. For example, the Welsh Office has acquired a comparable range of functions to the Scottish Office only recently. Consequently its scope for policy leadership was more restricted than that of the other territorial ministries.

Second, policy leadership depends upon the spillover effects of the policy. If its effects are confined to the particular nation, particularly when there is a tradition of autonomous action, the scope for policy leadership can be considerable. Education – especially teacher training and supply, curricula and examinations – in Scotland is a good example of an insulated policy area, as are housing, education and health in Northern Ireland.

Third, the territorial ministries have a range of organisational and informational resources at their command. They are the experts for their nation and this claim can legitimate the call for distinct policies. But perhaps even more important are the political resources of the ministries. Unlike any region in England, Scotland, Wales and Northern Ireland have a representative in the Cabinet. He can argue the case at the highest levels of government. Issues which are highly salient for one nation can be forced onto the agenda and the territorial ministry can become the lead department on the matter – e.g. fisheries in Scotland, water supply in Wales. And in the fight for resources, the secretary of state can call upon support from his national political environment, arguing for example that action is required to forestall electoral losses to the Scottish National Party.

One obvious indicator of the success of the territorial ministries in exercising policy leadership is their ability to gain a favourable allocation of public expenditure. Table 6.2 shows clearly that public expenditure is redistributed from England to the peripheral nations and that their share of such expenditure has steadily increased.

Policy leadership is probably greatest for organisational and administrative matters and 'self-contained' policy areas like education, and weakest for functional policy areas which overlap with general UK concerns. The degree of discretion ranges from autonomy to dependence, and varies between policy areas and over time, with the Scottish Office demonstrating a greater capacity to place territorial matters on the central agenda than the Welsh Office. In the case of Northern Ireland, the combination of one-party dominance, conservative ideology and a civil service with a long-standing tradition of autonomy has contributed to persisting variations in policy. It remains the most autonomous territorial ministry; a legacy of devolution and insulation from Westminster and Whitehall.

Its dependence on special factors like these gives territorial discretion a fragile base. It is exercised when the centre sees fit. But discretion there is; and if the centre has the power to intervene, these interventions do not necessarily amount to control.

Returning to Table 6.1, we now examine *Intermediate institutions*, the deconcentrated structures of central departments. The sheer diversity of structures both within and between departments demonstrates that functional and administrative criteria dominated decisions about boundaries. Their organisational pattern can only be described as a maze.

Table 6.2 Identifiable public expenditure in Scotland, England, Wales and Northern Ireland, 1960–80

Per head: United Kingdom = 100	Scotland	England	Wales	N. Ireland
1960–61	112	99*		99
1961–62	114	98		99
1962–63	114	98		103
1963–64	115	98	113	101
1964–65	113	98	114	100
1965–66	111	98	112	105
1966–67	112	98	113	105
1967–68	118	97	110	106
1968–69	124	96	113	119
1969–70	126	96	111	113
1970–71	117	97	104	118
1971–72	119	97	108	122
1972–73	127	95	110	127
1973–74	118	97	104	124
1974–75	117	97	104	134
1975–76	119	96	110	136
1976–77	120	96	112	144
1977–78	120	95	115	147
1978–79	119	95	112	150
1979–80	121	96	111	142
1980–81	121	95	125	138

Source: Parry, 1982, p. 100
* Joint figures for England and Wales until 1963

The primary tasks of intermediate institutions are managerial, i.e. enabling central departments to operate more effectively. They collect information, monitor the implementation of policies by local authorities, co-ordinate the activities of the several departments through the inter-departmental Regional Board, promote central policies and advise the centre on the development of those policies. To all intents and purposes, intermediate institutions are part of the central line bureaucracies: they are the agents of the centre and they have not been created to articulate territorial interests. The 'regional' level of 'government' in England has neither a constituency nor a political head. However, Young reports that regional offices of the Department of the Environment acted as the 'voice at court' for their areas, developed very close working relationships with local authorities and exercised some influence over the implementation of policy. They were 'classic middlemen', who had 'gone native' at least to a degree (1982: 89).

The contrast with the territorial ministries is sharp. Intermediate institutions, on occasion, can exercise some discretion but it is not their primary role. They express the dominance of functional politics in British government, serving the managerial (especially implementation) interest of the centre. They are a resource of the centre, embedded in multiple relationships, but with limited resources of their own which enable them sometimes to mediate between it and the locality. The degree of discretion is more limited than for territorial ministries with little or no legitimacy for their role as the voice of territorial interest. They warrant the label 'intermediate institutions' because they are neither bureaucratic agents nor decentralised bodies. Like Topsy 'they growed' and epitomise not the principled homogeneity of a centralised unitary state but the *ad hoc* heterogeneity of a differentiated polity.

If territorial ministries and particularly intermediate institutions can be seen as extensions of the centre rather than true examples of SCG, *non-departmental public bodies* (see, again, Table 6.1) are more obviously not of the centre. Indeed their very existence is a product of the latter's wish to distance itself from the functions concerned. The problem with this species of sub-central government is its sheer variety. The nationalised industries accounted for some 12.5 per cent of GDP and 9.4 per cent of total employment in 1980. Although privatisation has since reduced this figure substantially, it is still very large. Again, on the latest available figures, the National Health Service accounts for 6.2 per cent of GDP and 4.8 per cent of total employment.

Turning from the size of these bodies to the more elusive matter of relationships between them and the centre, only one conclusion is possible; accountability is opaque and confusing. For all their diversity, this group shares one characteristic; they are non-elected. Mechanisms for holding them to account for their actions are as complicated and otiose as they are ineffective.

In the case of the *nationalised industries* financial controls have been paramount. Traditionally they were required to cover their costs 'taking one year with another'; the break-even principle. This ostensibly simple rule encountered several problems, notably the inability of several industries to make any surplus and the indecision of the government on whether or not they were to be run on a commercial basis. Simultaneously, and in a wholly contradictory fashion, governments have asserted the need for the industries to be run on a sound commercial basis and intervened regularly – indeed it is alleged, daily – in their running – for example, on pricing policy. As Curwen (1986: 56–57) concludes, 'intervention has been piecemeal and unsystematic' opining that 'the concept of the public interest is very troublesome' and, in consequence, 'governments prefer to keep it as ambiguous as possible so that any choices are compatible with it'. The balance between public and private interests has never been found throughout the post war period, not even under the post-1979 Conservative Governments (see below).

The National Health Service is *sui generis*. It is a strange mixture of decentralisation by government departments and administration by nominated lay boards, perhaps best described as discontinuous hierarchy to make it clear that the centre does not have a direct line of command (Sharpe, 1977; Webb, Wistow and Hardy, 1986). Although the centre can set a ceiling to NHS expenditure, it has had considerably less success in influencing the distribution of these resources between both areas and specialisms. A complicated procedure for allocating funds – known as the Resource Allocation Working Party formula or RAWP formula – has been employed to give each Regional Health Authority (RHA) resources commensurate with its population and its need for services. It has made only a marginal reduction in the inequalities between regions. Similarly, repeated efforts to shift funds away from the acutely ill towards the 'Cinderella services' of the elderly and handicapped have resulted in only a limited redistribution. In law, the minister may be responsible for the NHS. In practice, the actions of the centre are confounded by the power of the medical profession which is without parallel in any other public sector organisation.

The remaining non-departmental public organisations or *fringe bodies* are those 'not a Government Department or part of a Government Department' with 'executive, administrative and regulatory functions'; with 'functions of a judicial kind'; and 'bodies whose principal function is to advise Ministers and their Departments' (Pliatzky Report 1980: 1 and 132–33). The ubiquitous term 'quango' is used in its original restrictive sense to refer to semi-private bodies or quasi non-governmental organisations. Whatever the preferred terminology, executive control of fringe bodies can only be described as 'blurred and spasmodic' (Johnson 1979: 388). The alliance of vague legislative standards and a measure of both operational and policy independence is a sure-fire recipe for ministerial actions that impinge on fringe bodies but do not achieve the stated purpose.

Local government is the pre-eminent sub-central organisation in the British system and it is the only one which commands the political legitimacy of direct election. The commonplace Westminster and Whitehall view of the British polity tends to equate local government with the English system whereas Scotland and Northern Ireland have distinct systems and there are additional significant variations within the English and Scottish systems. Table 6.3 provides a summary of the major types of local authority in the UK.

The picture becomes even more complicated when the widely varying distribution of functions between the different types of local authority is considered. The several systems also vary in their dependence upon grants from the centre. It is often argued that dependence upon central grants erodes the autonomy of local authorities. (As Table 6.4 makes clear, not only does the degree of dependence vary but it has been declining over recent years.) This presupposes that grant is the major determinant of the relationship between central and local government. In fact, the directly contrary point can be made: all local authorities have independent tax powers, and charge for many services. In consequence, they can finance their own decisions about the level of expenditure in individual areas and about the relative priority accorded to services. This independent tax capacity is the cornerstone of local discretion. Hence it is no accident that the centralising Conservative Governments of the 1980s have tried to restrict it by various devices. We discuss the impact of such changes, including the transition from property based to personal local taxes, below.

Given the variety of structures, functions and sources of finance, it should be obvious that the relationships between centre and locality are immensely varied. Table 6.5 provides a summary characterisation of the variety of relationships. Most of them are relatively obvious and will be summarised only briefly.

Bureaucratic relationships are widespread, having their roots in legislation – especially delegated legislation. They are particularly common in relation to the control of expenditure (see below) but by no means limited to it, for example, the

Table 6.3 Major types of local authorities, 1972–87: area and numbers

	London	England Conurbations	Shires	Wales	Scotland	Northern Ireland
Top tier authorities	Greater London Council*	Metropolitan Counties*	County Councils (39)	County Councils (8)	Regions (9)	Districts (26)
Bottom tier authorities	London Boroughs (32) City of London Inner London Education Authority	Metropolitan Districts (36)	County Districts (296) Parishes (7947)	County Districts (37) Parishes (682)	Districts (53) Islands (3) Community Councils (1343)	

* Abolished April 1st 1986 and with the exception of the Inner London Education Authority replaced by non-elected joint boards

Table 6.4 Sources of revenue income of local authorities, 1974–5 to 1984–5 (selected years): percentage by nation*

	1974–75	1975–76	1976–77	1980–81	1981–82	1982–83	1983–84	1984–85
Fees etc.								
England & Wales	18.8	19.4	20.5	21.2	21.4	21.3	20.8	21.2
Northern Ireland	15.0	15.2	14.7	16.2	15.9	15.1	15.9	17.6
Scotland	n.a.	15.0	16.6	17.3	18.5	19.4	19.3	19.5
Grants								
England & Wales	51.8	53.6	51.9	46.4	44.6	42.0	41.9	41.0
Northern Ireland	26	24.1	22.9	20.6	21.0	22.5	24.2	24.6
Scotland	n.a.	58.0	58.9	55.3	49.8	48.0	50.6	50.0
Rates								
England & Wales	29.4	27.0	27.8	32.4	34.0	36.7	37.3	34.3
Northern Ireland	59	60.7	62.4	62	63.1	62.3	59.9	57.8
Scotland	n.a.	27.0	24.5	27.4	31.7	32.6	30.1	30.5

Source: Connolly 1983, *Local Government Trends*, *Scottish Abstract of Statistics* and private correspondence
* The percentages for each nation do not always total 100 because changes in balances have been omitted

Table 6.5 Relationships between central and local government

Form of linkage	Basis of relationship	Key characteristics of relationship
Bureaucratic	Legislation, convention	Relatively clearly defined, predictable, regular, frequent
Technical	Requirements of the plan	Periodic, cyclical, financial
Professional	Shared expertise	Continuous, narrowly-based
Personal	Shared interests/problems	Irregular, very frequent
Informal consultative	Information transmission	Political, irregular, infrequent
Formal consultative	Information exchange	Overtly political, regular
Party political	Broadly common ideology	Infrequent, not always consensual, excludes officers

Source: Houlihan, 1984, p. 404

sale of council houses. Technical relationships become important with the introduction of policy planning systems in the 1970s. Thus, for functions such as housing and transport local authorities prepared capital expenditure plans and, in theory, the centre allocated funds for the period of the plan, leaving local authorities free to decide on priorities. Such plans generated considerable demand for supporting information and documentation. Professional relationships are almost a defining characteristic of central–local relations and occur between all levels of government, formally in advisory bodies and informally through individual contact as well as through common membership of professional bodies. Personal contacts at the officer level occur at both middle-level management levels, for example over the interpretation of rules and regulations governing the exercise of compulsory purchase powers, and at chief officer level, for example national discussions of shared problems such as the repair of system-built housing. Informal consultative relationships involve elected members and are less frequent than the personal contacts of officers, but more structured. It involves delegations to Parliament and central departments as well as more informal and social gatherings. Formal consultative relationships are a characteristic device of British government and central–local relations are no exception. The most publicised example of recent years is the Consultative Council on Local Government Finance wherein centre and locality meet to discuss the level and distribution of grant to local authorities. Finally, party political relationships have become prominent since the reorganisation of local government in 1974. Such relationships are episodic and are not confined to internal party committees or annual conferences. Indeed such points of contact are the tip of the iceberg diverting attention away from periods of intense intra-party lobbying such as occurred over the subsidisation of public transport or the re-allocation of functions to district councils.

One simple table cannot hope to capture the sheer variety of relationships between centre and locality. It does serve the important purpose, however, of demonstrating that relationships are not confined to bureaucratic links, belying popular perceptions to the contrary. And a key factor underpinning much of this variety is the changing political complexion of local government.

There are marked differences between the political resources of local authorities in the peripheral nations and in England. The former have their own centre with a minister of Cabinet rank. These territorial centres have a distinctive political environment and its relative compactness facilitates contact. There is an identifiable sub-central political system which provides easier, more frequent access for local authorities. In addition the secretary of state can articulate their interests at the highest levels of government. In this respect, the Department of the Environment is but a pale shadow of the territorial ministries and English local authorities have no equivalent friend or voice at court.

Perhaps more important, the political control of local authorities varies greatly. Table 6.6 shows the number of authorities controlled by the various parties just after the major reorganisation of 1974–76 and in 1985. It demonstrates a number of salient features of local political systems.

First, in England, the Labour Party had the upper hand in the conurbations and London whereas the Conservatives were strongest in the counties. However, and second, the Conservative ascendancy in the counties has been challenged by the rise of the Alliance grouping Liberals and Social Democrats. By the 1985 English county council elections, the Alliance's electoral interventions had created 23 (out of 39) 'hung councils' where no party had an absolute majority. Third, the pattern of political control is different in the periphery. The Conservatives are weak in Scotland and Wales, with political control shared by the Labour Party and the independents. In Northern Ireland local politics are *sui generis*, with control shared by Unionists, Unionists/Loyalists, SDLP/Nationalist/Independents. After the 1985 elections, Sinn Fein came to prominence also.

The history of the post-war period is one of ever more widespread partisan elections and ever more disciplined party organisation within councils. It is a mistake, however, to see local politics as simply dependent on the fortunes of national parties. A shared party label does not mean shared policies and priorities. Indeed the rise of the 'new urban left' in many areas represents a challenge to the old style of Labour Party politics. It seeks to demonstrate that socialism can work at the local level in order to effect a transformation in the policies of the national party. Quite clearly, this relationship is not one of superior and subordinate but one of rivalry. In consequence, no national government can rely on the support of like-minded local politicians. As the post-1979 Conservative Governments have found, the legitimacy bestowed by local election creates a platform from which to challenge the national government.

The final resources of local authorities are their national representative bodies. These form a legitimised grouping which is widely consulted over the drafting of bills and the implementation of legislation.

In sum, local authorities are embedded in complex networks of interdependence. This diversity may enable the centre to divide and rule local government. It is also a major stumbling block to effective central intervention. Post-war history provides many illustrations of the tension between the centre's desire for decisive action – the exercise of executive authority – and the inertia and recalcitrance generated by a highly differentiated governmental system characterised by interdependence.

Looking again at Table 6.1, the final set of actors to be considered are *sub-central*

Table 6.6 Political control of UK local authorities, 1976 and 1985

	C '76	C '85	L '76	L '85	A '76	A '85	I '76	I '85	NOC '76	NOC '85	Other '76	Other '85	Total
England													
non-metropolitan districts	163	139	30	54	n.a.	3	53	25	49	67	1	8	296
non-metropolitan counties	20	10	6	5	n.a.	1	1	0	12	23	0	0	39
metropolitan counties	2	0	4	6	n.a.	0	0	0	0	0	0	0	6
metropolitan districts	13	5	20	24	n.a.	0	0	0	3	7	0	0	36
GLC	0	0	1	1	n.a.	0	0	0	0	0	0	0	1
London Boroughs	13	13	18	15	n.a.	0	0	0	1	4	0	0	32
City of London	0	0	0	0	n.a.	0	1	1	0	0	0	0	1
Scilly Islands	0	0	0	0	n.a.	0	1	1	0	0	0	0	1
Northern Ireland[†]													
districts		0	0	0	0	0	0	0	6	1	20	25	26
Scotland													
regions	1	1	2	3	n.a.	0	2	2	4	3	0	0	9
districts	4	3	17	25	n.a.	1	18	16	13	5	1	3	53
islands	0	0	0	0	n.a.	0	3	3	0	0	0	0	3
Wales													
counties	0	0	4	4	n.a.	0	3	2	1	2	0	0	8
districts	4	3	11	16	n.a.	0	13	9	8	4	1	5	37

Notes

C = Conservative   L = Labour   A = Alliance (includes Liberal and Social Democratic Party   I = Independent
(including non party)   NOC = no overall control   n.a. = not applicable   controlled councils)

† In 1977, 17 councils had a Unionist majority, 3 had an anti-Unionist majority and 6 councils were deadlocked. In 1985, the figures were 16, 9 and 1 respectively with Sinn Fein gaining 59 seats overall

political organisations. Political parties, in England and the peripheral nations, the professions and the myriad of local pressure groups form an ever-shifting back-cloth for interactions between centre and locality/periphery. Thus, in spite of the nationalisation of party labels, heterogeneity not homogeneity characterises the relationship between national and local parties. The professions are an ever-present feature of sub-central government and fall into two main groups. The technocratic professions are concerned primarily with the services and lobby for their enhancement. Frequently, they have close links with their national counter-parts in the central department and, together, they can be said to form a policy community or a network characterised by continuity and stability which exer-cises a determining influence on policy formation. The topocratic professions are not concerned with any particular service but with the interests of their area as a whole. The most prominent ones are chief executives and directors of finance in local government. They too are prominent at the national level, on this occasion as actors within the national community of local government where they are disproportionately represented. The key consequence of their activities, in sharp contrast to the parties, is the nationalisation of standards. They have to be described as a non-local source of policy-making.

It is impossible to describe in any detail the political environments of the peripheral nations or the universe of local interest groups. One point only will be made: in both the periphery and the localities, politicisation is the order of the day. Whether we are talking of the rise of nationalist parties or the 'green movement' of environmental pressure groups, UK sub-central politics cannot be described as quiescent. Sub-central government has become pervaded by an effervescent heterogeneity of political organisations.

This reinforces the point already made, that British politics cannot be properly analysed on the basis of a simple, unitary state model, even though Thatcherite politicians have tried to act on this assumption. We now examine the way in which relationships have evolved in recent years. They form an instructive example of how the 'differentiated polity' has constrained the efforts of an un-usually active and determined central government to tilt the balance of power in its favour.

Changing relationships since 1979

If one single theme dominates the eighties, it is the search by central government for more effective instruments of control over the expenditures of sub-central government, in accordance with the overall economic strategies of monetarism and reduction of the public sector, noted in Chapter 1. Control is not, however, the only development of significance. The government has also sought to restrict the size of the public sector by privatisation, i.e. selling off enterprises and organisations to private firms and syndicates. Progress here was initially slow, but became a distinctive feature of Conservative policy. Whereas control and privatisation can be seen as an attack on the public sector – a means of curtailing its role in British society – the third feature of central policy involved the proliferation of non-departmental public bodies, thereby expanding the public sector and making it more complex. Certainly local government railed vigorously against its containment and bypassing in favour of non-departmental public bodies. The consultation so characteristic of the mid-1970s was replaced by bureaucratic direction and confrontation. (As Chapter 2 points out, this was also the case with interest groups, the trade unions and even business associations; part of a general more directive and authoritative stance by central government.)

For local authorities, government policy under the first Thatcher Government (1979–83) was to make local income and expenditure conform with national decisions. The achievements of the new regime can be described, at best, as mixed. Between 1979–80 and 1982–83, for example, total public expenditure rose as a proportion of GDP (Gross Domestic Product), i.e. all expenditure on goods and services within the country. Central government's expenditure increased sharply. The big spenders were not for the most part local government services and some local services declined dramatically; e.g. housing, as publicly-owned stock was sold off. The Conservatives cut central government's contribution to local services quite substantially – the proportion of net current local expenditure financed by central block grants fell from 61 per cent to 56 per cent. (Block grants are not tied to specific functions but made in support of services generally.) Local government manpower fell by 4 per cent in the same period. Most dramatically, local capital expenditure (expenditure, for example, on building projects and infrastructure like roads and drains) was subject to stringent regulation and was reduced by some 40 per cent in real terms from an already severely reduced base. And yet, in spite of the 'cuts', local *current* expenditure *increased* between March 1979 and March 1983 by 9 per cent in real terms. Even attempts to abolish superfluous non-departmental public bodies were conspicuously ineffective, involving some 240 bodies and a mere £11.6 million. The savings actually made were more than offset by the expansion of others – e.g. the Manpower Services Commission (MSC) designed to cope with retraining and unemployment. Equally unsuccessful were attempts to impose strict limits on what nationalised industries could borrow. Public spending in 1982–83 exceeded the plans of 1980 by some £1.75 billion (in real terms). Of the three prongs of government strategy only privatisation, i.e. the special sales of public assets, had any success, meeting the targets set since 1982–83 and totalling some £1.2 billion in 1983–84 (Riddell 1983; Steel and Heald 1984).

The bulk of central 'cuts' thus fell on selected services and on capital expenditures of local government, whilst, ironically, both total public expenditure and local current expenditure increased.

The consequences of Conservative policy during this first period were, first, a general failure to achieve the stated goal of reducing public expenditure; and second, the introduction of a generally antagonistic and confrontational style into relations between the centre and other bodies. This contrasted sharply, here and in other areas, with the Labour Government's 'neo-corporatist' consultative arrangements between 1974 and 1979. The new 'style' was more likely to produce unintended, negative consequences than the old, as the whole system was too complex to be controlled directly from the centre. The actions taken by local governments, 'quangos' and other autonomous bodies in defence of their own interests cut across or subverted central government initiatives.

One conspicuous example of the difficulty experienced in imposing controls was that the system of allocating central grants to localities, in support of services delivered there, took on no less than seven different forms in five years (1979–83). The failure of one change to produce the intended effects necessitated others to correct its failings. Ministers and civil servants, not to mention local authorities, had to take time from immediate problems to cope with the effects of continually changing legislation in the same area.

One attempt at direct intervention – the forced sale of publicly-owned houses by councils (and massively increased rents on those retained) – was extremely effective from the government's point of view. Others, however, such as the contracting-out of services previously done by a direct labour force, produced much more mixed results. This type of privatisation was in any case limited but it disproportionately exacerbated relationships between the various levels of government.

These relations had been worsened by central attempts at unilateral imposition of policy rather than consultation. As numerous conflicts broke out, particularly between the government and local authorities controlled by Labour, there was increasing resort to the courts to settle disagreements. Again, this reflected tendencies in other areas as the Conservatives relied on legislation to settle conflicts in their own favour (see Chapter 8 on how the courts themselves reacted in this situation). In the area of sub-central government an unprecedented number of key cases were tried. The incidence of litigation prompted a (probably hopeless) search for 'judge-proof' legislation by the government and legalistic stands on all sides.

The combined effects of an ever-changing grant system, unilateral alterations in the rules of the game and legal challenges created a climate of uncertainty in which sub-central budgeting became characterised by mid-year revisions, the use of large contingency funds and the continuous allocation (and re-allocation) of funds. In effect, local government did not know what money it had to spend and the centre did not know what local authorities would spend. Uncertainty has also bred an attitude of 'never do now what you can leave until later' and led to the development of a variety of strategies for avoiding the consequences of ever-changing government policy. These are the devices known collectively as 'creative accountancy', whereby for example expenditure on current services could be disguised as long-term capital expenditure, and vice-versa – thus in the end making sub-central politics even more opaque and further reducing accountability to anyone.

The continuous changes in the grant system and the failure to cut local current expenditure were probably the most serious unintended consequences from the central policy-makers' standpoint, but they were not the only ones. Two examples will suffice. First, capital expenditure did not just fall sharply in line with government plans. The tight revenue squeeze on local authorities made them reluctant to incur capital expenditure generally and to use the revenue from capital sales in particular. Moreover, the receipts from such sales were larger than planned. As a result, capital under-spending fell below the intended levels further exacerbating unemployment in the construction industry, and prompting (unsuccessful) calls from the centre for increased capital expenditure. Second, the resource squeeze on local authorities increased the cost of provision in other parts of the public sector. The mentally and physically handicapped remained in the more expensive National Health Service and were not transferred to local authority care, in line with government policy, because of the resource squeeze on the personal social services. Similarly, many rent increases required for council houses fell on the Department of Health and Social Security.

As the centre abandoned consultation for unilateralism, so local authorities abandoned co-operation for confrontation. Thus, Labour-controlled authorities increased their rates to compensate for loss of grant and their expenditure regularly exceeded government targets. The full-blooded adversary response focused on subsidised public transport. Following the House of Lords decision on the Greater London Council's (GLC) 'fare's fair' policy (see Chapter 8) the government introduced the Transport Act, 1982, to tighten its controls over public transport, especially the level of subsidy. This move was obviously partisan, provoked an antagonistic response and, once again, resort to the courts. Yet the level of subsidies remained high.

The Conservative election programme in 1983 included proposals (adopted at the prompting of Mrs Thatcher and her closest supporters in spite of misgivings among most other ministers) for abolishing the 'overspending', Labour-controlled Greater London and Metropolitan County Councils, and for taking powers to limit rate increases by individual local authorities ('rate-capping'). Abolition of the top-tier authorities in major conurbations could be carried through relatively simply, if messily, by legislation; they were finally abolished, in fact, in 1986. Their strategic, planning and co-ordinating functions were partly dispersed to 'lower-level' authorities, partly allowed to lapse altogether and partly transferred to non-elected Boards. Whether in the long run the need for co-ordinated approaches within socially and geographically integrated conurbations can effectively be tackled in that way remains to be seen.

The other commitment in the 1983 Conservative manifesto was to controlling local authorities' ability to increase rates – justified in part as limiting the burdens placed on local enterprises by councils opposed to the private sector. The power could be and was given by legislation but proved more messy in actual application than abolition of the metropolitan authorities.

The central objective of The Rates Act 1984 is to take away the power of local authorities to determine their own rate level. For this purpose, local authorities fall into two groups: those subject to selective limitation and the rest, subject to a general limitation on local rates as a whole – to be activated, should the need arise, by the secretary of state. To date, the latter has not been activated and will not be considered further.

Under the selective limitation scheme, the secretary of state chooses the local authorities to be rate-capped. He must specify the criteria for his selection: that is, they must be 'high spending' authorities. The local authority must exceed government-determined spending limits or £10 million for the year and its expenditure must be 'excessive'. For 1985–86, for example, 'excessive' meant that the authority exceeded the government-determined limits by 20 per cent and its target by at least 4 per cent. The secretary of state then stipulates a notional level of total expenditure for each selected authority. The authority can appeal against this total; that is, seek a derogation. When the total grant available to local authorities is known, the expenditure limit can be translated into a maximum rate, taking into account the financial reserves of the local authority. If the two sides agree on this rate, it becomes the legal limit. Assuming that the local authority does not agree with this rate level, and that it has not been able to renegotiate it with the secretary of state, the latter can lay an order before the House of Commons or impose, without parliamentary approval, an interim maximum rate. The local authority may not levy a rate which exceeds the maximum stipulated by the secretary of state.

This power means that the government can control both the income and expenditure of local authorities and therefore, sharply increased the degree of centralisation in British government. There are, however, a number of important caveats to such a bald assessment. Pre-existing problems of the financial system remained – for example, the rise in local expenditure and in the rates, repetitive legislation for unintended consequences, and instability and ambiguity. Others were dramatically intensified – for example, politicisation, technical complexity and inequity.

Between 1983 and 1985, local current expenditure continued to rise in real terms and to exceed government planning figures: by £770 million in 1983–84 and £850 million in 1984–85. By the government's own admission local current expenditure rose by 1.5 per cent per annum in real terms throughout the early and mid 1980s. Capital expenditure recovered slightly by 1986–87 although it remained at half the levels prevailing for the 1970s. The pre-existing trend towards reducing the proportion of local expenditure funded by grant continued; it fell to 49 per cent in 1985–86. The corollary was a substantial increase in the rates over and beyond the rate of inflation. Specific grants – tied to following a particular policy the government wished implemented – began to replace general 'block' grants in support of a general service as a further means of central control. Thus between 1981 and 1985, specific grants rose (as a proportion of all grants) from 17.6 per cent to 22.9 per cent (Grant 1986: 20).

The contribution of rate-capping to the reduction of 'over-spend' by local authorities was marginal. First, the government had to accept the existing level of expenditure of a rate-capped authority as the base for cuts; i.e. in effect it 'recognised' the over-spending of previous years. Given that total grant to local government was further reduced, the rate-capped authorities maintained or even increased their share of grant at the expense of other, primarily county, councils. The reductions in this base were not Draconian, in most cases it was simply 'frozen'; i.e. the 'cut' was equal to the rate of inflation. Some other authorities faced more severe cuts depending on the extent to which they had practised 'creative accountancy' in the past. Second, the number of councils affected was small: eighteen in 1984–85 and ten reselected (with two new additions) in 1985–86. The government was implementing a marginal reduction in a marginal number of local authorities and could not expect a dramatic reduction in overall local 'over-spending', let alone total local expenditure. Finally, rate-capping created pressures on other councils to increase their expenditure. High-spending local authorities, worried that they might be future candidates for rate-capping, levied rates to increase their reserves to ensure that they were cut back from the highest feasible level with money in the bank. Even 'moderates' found they had to increase their rates to cope with the additional functions inherited from the abolition of the GLC and the MCCs. The possibility remains that rate-capping, rather than reducing local expenditure and the rates, will actually cause both to rise.

As noted above, the Department of the Environment (DoE) had already been locked into a vicious circle of legislating for unintended consequences and rate-capping/abolition did nothing to break this circle. Because only one of the rate-capped councils was Conservative controlled, the government's action provoked a concerted campaign of opposition from 'victimised' Labour authorities which refused to set a rate. Consequently the government has legislated in the Local Government Act (1986) specifying a date for fixing the rate. The public relations campaign against both rate-capping and abolition was sophisticated and effective. Consequently, the government appointed the Widdicombe Committee to review, amongst other things, 'political' advertising by councils and, anticipating the committee's findings, it hastily introduced legislation to restrict such activities along with a code of practice (see *Local Government Chronicle*, 10 January 1986, p. 25) of such severity that it prohibited all sorts of other, clearly non-political, activities of councils, and had to be modified substantially. The continuing failure to control local expenditure, coupled with the embarrassment of a Scottish rate revaluation which increased assessments on owner-occupiers by enormous amounts, prompted another review of local government finance, the publication of the Green Paper, *Paying for Local Government* (HMSO 1986), and the 'promise' of a 'community tax' – better known as a poll tax – in the next Parliament. This list by no means exhausts the unintended consequences but it does demonstrate that in two short years the spate of legislative activity abated not one jot; repetitive legislation for unintended consequences is itself an important unintended consequence.

Another disadvantage of trying to impose direct controls is that each year the government is subject to fresh controversies and quarrels. To become embroiled often through litigation, in the budgetary details of eighteen or more councils strains organisational resources; provides opportunities for opponents to publicise errors and inconsistencies; and leads to the secretary of state imposing requirements to cut services and make redundancies – actions scarcely likely to enhance his popularity or gain him a good press. It is hardly surprising that the Conservatives did badly in the county council elections of May 1985 and subsequently lost control of the Association of County Councils for the first time ever, a result which further weakened consultative links between centre and locality.

Government proposals of the late eighties for a reform of the whole local budgetary system can be seen as an attempt to break out of this impasse. The proposals have three 'prongs'. One is to take major services such as police and education out of the hands of local authorities altogether and put them under central government, at least as far as finance and administration is concerned. The problem for the government here may be that in doing so it assumes (in the eyes of the public at least) direct responsibility for services whose deficiencies it has hitherto been able to blame on Labour-controlled local authorities. A subsidiary tactic is to force councils to 'contract out' most of their services such as waste removal, cleaning and catering to private firms, thereby diminishing their labour force and importance. Whole physical areas of inner cities may also be taken out of their effective control by setting up 'Enterprise Zones' or 'Development Areas' under special boards nominated by, and responsible to, Whitehall. Meanwhile, privatisation, self-management and 'opting out' will continue to reduce council housing stock and may be applied to any other services that remain in local hands.

A second 'prong' is to set a standard rate on business and commercial property throughout the country, reducing what Conservatives see as unfair discrimination by Labour authorities against the private sector in terms of unduly heavy property taxes. Should businesses then enhance their activity in inner cities, the Conservatives can claim this as a result of their policy.

The third 'prong' is to shift the rest of local taxation from a 'rate' on property, primarily affecting owner-occupiers, to a personal tax on each resident. This it is argued will make the cost of local services clearly apparent to each voter within the vicinity and thus act as a permanent financial restraint on local authorities of whatever political complexion.

Naturally such root-and-branch proposals have the effect of politicising local-central relations even further, especially since they further corrode the basis of Labour's local voting support which has consisted predominantly of council tenants and users of services, as against owner-occupiers and businessmen who support the Conservatives. Labour has scored an initial tactical victory by getting the personal charge labelled as a 'poll tax' (after the enaction which provoked the Peasants' Revolt in the 14th century).

More seriously for the Conservatives, the shift in the tax base will cause many administrative difficulties, chief of which are the problems of tracing and registering those who are supposed to pay it. The mobile, the homeless and the poor could create massive problems of evasion; escalating administrative costs for enforcement; defiance of recalcitrant authorities who enforce it laxly; and, ultimately, heavier costs for Conservative owner-occupiers who are easily traced. As those who do not pay tax will not be allowed on the voting register (and for obvious reasons will be anxious to keep off it) questions of constitutional and democratic propriety will also enter. Again therefore the attempt to deal with central-local relations in terms of a command model may have massive unintended consequences which create more problems than the ones they are supposed to solve.

Enough has been said to illustrate the problems associated with attempts to control local government in England (policies in Scotland, Wales and Northern Ireland have followed broadly the same lines, opposition in the two former cases being compounded by almost 100 per cent Labour control of the local authorities). During the period 1979–87 the Conservative Government also regulated non-departmental public bodies and privatised public corporations. Bypassing of recalcitrant local authorities meant creating or expanding single-function non-departmental agencies. The role of the Manpower Services Commission in providing employment mushroomed. The response to the crisis of the inner cities has been a profusion of special agencies – forerunners of the proposals now advanced. Abolition of the upper tier metropolitan councils produced a battery of quelgos (quasi-elected local government organisations) – joint boards only indirectly responsible to local electorates. Hand-in-hand with this expansion went a series of controls. The government sought to regulate the finance and staffing of the agencies; to develop corporate management techniques; to contract-out specific services as a way of imposing financial discipline; and to liberalise services (e.g. electricity production, express coaches).

The most distinctive policy was privatisation, which emerged to increasing prominence after 1983. A response to escalating public expenditure and frustration with the record of the nationalised industries, this policy raised massive sums of money for the exchequer but, paradoxically, also fostered a *re*-regulation (not *de*regulation) of public industry. The government remains the largest shareholder in many privatised enterprises with an effective veto over policy. It has also established new regulatory agencies – e.g. the Office of Telecommunication (OFTEL) – with more extensive (and precise) powers than existed before.

The post-1984 changes have made the British polity more centralised but, equally, the centre may lack the capacity to realise its objectives. If centralisation is effective (which it has not been to date) the system is likely to be complex, ambiguous, unstable and confused. The resultant policy mess will lead inexorably to further reorganisations of local government, as central interventions fail to produce their intended effects.

Understanding the differentiated polity

The attempt by the Conservative Governments of the 1980s to impose greater centralisation, dramatises the contrast between a unitary state characterised by partnership between all levels of government, local policy making and clear accountability, and a differentiated polity characterised by interdependence, non-local policy making, unclear accountability, and ambiguous and confused relationships in which centralisation and fragmentation co-exist. It is clear that a cardinal fault of the Thatcher Governments has been to employ a simplistic, unitary model of the British polity so at odds with the differentiated reality that failure was virtually guaranteed. Here we analyse various aspects of the present system which make for greater co-ordination or greater fragmentation on the one hand and greater or less public accountability on the other.

Partnership or interdependence?

For the bulk of the post-war period the relationship between central and subcentral government has been viewed as a 'partnership'. In this context the centre actively sought the co-operation of local authorities, avoiding compulsion. In its extreme form the partnership model sees central departments and local authorities as co-equals under Parliament and contains a strong normative component, being used to criticise central interference in, and control over, local affairs. Its major failing lies in its inaccurate description of relationships which vary over time and between policy areas. It had little to say about variations in the political process linking levels of government. A more satisfactory description has to be rooted in the analysis of patterns of interdependence; in a recognition that central dependence on sub-central units (and *vice versa*) is highly variable.

Patterns of interdependence in British government take the form of vertical, function-specific linkages. Policy networks are focused on central spending departments but incorporate a limited range of other actors, notably sub-central governments, the professions and selected interest groups who all contribute to shaping the 'departmental view' discussed in Chapter 2. Such networks differ in various ways including their degree of integration, membership, distribution of resources and extent of central dependence on sub-central units. It is not necessary to describe the several types of policy network to appreciate three important points.

First, fragmentation at the centre, already noted in Chapter 2 as a feature of central government departments, is sustained by the policy networks. Any minister who weakens in defence of his 'empire' will find his backbone stiffened by allies. The networks institutionalise interests in the structure of government, ensuring that their voice is ever-present, enhancing the effectiveness of any opposition and generating a pattern of policy-making characterised by incrementalism and inertia. Second, the networks are closed not only to citizens but also to Parliament. The act of aggregating and incorporating key interests into the structure of government serves to exclude a wide range of other affected groups, with a commensurate decline in accountability. Finally, the networks are the source of policy initiatives; indeed 'policy is its own cause' as the networks respond to their own past policies and the problems they have generated. In other words, much local policy-making has non-local origins. The networks provide the framework within which sub-central governments make decisions, specifying best practice and identifying ideas in good standing. This heresy that the home of local government has only limited local policy making warrants further consideration.

Local or non-local policy-making?

One common approach to policy-making in local government views each local authority as a discrete local political system with the capacity to initiate and maintain distinct policies. The problem with this approach is that it underestimates the importance of non-local sources of policy change. Quite obviously, the policy networks are one such non-local source but the professions and the corporate economy are also important.

The emergence of policy networks is a feature of the growth of the welfare state and allied to this form of differentiation was the process of professionalisation. The specialists in several policy areas became institutionalised in the structure of government. Dependence on expertise accelerated the employment (even creation) of professions which became key influences within the function-specific networks. Major examples include the medical professions in the National Health Service and engineers in the water industry. In both cases, the label 'professionalised network' can be used to describe their distinctive pattern of policy-making, where the profession, as a whole, insulated against outside influences by its peculiar expertise, has strong national institutions and effective communication channels for the dissemination of authoritative ideas.

To a marked degree, therefore, links between the centre and sub-central governments are now based on professional-bureaucratic contacts within policy networks. In marked contrast to the system of *cumul des mandats* in France, where mayors are often also national legislators and administrators, central and political elites in Britain have traditionally been insulated from each other. A dual polity has prevailed wherein the centre has distanced itself from sub-central governments, giving them operational autonomy in matters of 'Low Politics' (for example, public health) in order to enhance its own autonomy in matters of 'High Politics' (for example, foreign and defence policy) (Bulpitt, 1983, ch. 5). In the post-war period, functional politics prevailed over territorial politics and local policy making was dominated by technical criteria.

Corporate involvement in local policy-making is extensive. To take one example only, the sheer scale of the construction programmes mounted by local authorities virtually guarantees close contact with industry. In the evolution of high-rise housing, for example, the construction industry had a major interest in large-scale, technically sophisticated projects and, in consequence, had a regressive influence. Comprehensive urban redevelopment, motorway building and the switch to large district hospitals as well as high-rise housing all illustrate this preference for large-scale investment over the needs and interests of patients, the homeless and inner-city residents (Dunleavy, 1981).

There is thus a range of non-local sources of policy change which suggests that the capacity of local authorities for 'independent' policy initiatives is severely constrained. However, local authorities could still adapt policies to the needs of citizens. They are directly elected and presumably accountable to citizens and responsive to their needs. Such presumptions deserve closer scrutiny.

Accountability or confusion?

There are many dimensions to local accountability. At its simplest it could refer the two-party or Westminster model of local elections whereby the party with a programme of policies preferred by the electorate is returned to office and if it fails to act on its promises, or pursues unpopular policies, can be removed from office at the next election. Unfortunately for this view, turnout at elections is low, knowledge of local services is limited and voting is influenced primarily if not exclusively by trends in the fortunes of the national political parties. The kind of argument also presupposes that the electorate knows who is being held to account for what. Any discussion of accountability encounters the problem that the allocation of responsibility for services is ambiguous and confused, a point ably demonstrated by the Committee of Enquiry into Local Government Finance (Layfield).

The Layfield Committee (1976) was appointed to review the system of local government finance but defined its remit to include central–local relations as a whole. On this topic, it concluded that no firm financial guidelines were available to local authorities; government controls disrupted local budgeting; the cost of local services was not clear to councillors or the public; and the grant system did not make it clear who made the financial decisions. It argued that the central principle of the local government financial system should be 'whoever is responsible for deciding to spend more or less money on providing a service is also responsible for deciding whether to raise more or less taxation' (1976: 45–46 and 50). And by this criterion, the system was ambiguous and confused. This conclusion, as we have seen, remains entirely valid, with repeated changes adding instability to ambiguity and confusion. Whether the 'poll-tax' would help to clarify accountability remains to be seen.

If attention is switched from local government to sub-central governments in general, then the problem of accountability becomes even more acute. A major justification for *ad hoc* bodies is to distance ministers from particular services; to give managers a higher degree of operating autonomy. Consequently, accountability to Parliament becomes attenuated. Yet these bodies are appointed, not elected, and therefore not subject to any kind of local accountability. With some justification they have been described as 'the secret state' because of their immunity to direct political control (Dearlove and Sanders, 1984, ch. 5).

Only part of sub-central government is accountable to elected representatives therefore and, in the case of local government, that system of accountability is undermined by the failure to identify, in even the broadest terms, who is responsible for what. Confusion of responsibilities is tantamount to a breakdown in the system of accountability.

Local autonomy or fragmented centralisation?

Local autonomy is an elusive phrase. It can be defined as involvement in 'substantial activities over which it (local government) has a considerable degree of choice' and it can be seen as 'an essential element in achieving more responsible, responsive and accountable government'. The specific merits of such autonomy include diffusion of power; diversity of response to variations in local need; social learning through experimental means of service provision; and accessibility to citizens (Jones and Stewart 1983: 13–14). This and similar conceptions of local autonomy have to confront a key question; does local autonomy actually exist or is it an ideal to be striven for?

The impact of the foregoing analysis is to suggest that local autonomy has always been more an ideal than a reality. Thus, the phrase refers to local authorities, and yet in the differentiated polity there is a range of non-elected sub-central bodies immune to political control. Local choice is severely constrained by interdependence and non-local forces whilst the system of accountability is ambiguous and confused. Local autonomy has to be seen, therefore, as a yardstick for measuring the *defects* of local government, not for describing its merits. Any description of the relationship between the centre and sub-central governments has to start with the fragmentation of the centre into policy networks and the incorporation of selected sub-central interests into these integrated yet closed networks. Moreover, such networks are the major (non-local) source of policies. Consequently, fragmentation within the centre co-exists with centralisation based upon the individual policy networks. This pattern of relationships may be judged inferior to a system of local autonomy. But its existence constitutes a major obstacle to the revival of local self government and cannot be simply wished away by reformers.

The consequences of differentiation

Juxtaposing a unitary and a differentiated map of British government courts the twin dangers of over-simplification and over-statement. But the importance of an accurate map has been amply demonstrated since 1979 with Mrs Thatcher's Governments' ambitious attempt to create the minimal state and reduce public (especially local) expenditure. The centre has tried to impose its view of the nature of British government on sub-central governments. The map which guided its journey is best described as a command map; government was seen as a bureaucracy in which the centre's wishes were transmitted down the line to the lowest level. Bureaucracy was to be reduced by bureaucratic means. This command map confronted the messy reality of the disaggregated, differentiated polity. Rather than simplifying the government machine, the government made it more complex. The history of British government outside Westminster and Whitehall since 1979 is the sad story of a centre failing to understand the terrain it sought to traverse. Its map was faulty and the results can only be described as a policy mess wherein no one achieved their objectives.

Conclusions

To understand the sub-central government of Britain, it is necessary to accept that the idealised picture of a unitary state has been superseded by the reality of a differentiated polity. Rather than starting with local autonomy, the analysis of actual operations must focus on disaggregation, differentiation, interdependence and policy networks. To understand the system of sub-central government in the 1980s, three features require special attention.

First, the relationship between the centre and sub-central governments is one of *asymmetric interdependence*; that is, a combination of a strong executive tradition with disaggregated service delivery systems and 'hands-off' controls. There is a recurrent tension between interdependence and authoritative decision making by the centre. If the centre unilaterally determines the parameters of local action, then sub-central governments can delay and frustrate central intervention. The Conservative Government, despite its strong-arm methods, has been no more successful than any of its predecessors in resolving the problem.

Second, government action has undermined the long-standing political insulation of centre from locality and politicised inter-governmental relations. The government's determination to control individual local authorities has brought ministers into continuous conflict with local leaders. At one time inter-governmental relations could be described as government and politics 'beyond Whitehall'. Now they are part and parcel of the politics of Whitehall. Ministers have found that sub-central governments can impose high political costs on the centre and politicisation may yet prove to be the most significant change of the 1980s, the full impact still to be felt.

Finally, with the demise of the dual polity, the centre lacks an effective philosophy for the management of territorial politics. The idea that central government can simply command compliance is unrealistic. Tentatively, the government has experimented with populist methods of bypassing sub-central governments. It has appealed direct to citizens, vesting them with legal rights *vis à vis* local authorities (for example, by strengthening the ability of parents to choose a school for their children). But as yet no coherent strategy has replaced either the unwanted dual polity or the faulty command code. Without a coherent mode of operating, the phenomena of instability, ambiguity, and confusion, noted above, are destined to remain central features of the system, with the government locked into an ever more frustrating spiral of legislation for unintended consequences.

Chapter 7
The European Communities

Community institutions

Has membership of the European Community added another layer to the differentiated polity, blurring the lines of responsibility and accountability still further? Or has the necessity of producing a single British view to put to the other members helped reduce internal confusion? As we shall see, there is something to be said on both sides of this question.

We should note at the outset that the Community itself is not a single institution. At least four separate bodies are involved in the Community relationship with British governments. The best known is the European Commission, a body of seventeen technocrats located in Brussels; two nominated by each of the five big countries in the Community (Britain, France, Italy, Spain and West Germany) and one nominated by each of the smaller countries (Denmark, Ireland, Netherlands, Belgium, Luxembourg, Portugal and Greece). The job of the Commission is to initiate all Community legislation, and send its policy proposals for decision by the Council of Ministers (which we describe below). In making proposals, the Commission consults with the various national governments, interest groups, etc. It also mediates Council decisions. In addition, the Commission has the task of implementing numerous regulations emanating from the Treaty of Rome (the original agreement which set up the Community) and from previous Council decisions. The Commission sees that the Treaty is observed by member states, and any infringements may be reported to the Court of Justice of the European Communities, the second major community body which affects Britain and which sits in Luxembourg. The Court, consisting of one judge from each state, ensures the observance of Community laws. Its decisions are made by majority verdict, and are binding on members.

The Commission is often viewed as the community institution most likely to interfere in British affairs. It is certainly true that in the implementation of policy it is vested with authority that is independent of national governments. But the Commission is still tied by decisions made by the Council of Ministers. The more significant development is the supreme authority of the Court over British courts and over Parliament. Traditionally, courts in Britain have seen themselves as merely interpreting Acts of Parliament. To what extent this view is correct we shall see in Chapter 8. The explicit task of the European Court, however, is to ensure that the Acts of national parliaments or governments do not conflict with the founding agreements of the Community embodied in the Treaty of Rome. For the first time Britain has in this Treaty a written constitution that limits the supremacy of Parliament, a fact that renders the position of the Court very important.

The third major Community body is the Council of Ministers, which again meets in Brussels. The Council consists of a General Council and various technical councils. The foreign ministers of member states meet in the General Council, while ministers for particular policy areas such as agriculture meet in the technical councils. Associated with the ministerial councils is the Committee of Permanent Representatives (COREPER in Community jargon). COREPER I 'shadows' the Foreign Ministers and consists of the national ambassadors to the Community. COREPER II consists of the deputy ambassadors. Associated with it are numerous committees and working parties of appropriately qualified national civil servants. All these bodies carry out detailed preparatory work for the meetings of corresponding ministers.

The single-chamber European Parliament (whose members were first directly elected for 'Euro-constituencies' in June 1979; Britain has eighty-one such constituencies) is the fourth major community body. It meets for one part of the year in Strasbourg and for another part in Luxembourg, often holding committee hearings in Brussels. It does a great deal of its work in specialised committees like the select committees of the British Parliament. Although its members belong to six major party groups (Socialist, Liberal, Christian Democrat, Progressive Democrat, Conservative and Communist) and some small groupings, party divisions do not dominate its life as they do the House of Commons. This is partly because its competence is limited, so there is little as yet to divide over. Its major powers – to dismiss the Commission and reject the Budget – can be wielded only with a two-third majority. Its main influence is through publicity and investigation where it has extensive and increasing scope, particularly in regard to the Commission. Apart from the Parliament the main representative body is the Economic and Social Committee, but this is merely a consultative meeting of business and union interests with no formal powers.

Figure 7.1 graphs relationships between the European bodies. The outcomes of Community deliberations are expressed in directives, regulations, opinions and resolutions emanating from the Council of Ministers, and in judgements and opinions of the European Court. How far do these curtail the freedom of British governments to act independently or take the internal initiatives required, for example, by the need for economic regeneration? At the root of most British opposition to the Community (which divided both Conservatives and Labour, quite bitterly, in the 1970s) is concern over the political and/or constitutional implications of EC membership. The main issue has been the loss of sovereignty by national political institutions to the European Community. Given the controversies over this point, discussion is too often superficial and couched in political rhetoric. The actual situation is more like that of central and sub-central government inside Britain. Inevitably certain structural constraints are imposed by membership on British domestic and international policies. What is usually

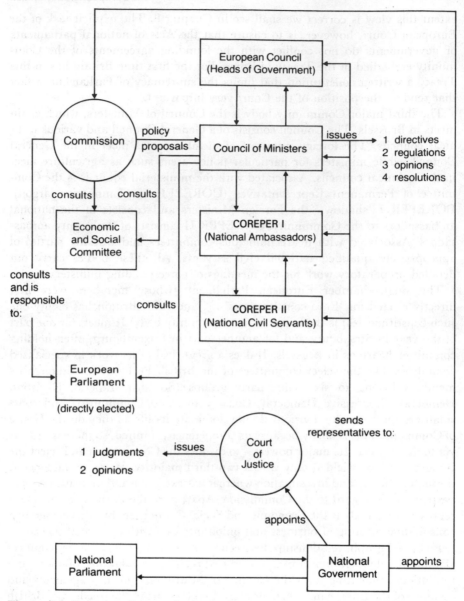

Figure 7.1 European Community institutions and their relationships with each other and with national bodies

not mentioned is Britain's considerable influence over Community policy through government participation in its decision-making bodies. In the remainder of this chapter we shall examine both aspects of the present situation.

The European Communities and British government

In acceding to the Treaty of Rome in January 1973, Britain was accepting a body of law which formally committed governments to certain common European policies, and to defined procedures for reaching decisions on these policies and enforcing their implementation. The Treaty of Rome, however, cannot always be taken at face value. Like many national constitutions, it often deals with prescriptions and intentions rather than hard realities. It is, too, a document that is subject to various interpretations, at least in areas where the European Court has not been asked to pronounce. Now it has also been supplemented by the Single European Act (see below). It is difficult, then, to pin down the precise characteristics of the European Community and the ways in which Community membership affects national governments. The EC is also an evolving organisation, moving when it can into new policy areas or those areas of common action designated by the Treaty of Rome and the SEA but not yet implemented. In some policy areas, the progress has been smooth and straightforward; in other areas, innumerable setbacks to common action have occurred. Equally difficult to describe generally are the decision-making structures. Sometimes, it is all too easy to point to the dominance of national governments in the making of common policies. But there are certainly instances in which Community institutions such as the Commission and the Court of Justice exercise considerable authority. Despite these problems in generalising about the characteristics of the European Community, it is useful to examine the effects of the EC on British Governments in terms of (a) the substantive areas of EC policy and action; (b) the EC policy-making process; and (c) implementation of EC policies.

Substantive areas of EC policy

The EC has moved with varying degrees of success towards the creation of a customs union, then a common market, and finally the harmonisation of social and economic policies. The final stage implies full political union. It is in the creation of a customs union that EC policies have been notably successful. Under the terms of the Treaty, the British government ceded its authority to fix quotas or taxes on imported goods (tariffs) and to subsidise exports independently. The General Agreement on Tariffs and Trade (GATT) is the international organisation under which tariffs and trading agreements are fixed. But GATT negotiations are now conducted by the Commission on behalf of Britain and other EC member states. Thus what was once an area of national competence has become an area of EC competence. The British government is not excluded completely from taking action on tariffs. But that action must be approved by the Commission and fit within the framework of GATT provisions negotiated by the Commission. Thus, in February 1980 the British government sought and gained permission from the Commission to fix import quotas on certain US synthetic textiles. The Commission allowed the British government to freeze 1980 imports at the level of the average volume for the previous two years. A similar request, however, to limit the import of tufted carpets into Britain from the United States was not allowed.

Though trading agreements for tufted carpets seem a world away from the controversies of high politics they are, nonetheless, part of a range of tariff questions which have vital importance for the British economy. As tariff negotiations have become the responsibility of the Community, so have national governments lost an important weapon in their armoury of economic policies. Governments ignoring tariff regulations and taking unilateral action can soon find themselves at odds with the Community and legally bound to pursue policies in accordance with the Rome Treaty. Where governments have in fact ignored Community directives, as in the case of France in the 1975 'wine war' with Italy and the 1980 surcharge on British lamb imports, there is strong Community pressure on the recalcitrant state to bring policies into line with common practice.

While the EC is firmly established as a customs union, progress has not been so rapid in the building of a common market. A common market implies a higher stage of co-operation than a customs union. It involves the free movement of labour and capital and the elimination of barriers to competition. The Treaty of Rome is quite clear in setting out the various provisions for the creation of a common market. But these provisions have been enforced quite haphazardly. Take the case of the free movement of capital. Throughout the 1970s, the British government placed limits on the amount of money that British citizens could send abroad either for investment or consumption. Though the limits placed on money sent to EC member states were higher than those for non-EC states, such limits were not sanctioned by the Rome Treaty. Yet the Commission did very little to force British compliance with the Treaty provisions. When in 1980 the Conservative Government finally abolished exchange control regulations, it was presented as an act based on economic doctrine (and probably North Sea oil wealth) rather than on a desire to comply with the Rome Treaty. Such a conclusion seems even more justified when we remember that all exchange control regulations were abolished, not merely those that applied to capital transfers to the European Community.

Progress towards eliminating the barriers to competition has also been haphazard. Fiscal harmonisation has proceeded to the point where there is a common turnover tax (VAT) throughout the European Community. But the British government, like other EC governments, has still retained its prerogatives in many other areas of taxation, such as income tax. Even where VAT is concerned, each government remains free to fix the rate at which tax is charged. Community control of certain discriminatory taxation policies has been more evident. British whisky producers, for instance, were pleased to see the European Court's outlawing of discriminatory taxation on certain kinds of alcoholic spirits. In some EC member states, such as Denmark and Italy, it had been government practice to impose lower duties (taxes) on home-produced spirits than on those produced elsewhere.

Other areas of competition policy also show uneven development. The granting of subsidies by national governments, for instance, is illegal under EC competition rules, except within the (officially defined) less developed regions. In Britain, these regions consist of Scotland, Wales, Northern Ireland and much of the northern part of England. The EC, through a ruling of the

European Court, was able in 1978 to prevent the British government from giving a subsidy to pig farmers. But, over the same period, there seemed much less willingness on the part of the EC to control the activities of the National Enterprise Board in giving preferential loans to British industry. Austin-Rover and British Steel are notable examples of firms receiving government aid which might be construed as illegal under the terms of the Rome Treaty.

The Commission has also been eager to achieve agreement on rules for awarding public sector contracts. While national governments continue to give preference to domestic firms in awarding government contracts, a common market cannot be said to exist. Understandably, perhaps, governments of the various EC member states have shown some reluctance in formulating a common policy. As a consequence, progress has been slow. The Commission has had more success in achieving agreement on Community-wide specifications for manufactured products. So long as each national government issues its own specifications, markets are defined by national boundaries. British electric fires, for instance, could not be sold in France because they did not meet French safety specifications for such appliances. Firms could compete throughout the EC only through the costly business of gearing production to meet the specifications of each member state. In such circumstances, home firms are distinctly advantaged in their domestic markets. Much of the energy of Community administrators is focused on common product specification and over 2,000 directives have been issued on this point.

The trade and industrial policies reviewed above represent only some of the directions in which the EC has moved in order to develop a common market within Europe. In the industrial sector, as we have seen, the process is by no means complete. There is a dual problem: first, that of reaching agreement on common policies, and then in enforcing those common policies. In the commercial sector of the economy, there has been still less progress. National laws, for instance, still prevent French and Italian citizens from purchasing life insurance, or indeed any other form of insurance, on the British market. It is only in the agricultural sector that the EC has made major progress towards the creation of a common market, through the Common Agricultural Policy (CAP). In this case, the common market has been achieved by an EC price support system covering most agricultural products. Prices are fixed at the Community level.

The CAP represents one of the few instances of the successful harmonisation of national policies at the European level. It has been criticised in Britain because of the effect of the price support system in raising consumer food prices. Nonetheless it provides, or is intended to provide, basic income security for large numbers of poor agricultural producers throughout western Europe. Britain is unusual in having the smallest agricultural population in western Europe. The tiny inefficient farms found in many parts of continental Europe and Ireland are rare in Britain. Thus Britain gains little from the redistributive impact of the CAP. Since the early 1970s, the EC has been keen to promote other redistributive policies. On the initiative of Willi Brandt, then Chancellor of the German Federal Republic, the October 1972 summit of the EC heads of government in Paris called for vigorous Community action in the social field. The summit demanded a programme of action on employment training, work conditions, workers' participation, consumer protection and regional development. In 1974 a programme was approved signalling a more interventionist phase in the Community's development. Since then, further grants have been available for the restructuring of industry and the development of infrastructure, channelled through such bodies as the European Regional Development Fund and the various funds of the European Coal and Steel Community. Loans at preferential interest rates have also been made available through the European Investment Bank and similar facilities.

The supporters of these new initiatives hoped that the EC would cease to be identified merely as an organisation facilitating trade and investment for European businessmen. They hoped also that agriculture would cease to be the only major area into which EC resources were channelled. With the passage of the Single European Act by the European and national Parliaments in 1986–87, coupled with the budget crisis as expenditures outgrew the tax base, some of these hopes came closer to being realised. The budget crisis prompted demands for more taxes to be raised for the Community through an extension of VAT, but also involved heavy cuts in farm subsidies, with diversion of revenues to the social programmes and the promotion of new technology. The Single European Act was a modest step towards a more efficient Community; it gave slightly increased powers to Commission and Parliament: provided for more majority voting on the European Council, endorsed new policies for research and environment, made a formal commitment to abolish trade barriers by 1992, and provided a more stable basis for Community co-operation on foreign policy, including a small new political secretariat operating in Brussels. The Act was perhaps more important symbolically than in terms of practical effects. It showed that the structure of the Community could be modified in a more federalist direction, in spite of the apathy or downright hostility of some national governments, and that Community-wide initiatives could be taken on some of the more pressing economic problems, such as the development of information technology.

The development of Community initiatives is still spasmodic and uncertain however. In very few areas have EC policies effectively replaced national policies. There have been interminable delays in formulating common policies, and also inconsistencies in their enforcement once they have been agreed. As far as British government is concerned, there are some areas of policy, such as tariffs and agriculture, which were once dealt with at national level and are now almost exclusively handled at Community level. This means that government departments like MAFF (Ministry of Agriculture, Fisheries and Food) have a very important European dimension to their work. But such has been the range of EC initiatives that there is hardly a government department that is not in some way involved in EC activity. Certainly, departments such as those of Trade and Industry are affected by EC membership; both are concerned with tariff policy, and must clearly bear in mind EC legislation when considering, for example, policies involving government aid to industry. Even the Home Office is affected by EC membership. As the department responsible for the issue of visas and work permits, it has been very much affected by the EC policy on the free movement of labour within the member states. Treasury policies are affected by EC policies on spending and fiscal harmonisation, etc. The list can go on. The Foreign and Commonwealth Office (FCO) is also heavily involved as the harmonisation of foreign policies has been an unexpected and spectacular success of the Community. It also acts as the main liaison between national ministries and the EC organisations.

In terms of substantive policies, there can be little argument that Britain has become deeply enmeshed in the European Community. Though the depth of involvement differs among various policy areas, it nonetheless covers an extremely wide range of government activity. How, though, have the *processes* of British government been affected by EC membership? To answer this question, let us now look at how policies are made in the Community.

The EC policy-making process and British politics

One of the persisting doubts (among the doubters) about British membership of the EC concerns the extent to which the British government has ceded its authority in important areas of national policy to a *supranational* organisation. When Britain joined the EC, she was already a member of several other international organisations: the United Nations, The North Atlantic Treaty Organisation (NATO), the Organisation for Economic Co-operation and Development (OECD), the International Monetary Fund (IMF), etc. All these organisations involved, to some extent, an international commitment by the British government, even to the point of declaring war. The perceived difference, however, between the latter organisations and the EC is that they are *inter-governmental*. Decisions within these international organisations are made by agreement among national representatives. No government is obliged to agree to a policy that it does not want to accept. The British government, therefore, could not be told what to do and be obliged to comply. In the EC, it could be told what to do. In principle, the EC has authority over the British government.

A supranational authority was exactly what the original founders of the EC had wanted. In practice, however, the way in which policy is made in the Community shows that national governments have lost very little of their authority. The EC's founding fathers had envisaged that the *Commission*, which is the executive body, would share authority with the *Council of Ministers*, which is the decision-making body representing the various member states. One of the jobs of the Commission is to initiate all EC legislation. It formulates various policy proposals by consulting with national governments and interest groups, and then submits these proposals for consideration by the Council.

As noted above the Council consists of a General Council and various technical councils. The foreign ministers of the various member states meet as the General Council, while ministers for particular policy areas, such as agriculture, trade, social security, etc., meet in the technical councils. The decisions of the Council are issued in the form of regulations, directives, recommendations, and resolutions. Regulations have the immediate force of Community law. Directives, on the other hand, though binding on member states, leave national governments free to determine the means of carrying out the policies concerned. Thus the Community directive on direct elections to the European Parliament necessitated the British government putting its own Bill on the elections through Parliament and adopting the single constituency, simple plurality method of election as opposed to the PR systems used by its partners.

Though the above outline approximates to the formal procedures for EC policy-making, it conceals the developments since 1966 which have brought about a considerable increase in the power and authority of the Council. The Rome Treaty neither provides for the effective voting system used in the Council, nor for the growth of two important institutions linked to the Council: COREPER (The Committee of Permanent Representatives) and the European Council.

Under the terms of the Rome Treaty, a weighted voting system is used in Council decision-making, which allows policies to be determined by majority decision. In practice, however, ever since the Luxembourg Compromise in 1966, which ended a French boycott of Community institutions, any member state has been able to exercise a technical veto on a policy which it feels will threaten its vital national interests. In such cases the veto works simply by not putting the proposal to a vote. The veto powers enjoyed by each member state are extremely broad for there is no precise definition as to what constitutes vital national interests. Few governments would presume to define the vital national interests of another, or be prepared to have others judge their own. On more than one occasion the British government has successfully argued that the mesh size of fishing nets is a matter of vital national interest to Britain.

The only occasion when the Luxembourg compromise has broken down and 'vital national interests' have apparently been ignored was during the May 1982 meeting of Community agricultural ministers. The British Government was the last one to hold out on the 1982 farm price increases, already agreed by the other nine community members. Amidst growing frustration with British intransigence, the farm deal was put to the vote by the Belgian President of the Council, receiving the support of all but the British, Danish and Greek representatives. Accordingly, the price increases were approved by qualified majority. This practice will become more common with acceptance of the Single European Act described above. However, the more significant point is that in the period from 1982 to the passage of the Single Act, not one other decision was made in the Council by majority voting. A majority of member states, including all the large ones, seem unwilling to see the 1982 vote as setting a general precedent. They point to the particular circumstances surrounding it. First, and most important, Britain had no objection in principle to the proposed price increases. By holding out on the issue, Britain was hoping to obtain agreement on completely different and unrelated issues, namely her budget rebate for 1982 and trade sanctions against Argentina; thus it could be claimed that on the question of farm price increases there was no threat to British interests. Second, Britain had delayed agreement on the farm deal far longer than in previous years. Governments in the other member states faced considerable political pressure at home to bring the issue to a speedy conclusion.

On the whole, the particular way in which decisions are made within the

Council has meant that Britain and the other member states have increasingly viewed Community decision-making as a bargaining process. It has been in the interests of the British government to define its national interests carefully and then engage in horse-trading both within and across policy areas. The result has been an enormous expansion of the number of bodies in which trading takes place. When a Commission proposal arrives at the Council, it is immediately sent to one of the committees or working parties attached to COREPER. These committees and working parties consist of civil servants representing each member state. Some are permanent, such as the Article 113 Committee which assists the Commission in trade and tariff negotiations, and the standing committees on agriculture and employment. Many of the working parties, however, are set up on an *ad hoc* basis; on average there are approximately fifty in operation. It is in these committees and working parties of national civil servants that the major part of Council business is handled.

It is only when a proposal cannot be agreed at the level of COREPER's working parties that it is passed up for negotiation at a higher level. In such cases, the function of the working parties will be to determine the major points at issue between the various parties. From the working parties, the proposals go first to Part II of COREPER, consisting of the deputy permanent representatives of the member states (i.e. the deputy ambassadors). If necessary, it will go to Part I of COREPER, consisting of the full permanent representatives. It is only when a matter has not been agreed at this level that it will go for discussion in the full session of the Council of Ministers.

It is in the nature of EC bargaining that disputes between parties tend to involve trade-offs across a whole range of issues. Such bargains can be struck most effectively by those at the centre of the policy-making process. It was a natural progression, therefore, that the European Council should have been set up in the early 1970s. The European Council is the thrice-yearly meeting of the European heads of government. Each member state takes its turn in hosting the meeting. Though having no formal basis in the Treaty of Rome, the European Council is the forum in which agreement can best be reached on the most intractable issues within the Community. It is rarely concerned with the fine details of an issue. These are left to the various technical councils and the working parties of COREPER: the Council instead seeks to influence the broad direction of EC policy and to iron out disputes among the member states. It was the natural forum in which the countries like Italy, which were most anxious to see progress towards more integration, could get agreement to initiate the process leading to the Single European Act – substantially watering down the proposals, however, to get the agreement of more reluctant federalists like Britain. A typical meeting will trade concessions in one area for progress in another; in 1979–80 for example the European Council discussed, among other items, Britain's budgetary contribution to the EC, which the British government claimed was disproportionately large compared to the budgetary contributions of other members. The deal that was eventually worked out to solve this problem involved the British government's agreeing to an increase in EC agricultural prices (something unpopular with British consumers), and also the rechannelling of Community money to Britain through the regional aid programmes. In this instance, then, a bargain was struck which involved three major areas of policy.

It could be said that the bargaining over Britain's contribution broke down in May 1982 when the British government was outvoted on the farm price increases. Farm prices could no longer be kept as a bargaining ploy in negotiations over budget contributions and economic sanctions against Argentina. More to the point, however, is that Britain overestimated the strength of her bargaining hand. The fact that unlimited sanctions were agreed by eight members of the Community and that a budget compromise was also agreed just a few days after the farm vote, suggests that bargaining still has an important place to play.

As things stand, there is little doubt that the Council of Ministers and the other institutions representing member states dominate the EC decision-making process. Though the Commission has been eager to take initiatives on common policies, it has usually found itself playing a mediating role. The Commission has been obliged to accept a much more gradualist view of European integration than the one it had adopted in the early days of the Community. As studies of EC policy-making have indicated, the formulation of common policy has depended far more on the strength of support among national governments for a particular policy than upon the activities of the Commission. Even where strong support is forthcoming, determined opposition from another member state can effectively stifle the legislative process. It is for this reason that we are likely to see a continuation of existing constitutional practices within the Council of Ministers.

The direct election of the European Parliament (the first elections were held in June 1979 and a second set in 1984) has also made little difference to the policy-making dominance of the Council of Ministers and its associated organisations. Like the appointed European Parliament before it, the present parliament has few powers with which to challenge the authority of the Council, though it has become more assertive in recent years in delaying approval of the Community budget and in putting pressure on national governments (e.g. by passing a form of the Single European Act before it was approved by the European Council).

What consequences, overall, has the EC policy-making process had for the processes of British government? First, it is clear that the *executive branch* of British government is very closely involved with the Community decision-making process, at all stages. It is consulted by the Commission when the latter formulates its policy proposals; it is also, with the executives of the other member states, at the centre of the Council decision-making process. As a consequence, British government ministers and civil servants now make frequent trips to Brussels, engaging in meetings both with the Commission and their counterparts from other member states. Prime Ministers meet in the European Council, ministers in the Council and its technical councils, and civil servants in working parties of COREPER and other committees.

Besides the home civil servants making frequent trips to Brussels, there are also significant numbers based for longer periods at the United Kingdom Permanent Representation to the European Communities. Though this office is headed by officials from the Foreign and Commonwealth Office, approximately two-thirds of its staff consist of home civil servants from other government departments. In its own way, the Permanent Representation is a mini-Whitehall, and is thus quite different from the usual British embassy abroad. The home civil servants are seconded for approximately two-year periods. They make up many of the regular staff of COREPER's working parties. Though formally accountable to the FCO, they maintain close liaison with their home ministries.

The close involvement of the executive branch of British government in the EC policy-making process stems, of course, from the fact that policy is determined by a process of bargaining between national governments. These circumstances in turn affect the way Britain's EC policy is formulated. Clearly, in many areas of policy, British officials do not think of their role in terms of formulating a bargaining position. Relationships between the British government and the EC are very much an ongoing process, day by day and minute by minute. In this way, relationships between departmental civil servants and their opposite numbers in Community secretariats are rather like those they have had in the past with some domestic interest groups (Ch. 2).

From the British point of view, much EC legislation and activity is entirely non-controversial. However, the fact that policy is decided through negotiations between national governments and that there are, on occasion, questions which arouse considerable controversy, pervades the entire policy-formulation process. The British government thus tends to define and defend its interests in relation to the Community as a whole and the other member states. The simple result of these perceptions is that the Foreign and Commonwealth Office, which traditionally represents British interests abroad, has become the central co-ordinating ministry for EC policy. It organises the UK Permanent Representation in Brussels and acts as the link between the home civil servants based in Brussels and their counterparts in the Whitehall ministries. The European Communities Section in the FCO is responsible for most of the co-ordinating work; it consists of several desk-men covering different EC policy areas.

European Community membership has meant that the FCO has come to play an important new role in the domestic policy process. The importance that the FCO attaches to this is illustrated by the fact that in 1982 the Permanent Under-Secretary and the Deputy Permanent Under-Secretary of the FCO were Britain's last two ambassadors to the European Community. It might well be argued that the FCO has found a convenient new *raison d'etre* at a time when Britain's influence in the world, and therefore the role of the Foreign Office, was declining.

Though the FCO plays a co-ordinating role in formulating Britain's EC policy, it does not have the technical competence to determine that policy by itself: in discussing, for instance, the specifications of an industrial product, it is hardly within its competence to make an effective contribution. Thus there is considerable reliance on the functional ministries which do possess such expertise. Departments closely involved in formulating British EC policy in their areas of competence are the Treasury, MAFF (Agriculture and Fisheries), DoE (Environment), Trade, Industry and Energy. Most of these departments have EC sections co-ordinating their involvement with the Community.

Departmental representatives liaise with the FCO, but also participate directly in meetings of specialists held under the aegis of the Commission; in the working parties and associated committees of COREPER; and also in *ad hoc* committees shadowing Council and European Council meetings. The functional departments also play a major role in the preparation of briefs for Council meetings.

Co-ordination of British policy is achieved for the most part through a series of informal telephone contacts among officials from interested government departments. But there is also a committee system through which EC policy can be discussed. At a basic level, there are a series of interdepartmental committees in the major policy areas. There is also considerable scope for the creation of *ad hoc* committees, bringing together the people most immediately concerned with a particular policy issue. Usually, these *ad hoc* committees are organised at the instigation of one of the functional departments. Its composition might vary widely. A committee meeting on shipbuilding subsidies, for instance, would be chaired by a representative from the Department of Industry, and include officials from the Treasury, the Department of Employment, the FCO, and possibly the Welsh, Scottish or Northern Irish Offices. Only the FCO would be represented on every committee.

Above the specialist policy committees is a European Communities Committee that oversees the preparation of briefs for the Permanent Representation and the Council meetings, and is generally responsible for the co-ordination of Britain's EC policy. There has also been an even higher level committee of top civil servants who have discussed the longer-term issues involving Britain's membership of the European Community. Almost certainly, when the Labour Party was proposing, in the early 1980s, to withdraw Britain from the EC, there was high-level discussion of the implications (economic, political, etc.) of withdrawal.

In its capacity as a central co-ordinating body, the Cabinet Office also plays a significant role in the formulation of Britain's EC policy. Officials from the Cabinet Office attend the regular committee meetings on the EC, and are very closely involved in the more controversial Community issues. They also play a mediating role in ironing out differences between government departments: such a mediating role is especially important in EC policy, where the government tries to present its views in Council meetings in terms of a national consensus.

Besides all the interdepartmental civil service committees concerned in formulating Britain's EC policies there are, too, political interministerial committees. These include a Cabinet Committee composed of the ministers most affected by EC activities, which regularly discusses EC issues and which is chaired by the Foreign Secretary.

Many of these arrangements for co-ordinating policy form an extension of the inter-departmental committees and negotiating sessions already described in Chapter 2. What is new is the central co-ordinating role of the Foreign and Commonwealth Office, and the opportunities for civil servants from different Ministries to work closely within the same organisation in Brussels, at the British Permanent Representation. With the additional complexity of the

Community bureaucracy to contend with, we might have expected the existing fragmentation of British administration to increase. In fact, the negotiation of additional Common Market agreements seems to have been assimilated into the existing structure with considerable ease.

This may of course stem from the ability of a loose-jointed structure to adapt comfortably, but still loose-jointedly, where a tighter-knit organisation might have had to recast its entire procedures. And as we have seen, change towards greater co-ordination in British administration might have been no bad thing. It is typical that Community membership has not strengthened the hands of the Treasury, the traditional co-ordinating department; nor has it produced a notable expansion in the role of the Cabinet Office, which might have been expected to plan centrally for all the activities of government. Instead a third co-ordinator has arisen in this specialised area, one without much technical expertise and with a traditional, rather cautious, attitude. With this development the fragmentation at lower levels of British government is also reflected among the co-ordinating agencies.

The Community structure also adds substantially to the points at which agreements from other parties have to be obtained in the process of making policy. This increases the already large number of bodies with inherent blocking abilities which exist inside Britain and which we examined in the last chapter. The greater the number of decision points, the less likely is a policy to be agreed and implemented – though conversely the more extended opportunities are for affected interests to make their views heard. In light of the much greater complexity of the Community structure it is surprising and reassuring that British administrative processes have adapted to it with relative efficiency. While membership has done nothing to reduce fragmentation in British government, it has not notably increased it.

One reason for this lies in the tendency of British interest groups to work directly with departments in London rather than negotiating at one remove with Community agencies in Brussels. It is certainly true that such groups, whether employers' associations, trade unions or others, have developed links with European organisations representing their respective interests, but co-operation still seems minimal. Some interest group representatives are formally involved in EC organisations through their membership of such bodies as the European Economic and Social Committee. The latter, however, has only consultative functions. Other British interest groups have sent delegations to the Commission and the European Parliament when they have wanted to have their say on a particular issue. The problem is that policy is made in the Council through the process of bargaining between member states. Thus interest groups have found it to their advantage to focus their attention on their own national government and, indeed, on the particular government department responsible for their own policy area. The National Union of Farmers therefore seeks to influence the Common Agricultural Policy through the Ministry of Agriculture. At best, the Commission or the European MPs will be viewed as an important ally in obtaining the desired outcome. There is no doubt, though, that in the ordering of priorities the Whitehall department most immediately concerned is the first group that needs to be convinced of a particular policy.

The focus of interest group activity, then, has changed little since Britain joined the Community.

The picture that emerges from our analysis of British involvement in EC policy-making is one of the dominance of the national government. For the British Parliament, the picture is not so satisfactory. Indeed, it could be argued that one of the major consequences of EC membership has been the burgeoning power of the British executive. There has certainly been a problem in exercising public control over decisions made by national governments in the Council of Ministers. From the point of view of the British Parliament, the mere fact that decisions having the immediate force of law can be made in the Council of Ministers means that Parliament is no longer the supreme law-making body in all areas.

The best that Parliament can hope for in controlling EC legislation is to exert control over the British government's negotiating position within the Council, the European Council, or COREPER. In practice, the experience of Parliament in trying to exert this control has been less than happy. When Britain joined the European Community, the Foster Committee in the House of Commons and the Maybray-King Committee in the House of Lords were set up to report on appropriate methods of scrutiny. In the Commons, the Committee on European Secondary Legislation was formed in May 1974; it consisted of sixteen members. From the beginning, it was clear that the Committee would be hard pressed to fulfil its functions of scrutiny. The Committee has the right to examine draft proposals submitted by the Commission to the Council of Ministers. These documents are supplied by the relevant Whitehall departments. However, the Committee has extremely limited powers once it has received the documents. It is *not* empowered to debate the merits or demerits of a Commission proposal; all it may do is to recommend that a particular proposal be referred for debate to a standing committee or, in certain important cases, to the House as a whole. With thirty to forty documents arriving at the Committee every day, there are few that either merit or can be given further consideration.

Once an issue has been earmarked for debate, there still remains the problem of how Parliament is to influence the government's Council negotiating position. No specific amendments are allowed to be made to the Commission proposals, and the House or standing committee may only debate on a 'take note' motion. Additional problems arise from the fact that a maximum of ninety minutes is allowed for a debate, and even this small amount of time is not made available until two hours before midnight.

From 1974 to 1976 the government was prepared to listen to the views of Parliament on EC legislation, though it would not submit its own views to scrutiny. By 1976, however, the government was no longer prepared to grant even this meagre concession in all circumstances. Michael Foot, then Leader of the House, stated on behalf of the Government:

'Ministers will not give agreement to any legislative proposal recommended by the Scrutiny Committee for further consideration by the House before the House has given it that consideration, unless the Committee has indicated that agreement need not be withheld, or *the Minister concerned is satisfied that agreement should not be withheld for reasons which he will at the first opportunity explain to the House.'*

(The italic type emphasises the considerable freedom of action which the British government has been able to reserve for itself). The Committee faces further scrutiny problems when the Commons is in recess. No debate can be called and the Committee cannot even meet. The chairman cannot act on his own initiative to scrutinise legislation. The fact that the parliamentary timetable is not co-ordinated with the timetable of the Council of Ministers means that the Committee is often in a position where it cannot carry out its functions. When an instrument is adopted in Council before it reaches the Committee, the limit of the government's obligation is 'that the Committee should be informed, by deposit of the relevant document and by submission of an explanatory memorandum, of instances where fast-moving documents go for adoption before scrutiny can take place'.

In view of the unfavourable procedures for adequate Commons supervision of EC legislation, it is hardly surprising that there is little rush among MPs to serve on the Scrutiny Committee. There have also been persistent calls by those serving on the Committee for an improvement in the scrutiny procedures.

The House of Lords provides a far more successful example of parliamentary scrutiny of EC legislation. Like the Commons Committee, the Select Committee on the European Community in the House of Lords was set up in 1974. It has twenty-three members on the main committee, and some eighty peers who are involved with the seven specialist subcommittees. Unlike the Commons Committee, the Lords Committee is able to call expert witnesses and debate the merits of the proposal before it. The chairman can decide which issues to put before the Committee, and in addition the various sub-committees allow the Committee time to deal with the more important business. As in the Commons, however, debates held in the Lords on Commission proposals are limited to 'take note' motions.

The limited influence of Parliament over EC legislation cannot be laid entirely at the door of the European Community. To be sure, the fact that ministers go to Brussels to bargain in the Council of Ministers means that it is difficult to tie them down to a particular line. The policy that emerges in the Council will almost certainly be a compromise, and Parliament cannot anticipate precisely what it will be.

Denmark, in contrast, provides an interesting example of a national parliament (the Folketing) exerting considerable authority over EC legislation. The Folketing secured its position during the debate on EC membership. Under the Danish Act of Accession, the government is required to make an annual report to the Folketing and keep Parliament informed of Council business. General debates on the EC are held at regular intervals, and special debates also take place. The main mechanism, however, by which the Folketing controls the government's negotiating position in the Council of Ministers is through the Market Relations Committee. The committee system is extremely well developed within the Folketing, and committees enjoy considerable authority. The Market Relations Committee is the most authoritative of all the Folketing's Committees. It is also the most prestigious. Its seventeen members, elected proportionately from the various political parties, include many former Cabinet ministers. Under the rules of procedure, the government is committed to consult with the Market Relations Committee on all Council business. The Committee meets weekly and may question ministers and civil servants involved in EC policy. The government is obliged to seek mandates from the Committee before important Council decisions. In many council sessions, Danish ministers have had extremely narrow mandates, and have, on some occasions, had to seek new mandates from the Committee before reaching agreement on a particular issue.

In the light of Danish experience, the inability of the British Parliament to control its government's negotiating position should perhaps be put down to the more general decline discussed in Chapter 3, and attributable to the dominance of a single party in government at any one time, government control of the parliamentary agenda, and the poor access of parliamentarians to information. What seems also to be the case, however, is that in Britain EC membership has allowed the executive even greater licence to escape legislative scrutiny. It seems unlikely that Parliament will be able to regain its authority. In the case of EC legislation, the European Parliament will very likely inherit it. Already, that body is a growing thorn in the side of the Council of Ministers as it attempts to exert authority over the Community budget and to take popular initiatives.

As things stand at the moment, there is neither European parliamentary control nor British parliamentary control over the EC policy-making process. As a result, British EC membership has resulted in a considerable increase in executive power. It might even be said that the increase has been in bureaucratic power. It is surely significant that the only British representatives permanently based in Brussels are civil servants.

The implementation of EC policies

The last of the ways EC membership has affected British government is in regard to the implementation of policy.

Once the Council of Ministers has made a decision, it may issue a regulation or a directive. The matter then passes out of the hands of the Council. In its capacity as guardian of the Treaty, it is now the Commission's task to ensure that Community law is observed, and that national governments carry out the obligations agreed in Council. Where a directive has been issued, the Commission may find itself in the position of having to cajole a government into enacting the necessary national legislation. This happened with regard to a 1976 Council directive on the use of tachographs in the cabs of long-distance lorries. Faced with British unwillingness to enact the directive, the Commission took the British government to the European Court which ordered the British government to comply.

In enforcing the observance of Community laws, therefore, the Commission can call for a judgement from the European Court. It also has the power to impose sanctions directly on firms that violate EC competition laws – for example, Pioneer was fined $6.2 million for operating a discriminatory pricing policy within the European Community. This fine amounted to 4 per cent of the company's turnover. This powerfully illustrates the point made above, and expanded in the next chapter, about the legal enforcement of policies inside Britain.

It is, indeed, the role of the European Court that may be of most significance for domestic politics. In acceding to the Treaty of Rome, EC law immediately became supreme over domestic law. For Britain, this change was particularly dramatic. Britain has never had a written constitution and Parliament has always been regarded as the supreme law-making body. There were no British courts formally empowered to consider the 'constitutionality' of a law passed by Parliament. As part of the EC, Britain is subject to the rulings of the European Court which has the authority to determine the 'constitutionality' of a British Act of Parliament (although paradoxically an Act abrogating British adherence to the Treaty would not be subject to review).

The supremacy of the European Court has made it an important influence on social and political change in the member states (including Britain). In the case of *Smith* v. *Macarthy* a Mrs Wendy Smith employed by a pharmaceutical company brought a case against her employers who were paying her £10.00 less than a man who had previously been employed in the same job. The firm was found in violation of article 119 of the Treaty of Rome. No doubt the firm would also have been in violation of the EC's 1975 directive on equal pay. An interesting aspect of the case was the claim by the advocate-general that a woman should be paid the same as a man even where only a hypothetical comparison could be made. As was noted at the time, a finding of this type would go further than Britain's own equal pay act. Not just on equal pay but also on consumer and environmental protection, action in the European Court may well represent a route whereby individuals and special interest groups can effect change. Accordingly, the European Court, in a similar way to the Supreme Court in the United States, is well able to take an important part in British politics. The slowness of the decision-making process within the Council of Ministers may actually push it into doing so.

Chapter 8
Judicial decision-making

British governments have complied not only with judgements of the Court of Justice of the European Communities (to give the 'European Court its full name), but also with the more controversial rulings of the Commission and Court of Human Rights. This was set up at Strasbourg under the European Convention on Human Rights to which the British government is a signatory. Its doubts on the validity of terrorist interrogations in Northern Ireland in the early 1970s moved governments to amend procedures and instructions on this point to provide more safeguards for the suspect, even though the court has mainly moral authority on its side rather than the economic sanctions of the Community. In 1982 the Court ruled that children whose parents disapproved of their corporal punishment should not be caned or strapped in British schools – a decision which materially affected the structure of authority in education and was followed by government circulars designed to restrict the practice so severely as almost to extinguish it.

In all, the British government was found in the wrong on no less than eight occasions by the Court of Human Rights in the period 1975–82, on matters ranging from the retention of flogging in the Isle of Man to restrictions imposed by the Home Office on prisoners' rights to communicate with their lawyers. In all cases the condemnation prompted some action by the government – sometimes a substantial modification in the offending practice if not its outright abolition.

Despite the more publicity-worthy activities of the Court of Human Rights, it has no guaranteed long-term power in Britain. For one thing, the rights of citizens to bring cases before it depends on the UK government's periodic consent. Although as yet no UK government has failed to renew this right, there is no general sympathy for entrenched and legally enforceable civil rights in British politics, as witness the strongly-held opposition on all sides but especially on the left, to legislating a domestic code of civil rights. The same cannot be said for the European Court. With Britain's accession to the Treaty of Rome in 1973, an entirely new legal principle was incorporated into the British system. It is now no longer strictly true that a British court could never overrule an Act of Parliament, as had previously been the received wisdom.

If a British statute seems to a court now to contradict some directive of the

European Commission, or an article of the Treaty of Rome, the court would have to give precedence to the European ruling. So far there has never been a clear need actually to overrule a British statute, but many cases of potential conflict occur. When this happens any court *may*, and the final court of appeal *must*, refer the matter to the Court of Justice, under Article 177 of the treaty. This will then rule on the applicable law, which the British court in question has to apply. Although applications under Article 177 are nothing like as common in Britain as in Germany and Italy, the British courts have shown themselves perfectly willing to obey the procedure, and if necessary to interpret the statute or rule as instructed. Because the European Court is itself increasingly moving to extend the civil rights it deems the Treaty of Rome to include, there is more chance of effective legal protection this way, and by direct citizen appeal to the European Court, than is ever likely to come from Strasbourg. Recent European cases involving equal rights over retirement ages for women have already, for example, pushed the British government in directions it had shown no previous interest in pursuing.

Is the political influence of the European courts matched by the British courts within their own domestic jurisdiction? In many respects, the courts are yet another 'alternative government' with extensive areas of independent decision-making. Given the division of power we have seen existing between central departments on the one hand, and Quangos and local governments on the other, it would be very surprising if the courts did not have similar scope. We shall examine this point below, along with the criteria used to decide cases, to see how far this contributes on the one hand to the fragmentation of policy-processes, and on the other to the protection and representation of the individual.

Court structure and work

First, however, we shall summarise the way in which courts are organised and the broad nature of the work they do. As with local government, there are different court systems in different areas of the United Kingdom: one for England and Wales, one for Northern Ireland and one for Scotland. The English system (also covering Wales) is by far the most important in terms of numbers of cases and people dealt with. Table 8.1 summarises its main features. The bottom tier consists of a fairly unique institution, the magistrates' courts, where men or women without legal training (justices of the peace: JPs) have basic criminal jurisdiction (involving violence against people and offences against property such as theft) and some social and family cases (involving disputes between husbands and wives, for example). The magistrates are unpaid and work part time. Local notables such as doctors, clergy and trade unionists are appointed through a secret committee for each area, but the quickest route is through nominations from local political parties. Partisanship on the bench is strongly disapproved, however, and almost unheard of. Since most political activists and local notables are middle-class, so are the magistrates. They deal with the vast majority of legal cases. As there is little central supervision of their actual work, other than the small numbers of cases

Table 8.1 The modern English court system in outline

Court	Functions Criminal	Civil	Number of courts	Annual case load	Composition	Additional comments
Magistrates' Courts	Petty crime	Very limited	Several hundred	Vast	Part time lay JPs	Apart from trying minor crime, these courts vet all prosecutions in remand hearings
County Courts	None	Extensive case load for all civil law cases subject to financial limits	Over 100	Nearly 2 million cases started each year; less than 5% come to trial	Circuit judges and Recorders (more than 500)	Most civil cases start and finish here, and much of the work is small claims business
Crown Courts	All	Some limited areas	Technically one court, with 97 centres	Approximately 60,000 cases put down for hearing	High Court and Circuit judges and Recorders	This is the main criminal court. It has three tiers; in the first High Court judges sit to try the most serious crimes, in others circuit judges try more minor offences. It also hears appeals from magistrates' courts and passes sentences on certain cases where conviction has taken place before magistrates
The High Court A: Chancery Division	None	Trusts, wills, tax law, company law, property, etc.		Approximately 700 trials	12 High Court judges under the Vice-Chancellor	
B: Family Division	None	Family law in general		2/3,000 defended cases	17, under the President	All divorce cases start in the County courts but defended ones may come here; as with adoption procedures

C: Queen's	Some appeals, mainly in public law from tribunals and magistrates courts	All civil law not dealt with elsewhere, especially contract and tort	1,500/2,000 full trials	44 judges under the Lord Chief Justice
Court of Appeal A: Criminal Division	Most criminal appeals	None	6/7,000	It consists usually of one or two judges from the court of appeal sitting with judges from Queen's Bench Division in a bench of three
B: Civil Division	None	Most appeals from anywhere which are not strictly criminal law	c.1,500	The Master of the Rolls and 16 Lord Justices of Appeal. Usually operates in 3 man benches
The House of Lords		Appeals from any court in England and Wales on any matter, and from Scotland and Northern Ireland in many cases. Most of the work consists of civil appeals from the Court of Appeal	50/60	Between 10 and 12 Lords of Appeal, under the Lord Chancellor (who will very rarely sit). Usually works in five-men benches
The Judicial Committee of the Privy Council		Basically this is a group of Law Lords acting as a Supreme Court of Appeal from some parts of the Commonwealth		

Note A. Case loads are very difficult to estimate because the bulk of civil cases are resolved either before coming to trial at all, or before the trial is over. The figures given are rough estimates of the number of cases that actually do come to trial, whether they are actually brought to judgment or not.

Note B. The various divisions of the High Court all play some appellate role over cases in their areas from lower courts and from tribunals. This is particularly so for the QBD which has an overall responsibility to supervise all inferior courts and tribunals.

appealed to higher courts, there is considerable variety in their decisions between different areas, notably on sentencing and fines. Above the magistrates' courts are the crown and county courts, staffed by professional judges, which hear more important civil and criminal cases.

Although the magistrates' and crown courts deal with most people, they are not important enough nor central enough to affect policy. This is the sphere of the higher courts located in London. They are collectively known as the Supreme Court of the Judiciary.

The first of these is the High Court, comprising about one hundred judges sitting in three different divisions and dealing both with criminal and civil cases of the greatest importance. The first of these is the Family Division, which covers matters like property settlement after divorce, adoption, child care and so on. While decisions in these areas are not what is usually seen as 'politics', making and applying rules governing our behaviour in such intensely private and sensitive areas can plausibly be seen as an exercise of power that has more real or potential impact on the lives of ordinary people than anything that a backbench MP could ever expect to have, and perhaps an impact of greater force than more clearly political matters such as the budget. The best example of this power is the way Lord Denning, for many years Master of the Rolls (the third ranking Judicial Office), managed to ameliorate conditions for women deserted by their husbands, by his personal interpretation of their rights, doing more in this direction than any Act of Parliament passed this century. Such power is by no means necessarily used in a 'liberal' fashion. The rights of 'gay' fathers to have access to their children were severely restricted in one case where the presiding judge gave an insight into a, hopefully untypical, judicial ideology by announcing that a 'reasonable homosexual' would realise he 'had nothing whatsoever to offer his son'.

The Chancery Division deals with tax matters. While it may make decisions from time to time which run counter to government policy, these can be rapidly changed in the annual financial legislation passed by Parliament.

Politically, the most important part of the High Court is its biggest division, the Queen's Bench Division (QBD). This owes its importance to three roles. First, it essentially guides the development of the criminal law, both in the definition of crimes and of rules of evidence (which are usually left to common, judge-made, law) and in sentencing patterns. Second, it deals with most important cases in civil law, and even where these are actually controlled by statute (i.e. Acts of Parliament) rather than common law rules, the statutes are usually based on existing common law traditions. If this sounds innocuous, consider how vitally political is the question of when you should be liable for injuries your carelessness causes strangers. It was, for example, a civil law case coming from QBD that did more than any government managed to do up to 1982 to make the wearing of seat belts compulsory. Because of that decision, anyone injured in a car crash who was not wearing a seat belt would get damages much reduced from what he would otherwise have received, however much the other driver was at fault. No government ever contemplated a fine for not wearing a seat belt that would be anything like so punitive.

Thirdly, the most important reason for regarding the Queen's Bench Division as politically crucial is that it is the nearest thing in Britain to an Administrative Law Court of the sort found everywhere in Europe and modelled on the French Conseil d'Etat. Administrative law, the very existence of which in England is a moot point, is that branch of law which controls the behaviour of officials towards the ordinary public. Thus it is deeply involved in civil rights problems of all sorts, and also in the question of how, in a democracy, one makes sure that governments only do what they have been authorised to do by Parliament. England has no legally effective Bill of Rights, and there are no courts specially charged with ensuring that civil rights are observed. But the Queen's Bench Divisional Court will hear cases arising from alleged improper behaviour by governments and their agents under the traditional protection of common law rights. Some enthusiasts in fact claim the Divisional Court is the nucleus of a future fully-fledged Administrative Court – this point is discussed further in the section on tribunals and administrative law. But what sort of 'rights' in general will the courts protect?

They can be very trivial or very vital, and are usually somewhere between; important for the individual concerned but of no earth-shaking consequence, *taken singly*, for most of us. Cumulated, however, the public law decisions of the QBD and the Appeal Courts set the pattern of democratic rights against public authorities. For example; a market trader urinated against a wall in the market place, and promptly had his trading licence taken away by the local council. The court gave it back to him. (Should a man's livelihood be put at risk by the arbitrary reaction of local authorities to his natural functions?) In 1976–77 a Cabinet minister gave instructions to the Civil Aviation Board not to allow Mr Laker to fly people cheaply over the Atlantic, in a way that Mr Laker claimed the enabling legislation did not allow. (Should ministers be able to interfere with entrepreneurial spirit so easily unless the legislature is very clear that it wants this restriction? The courts agreed with Mr Laker.) The Home Secretary found out that people, knowing their TV licences were going up in price soon, were rather sensibly buying their next licence early at the lower cost. The BBC was losing money by this, so he tried to stop them doing so, and indeed to claim back extra money from those who had got away with it. The court did not let *him* get away with it. In these ways the court sometimes protects, sometimes opposes, the private individual against the state.

Such decisions do not go unchecked as any politically novel and potentially influential case will be appealed to a higher court. Appeals, moreover, are often granted; indeed a counter-appeal after the appeal is often granted too, returning the situation to base. There are two levels of appeal. A case decided in the High Court can be appealed first to the Court of Appeal, in either its criminal or civil division. The civil division, presided over by a senior judge known as the Master of the Rolls, hears about 1,000 cases a year, sitting in benches of three. All but a tiny minority of cases stop here; the next stage of appeal is to the Judicial Committee of the House of Lords which is entirely separate from the House of Lords as a legislative body. The Court of Appeal has usually only about thirty members, the Lords about twelve. We have a tiny judicial élite: counting the whole of the High Court, less than 200 important judges.

It is interesting to note that the recruitment area is similarly restricted. All senior judges must have been barristers and usually Queen's Counsel; and we have possibly less than 3,000 practising barristers in this country at any one time. Britain is peculiar in distinguishing between solicitors, charged with routine legal business, and the barristers (advocates in Scotland) whom they brief for major cases and who alone are entitled to appear in important courts for the opposing sides. Queen's Counsel are the most senior and successful barristers; the number with the age and experience to consider themselves suitable for judgeships in any generation is naturally much smaller.

It is in the Court of Appeal and the Judicial Committee of the House of Lords that the vital decisions are made which often have political bearings. Though the decision of course may merely ratify a decision of the High Court, which itself may ratify a decision of a magistrates court or a special tribunal, it may alternatively mean overthrowing a decision that has been agreed on by all the previous tiers.

There are in addition two other legal structures which give to English judicial officers a potential impact on politics. At a level lower than the High Court are innumerable tribunals and appeal tribunals, with which we deal separately. Finally, there exists something called the Judicial Committee of the Privy Council. In fact this is the Law Lords under another name. This committee acts as a final court of appeal from certain commonwealth and colonial countries. As such it often acts as a fully fledged supreme court interpreting a written constitution. The Privy Council has, for example, decided on the constitutionality of the death penalty in Singapore. But it is of little importance in British politics.

Courts in Northern Ireland, though separate, closely resemble the English, with less of an emphasis upon lay magistrates and juries. The law administered there derives largely from English common law, modified for Irish conditions and shaped to some extent by Acts of the former Northern Irish Parliament between 1922 and 1972. There is an Appeal Court in Belfast, but the judicial House of Lords has ultimate jurisdiction.

The Scottish system is more distinctive. While there are district courts with lay magistrates, the major court of all work is the Sheriff Court, with jurisdiction over a considerable population and area, and powers to try all but major criminal and civil cases. The sheriff is a professional lawyer, like the judges in the Crown Courts in England. At the centre of the system are the eighteen senators of the College of Justice in Edinburgh, who man both the chief civil court, the Court of Session, and the chief Criminal Court, the High Court of Justiciary. Other senators than those who tried the original case sit as a Court of Criminal Appeal, which is the final authority in criminal cases. There are also appeals in civil cases from the Outer to the Inner House of the Session, but the final authority here is the (judicial) House of Lords, sitting with two Scottish Lords of Appeal out of the five judges.

These institutional differences are reflected in the different nature of the law administered in Scottish courts. This diverges from the English system in two major ways. The actual law, in the sense of the legal rules applied by courts, is often different from equivalent rules in England. Property law, for example, retains much more of the feudal inheritance than does the English law of real estate. Secondly, the sources of law, and the general theory of law is different. Although this difference can easily be exaggerated, Scots lawyers operate under a system heavily influenced by Roman law, as is true in continental Europe. There is no room here to discuss Scotland separately. Much of what is said below will still be true of Scottish courts and judges, but not all. It will certainly be the case, however, that any conclusions about the autonomy and political importance of English judges will apply equally, if not more, to Scottish judges (and for that matter to Northern Irish judges).

A last general point about all the legal systems is the exceptional degree of autonomy which lawyers as a profession enjoy. With regard to the practice of their profession and its ethics, they are totally self-regulating under their elected councils. Since legal ethics determine the conduct of business in court, and much of the interpretation of law, the self-government of lawyers is even more important politically than the self-government of other professions like doctors; it reaches out to the substance of law in the proceedings of the (separate) Law Commissions for England and Scotland. These are quangos charged with revision of law, and composed wholly of lawyers. Formally they deal with technical revisions of law – cleaning up obscure language, consolidating and codifying branches of law, repealing obsolete statutes – and everything they recommend has to be approved by Parliament. In practice, the matters being technical and non-controversial, their recommendations are accepted with little debate. Although technical, such revisions can have enormous importance for individuals as when they changed the basis of Scottish landholding to absolute freehold from a form of tenure where the superior still retained certain rights (such as mineral rights) and could prohibit development, for example. In some areas the Law Commissions act like a mini-legislature, except that they are nominated, not elected bodies, and are responsive to legal opinion much more than to any other influence. One very good example of the influence of the Law Commission is discussed elsewhere in this book. The new 1986 Public Order Act was the cause of much parliamentary furore and lobbying by such bodies as the Police Federation and the NCCL. Looked at closely, however, the act hardly deviates at all from the draft Bill published by the English Law Commission in 1983.

The political role of the courts in a system without judicial review

It is clear from what has been said in the two previous chapters about a growing recourse to legal action to resolve political disputes, that the higher courts have an important mediating role between central and sub-central government on the one hand; and between both of these and Community institutions on the other. Conservative legislation of the 1980s, particularly the laws regulating industrial relations and trade union activities, have also extended the supervisory and decision-making powers of the courts into new areas, where they could potentially find themselves in conflict with powerful political interests.

All this has happened in a system where the courts lack what has often been taken as the distinguishing mark of a 'political' jurisdiction – that is the power of 'judicial review'. 'Judicial review' in its layman's sense means a system in which laws and other acts of the legislature can be overruled by a court if they are held to conflict with constitutional rules, basic human rights, or any other laws treated as superior to ordinary legislation. In the United States the Supreme Court can invalidate Acts of the Federal Congress or the state legislatures if they contradict the constitution. Courts with similar powers exist in Canada, Australia and West Germany among other countries, and as we have seen the European Court has similar powers in countries of the Community.

When this sort of power belongs to a court, its judges are clearly of political importance. Most experts would agree that no such power belongs to English courts: no Act of Parliament can be brought before a court and challenged as to its basic lawfulness (Scottish courts have asserted vague claims to do this on occasion, but have never actually done so). This is part of the general doctrine that Parliament is supreme and knows no constraint at all. (Except, as mentioned, from the consequences of UK membership of the European Communities.)

This formal supremacy of Parliament also applies, of course, to governments, quangos, local government, and all the other bodies considered in Chapter 6. Nonetheless these can by their actions render parliamentary or even governmental action ineffective, and sometimes a dead letter. Thus it does not follow that, because the courts cannot overrule state law, they therefore lose their political relevance. It is useful in this regard to note a seldom-mentioned fact about other national courts that do have the power of judicial review. They seldom use it. Only a handful of Congressional Acts have been overruled in America since the 1930s, and in Canada, Australia and West Germany the use of a court to veto legislation is even rarer. But no one will try to argue that these supreme courts have stopped being politically important.

The truth is that judicial review is only one of a series of powers that courts everywhere exercise, and arguably is not the really important one anywhere. Let us list briefly the possible areas of power of our courts, the better to consider this matter. To start with, the only thing the courts in England cannot do is to say that a parliamentary Act is not valid law at all. But how restrictive this is depends on another matter: how much of the work of governing England is carried out by parliamentary Acts? The detailed answer to that question is found elsewhere in this book. Here it is enough to say that much of the exercise of power and control by the state in Britain does not involve the application to a citizen of statutes passed by Parliament. For one thing, local authority by-laws are controllable by the courts, who may overrule them if they do not fit with the parliamentary legislation authorising them.

For example, a whole series of important cases in England during the 1960s involved the 1961 Caravan Sites Act. Under this, local authorities were given great powers to plan and control the development of caravan sites, but their effective power to do so was severely limited by the (judicial) House of Lords, who used the empowering legislation, the parliamentary Act, to curtail and alter what the local authorities wanted to do. In this and similar ways the whole of England's planning law is subject to control by the courts, and planning law is hardly a trivial matter.

Next we ought to note that many parliamentary Acts do little more than empower ministers to make detailed regulations roughly in conformity with a (very often vague) general intention. This discretionary power is entirely subject to control by the courts, with the effect that though an Act may not be overruled, most of the steps necessary to make the Act *do* anything can be. One case to hit the headlines in the late 1970s shows this: the Tameside case, where the (Labour) Secretary of State for Education tried to stop a local authority changing from an original plan to go comprehensive in order to retain its grammar schools. The Act certainly gave him, in general, the power to intervene in such situations. But the local authority and parents took the minister to court and succeeded in getting a ruling that what the minister was trying to do was illegal. One might well ask 'who needs judicial review?' in situations like this! Very few Acts can be so specific as not to need ministerial discretion, or not to involve the passing of delegated legislation, both of which can be and are checked by the courts.

Next, although courts cannot overrule an Act of Parliament, that does not mean Acts do not come before the courts. The vast majority of law cases, whether they are between private citizens or between a citizen and the state (either as criminal cases or otherwise) involve statutes. No one asks a judge to say a law is not a law at all in Britain, as they sometimes do in America. What they ask is what the law actually means. This process is called interpretation, or 'construction'; it is in interpreting the meaning of the Act, often a matter of dealing with very vague or general phrases, that judges have most of their power. The whole thrust of a piece of parliamentary legislation can be changed or bent or reduced or increased in impact in this way, and all entirely legally, but without recourse to 'judicial review'. For example, the 1971 Race Relations Act was very considerably reduced in its ability to prevent discrimination between citizens of different racial backgrounds by two decisions of the House of Lords which were presented as simply matters of 'interpreting' what the words in the Act actually meant. In one case a local authority was allowed to refuse to give a council house to a man who had the legal right to live permanently in Britain, and who had done so for twenty years, and who was otherwise entitled to a house, simply because he was, in origin, a Pole. The court 'interpreted' 'race' to mean only colour, not nationality, so it was acceptable to discriminate between whites from different countries.

In another case a political club was allowed to refuse membership to a card-carrying member of the relevant party because he was black. They 'interpreted' a clause that forbade discrimination by anyone 'providing services to the public or a section of the public' in such a way as to allow this discrimination, though no one could possibly have thought Parliament wanted to let political clubs off the duty to be unprejudiced.

Finally our courts have enormous influence over the rules we all have to obey in our relations with each other, because much of criminal law and most of civil law does not come from parliamentary Acts at all, but from what is known as 'common law'. Common law is overtly made by the judges. It was the original law of the country before parliaments either existed or bothered much about regulating private activities. It is a matter of tradition, a slow developing of rules based on previous cases known as 'precedents.' Most of the law of contract, for example, which regulates business activities, is still common law; what rule shall govern a contract drawn up between two private parties is essentially up to the judge and his ability to understand or to change the rulings in previous similar cases.

In criminal law too this judge-made law is often important. When can a policeman break into your house and search it? Is someone who burns down a house in revenge without realising that there is someone in it who consequently dies, guilty of murder? The answers to questions like this cannot be found in any statute. Parliament has never legislated on the matter. But hundreds of judges over the centuries have made decisions which can be seen as containing rough and changeable rules.

All these powers go together to suggest that courts and judges in England are very important indeed; if the judges can create rules that we have to obey, or can alter rules created by Parliament, or can control the exercise of powers given to ministers and authorities *by* parliamentary Acts, are they not actually governing us? And is not governing precisely what makes an institution 'political'?

There is one (and only one) argument that says no to that question. At any time, if Parliament does not like what the courts are doing, it can change the law by passing a new, clearer, more specific Act which the courts will have to obey. The chapters in this book on Parliament and the executive have shown why this is a less than powerful argument. How much time can be spared, how much attention can the Cabinet give, to checking what the courts do? In criminal law there has only been one major example since the war of Parliament passing an Act which was intended, partially, to change a ruling that the court had made. In 1963 a murder conviction was upheld by the House of Lords on a man who had killed a policeman by driving fast and dangerously as the officer, trying to arrest him, clung to the running board of his car. It was fairly clear that the driver (who, incidentally, was a personal friend of the policeman) had never intended to kill him, and had not realised he was likely so to do. This was thought so unfair that some years later an Act, the 1968 Criminal Justice Act, instructed courts to take more notice of what alleged violent criminals thought they were doing. It is interesting to note in passing that most criminal lawyers believe that the wording of that Act is still so vague that it probably does not prevent a court repeating the original decision that produced it.

The power of the courts does not only exist because Parliament has never tried to curb it, nor has Parliament always been successful when it has tried to change a court's ruling. A celebrated administrative law decision called *Anisminic* in 1969 involved a case where a company which felt itself aggrieved by the refusal of the Foreign Compensation Commission to recoup it for being forced to sell its property in Egypt to the Egyptian government at a loss. The statute that set up the FCC *specifically* denied the right to appeal against any decision of the FCC to *any* court. Nonetheless the Law Lords heard the case, refused to accept that they could be excluded from hearing it, and decided in favour of Anisminic. For some time the government attempted to pass legislation to reverse this but were held up in the House of Lords and finally gave up.

If these examples mean anything, they mean that the role of the courts is not seriously constrained by Parliament's theoretical power to change the law and overrule them. Though there are certainly isolated examples of governments doing so, these are rare, and less important than the general point that Parliament is far too busy and preoccupied to monitor what judges are doing in their vast areas of discretionary power over our lives.

There is another, rather less formal aspect of the power of our judiciary. For many years now Home Secretaries, civil servants and eminent criminologists have tried to introduce reforms in sentencing policies in our criminal courts. Not only have they had pragmatic policy changes in mind, they have been more generally concerned to introduce a formal punishment theory accompanied by suitable training for new criminal court judges prior to their handing down their first sentences.

Despite the essentially non-partisan nature of this attempt, almost nothing has been achieved in the face of intransigent, if often well argued, opposition by the judges. This came to a very public head in the autumn of 1981. The Home Secretary was faced with desperate overcrowding in prisons, to such a point that his own prison governors had started writing letters of complaint to the press. To reduce the problem he was contemplating a reform of sentencing policy designed to cut the prison population by giving nearly all prisoners an automatic parole after they had served a part of their sentence.

The Lord Chief Justice called a meeting of all High Court judges. The Home Office proposal was dropped. Very simply the judges had told the Home Secretary that if he implemented his reform they would merely increase the sentences they handed down so that, even with the automatic parole, prisoners would be serving sentences as long as they had in the past.

This sort of judicial power is not inescapable. Other jurisdictions have much tighter control over what happens to criminals. But in Britain the very assumption of the non-political role of the judiciary in some ways increases their power. For where the official ideology of crime and punishment has for so long been removed from party politics and placed in the hands of men – the judges – clearly identified as politically neutral, they seem justified both to themselves and to the public in asserting their autonomy in their own sphere. This special public image has ramifications throughout politics. If the government wishes to neutralise a potentially serious incident, they appoint a judge to investigate it. Whatever he may find, few will dare to challenge or ignore his conclusions because to do so would appear as an unseemly intervention of power or politics into a 'professional' zone. The same Law Lord (Scarman) – just one example – was given the tasks of investigating the killing by British troops of thirteen Ulstermen in a riot, the death of a demonstrator in London, and the disastrous Brixton riots of 1981 in London.

As the judges are elevated to such an important role by governments, it is not surprising that they should be able to control many legal matters behind the scenes, whatever the executive might wish.

Administrative law and administrative tribunals

Quite apart from the courts, there are innumerable bodies called tribunals (though some tribunals are called committees!) set up by various Acts of Parliament to oversee the decision-making of civil servants exercising the wide discretionary powers given them by modern legislation. Though seldom in the public eye until recent years, such quasi-courts go back to the beginnings of the welfare state, because it is largely in provision of welfare and allied rights that they have their role. Probably the first modern tribunal was set up under the 1911 National Insurance Act to hear appeals about the provision of unemployment benefit.

Judges have never liked tribunals, which they see as encroaching on their own powers, and have always insisted, usually successfully, that the courts have a historic supervisory right in common law over them. In 1958 the Franks Commission on Tribunals regulated them, and the principles of this regulation, now enshrined in the *Tribunals and Inquiries Act 1971* have made the tribunals as independent as possible of the minister heading the department over which they exercise oversight. Typically they consist of a legally-qualified chairman appointed by the Lord Chancellor, and two laymen.

Tribunals, though largely ignored by political scientists, are crucially important because it is to them, rather than to courts, that ordinary people are most likely to turn for justice. They are many and varied, and we can do no more here than list a few of the more important. The most important, because the busiest, are probably the Social Security Appeal Tribunals, dealing with around 100,000 cases a year, on all aspects of social security entitlements. Appeal can be made from these to the Social Security Commissioners, and from there to the Court of Appeal, ensuring that social security law develops in a way broadly compatible with the rest of civil law. Industrial Tribunals, dealing with unfair dismissal, and discrimination on sexual or racial grounds, hear another 40,000 cases a year, and like the Social Security Tribunals have their own appeal system, the Employment Appeal Tribunal, again linked into the Court of Appeal. Rent Assessment Committees work in the highly complex area of housing law, hearing 16,000 cases, but with no proper appeal procedure.

Politically the most sensitive area in the field of tribunal law is that of immigration, which is a less wonderful example of the liberalism of the English legal system. There are nine centres around the country where *Immigration Adjudicators*, sit (unlike most tribunals) as one-man courts to hear appeals from immigration officers and the Home Office on matters like refusals to grant entry or the making of deportation orders. Though these adjudicators can be appealed to the Immigration Appeal Tribunal, there is no right of appeal to the courts! Of the 11,000 appeals to Immigration Adjudicators, leave to appeal to the Immigration Appeal Tribunal is allowed in only 500 of the 4000 cases where it is sought.

However, the absence of a right of appeal to the courts is not as final as it may seem. As a result of the judges' insistence on their supervisory role, an increasingly important doctrine has developed called, confusingly, 'judicial review' (which has nothing at all to do with the usual sense of judicial review of Acts of Parliament used earlier).

Judicial review of administrative decisions, which is increasingly resorted to by people unhappy with their lot in any tribunal, gives the right to go to the Divisional Court of Queens Bench. This is a group of about a dozen judges who specialise in administrative law, and usually have considerable experience as barristers working for government departments before elevation to the bench. Though there are important technical distinctions between appealing a case on a matter of law, and seeking judicial review of procedure, the latter is often the best hope for complainants, and in some cases is the only avenue. It is clear that governments try to restrict appeal rights when they do not really want to extend legal protection. This applies not only to immigration but also rent cases, those unsuccessfully seeking release from a mental hospital from a Mental Health Review Tribunal, and those dissatisfied with the Vaccine Damage Tribunals, who oversee payments under the Vaccine Damage Payments Act 1979 (an act the government was very unwilling to pass in the first place).

Given the complexity of the tribunal system, the manifest fact that the judges are not going to allow tribunals to work out their own law, and the presence of a growing expertise and authority in the Divisional Court, there are increasing demands that Britain give up its age-old objection to administrative courts and actually create one, from which all those denied justice by anybody dealing with public law rights could go. This would be a step towards recognising overtly the political role and responsibilities already assumed by the courts.

The ideology of English judges

The autonomy and political power of the courts render specially important the nature of the legal culture – the criteria according to which judicial decisions are made. Specifically, how far does it reflect popular attitudes and interests, or how far act against them?

Judges themselves conceive the courts as neutral appliers of law, thinking of their function as 'deciding disputes in accordance with law and with impartiality'. The law is thought of as an established body of principles which prejudges rights and duties. Impartiality means not merely an absence of personal bias or prejudice in the judge but also the exclusion of 'irrelevant' considerations such as his religious or political views. In contrast it has been claimed that judges' real view of the public interest contains three elements: 'first, the interests of the state (including its moral welfare) and the preservation of law and order, broadly interpreted; secondly the protection of property rights; and thirdly the promotion of certain political views normally associated with the Conservative Party' (Griffiths 1977: 195).

This assertion has been buttressed by a demonstration that the family and social background of judges is extremely privileged and atypical of the population; they come from wealthy professional, upper-middle-class families, were predominantly educated at exclusive schools and Oxford or Cambridge, and are forty or fifty when first appointed and in their sixties before they attain a really powerful position in the House of Lords or Court of Appeal. With a more formal training system for barristers, and with adequate incomes to be earned soon after admission to the Bar, the system of recruitment should be less exclusive in the future, but most barristers and hence most judges will even then be far from men of the people.

The same can be said of the personnel of all the key institutions in Britain, including the Labour Party. So a more exclusive background is not necessarily associated with Conservative opinions. In any case, the definition of the Conservative side varies. Upholding the right of neofascists to speak in public could be a Conservative, not to say reactionary, position; or it could proceed from a 'progressive' concern with civil liberties which also uphold a Communist's or homosexual's right to do likewise. But the main reason for background not affecting decisions is that it is such a remote influence. Decisions are more likely to be affected by intensive professional training, professional traditions, and the views of one's working associates.

If we accept this, what are the main tenets of the legal profession which influence judges? The first and perhaps most important is to stick to clear and unambiguous precedents. Judges themselves do not see themselves as free, and often give decisions that go against the grain. Hark to Lord Hailsham, who as a member of several Conservative cabinets can be unambiguously categorised politically. He was giving judgement in a case where a woman was being prosecuted for breaking regulations governing overcrowding in boarding houses, though actually she was running a refuge for battered wives:

At the beginning of this opinion, I said that my conclusion, though without doubt, was arrived at with reluctance . . . This appellant . . . is providing a service for people in urgent and tragic need. It is a service which in fact is provided by no other organ of our much vaunted system of public welfare . . . When people come to her door, not seldom accompanied by young children in desperate states and at all hours because, being in danger, they cannot go home . . . the appellant does not turn them away . . . but takes them in and gives them shelter and comfort. And what happens when she does? She finds herself the defendant in criminal proceedings at the suit of the local authority because she has allowed the inmates of her house to exceed the permitted maximum, and to that charge, I believe, she has no defence in law. My Lords, this is not a situation that can be regarded with complacency by any member of your Lordships' House, least of all by those who are compelled to do justice according to the law as it is, and not according to the state of affairs as they would wish it to be (Lord Hailsham, at page 443 (1977) 2 All ER 432).

He then cast his vote against the side he undoubtedly favoured.

Similar examples are too numerous to mention; the extent to which judges do believe that they are restricted by precedent and by a duty to follow Parliament is something that could not be exaggerated were it not that the orthodox view in English law unfortunately has exaggerated it. Perhaps there is no better example of this role belief than the voting in one case in 1972, *Jones v.*

Secretary of State for Social Services, which, as far as facts went, was a nearly identical replay of a case in 1967. In the Jones case at least two Law Lords voted for Jones, in order not to overrule the earlier case, *even though* they felt that both Jones and the earlier plaintiff were not entitled to win, and *even though* they acknowledged that the House has the right to reverse itself. So strong was their adherence to the principles of certainty and *stare decisis* (letting previous decisions stand).

The law, however, is often not clear, and judges have wide areas of discretion. What legal values guide them in this case, and are they systematically biased towards one political side rather than another? It is certainly the case that judges (and lawyers generally) are professionally trained into notions of restraint, caution, restriction, respect for property and family, and obedience for law. Probably they also have a leaning towards conventional moral values. These are attitudes congenial to Conservatives in Britain and, as we have shown in Chapter 4, they are also values cherished by most Labour supporters. In other words, to equate generally conservative attitudes (with a small 'c') with politically Conservative attitudes on the part of judges also implies categorising the British population as a whole as Conservatives, which is obviously not correct. The striking similarity between legal attitudes and those of the population suggests on the contrary that the courts may reflect rather well the underlying preferences of most citizens.

One can put the idea of a politically Conservative bias on the part of judges to a partial test by examining their actual decisions on a number of cases. Judges who regularly vote in a way that, for example, protects individuals against state intervention by holding against tax inspectors and planning bodies and so forth, but who very frequently vote to uphold criminal law convictions, might be seen as revealing pro-Conservative sympathies. If most judges voted in this way the bench collectively might be seen as Conservative. In fact even a partial check on decisions of a few leading judges (Table 8.2) reveals considerable differences between them. It is hard to explain why these should exist if we have a consistently pro-Conservative bench. Using the figures in the table to infer different judicial ideologies along the lines of pro-state/anti-state, pro-law and order/anti-law and order, Lord Pearson might be characterised as most Conservative in inclination (though his record in that respect is not consistent). In other cases there is either a balance with about 50 per cent of decisions on both sides, or a judge must be characterised as Conservative in some areas but not so in others (as for example Lord Reid on votes against criminal prosecutions, or Lord Dilhorne in upholding the weaker side in unequal civil cases). But if judges divide among themselves (or incline to different sympathies on different issues) they are doing no more than reflecting general tendencies among the population and can hardly be singled out as politically biased on that ground.

This is not to deny, of course, that judges often decide on the basis of their own values and that these are generally conservative (with a small 'c'). However, rather than seeing this as a deliberate attempt to impose their own views on the rest of us, it can more usefully be seen as evidence of weakness in the structure of our laws. When a judicial decision is not strictly determined by the legal/factual

Table 8.2 Voting records of certain Law Lords in 'difficult' cases*, 1965–77: percentages

Name	Votes for prosecution in criminal cases	Votes for Revenue in tax cases	Votes for state in public law cases	Votes for 'more powerful' side in unequal civil cases
Reid	49	38	71	70
Morris	64	55	65	40
Wilberforce	50	57	48	50
Pearson	77	46	56	53
Diplock	76	53	33	46
Dilhorne	74	65	44	37

Percentages are based on very small sample sizes and are not reliable in many cases: the table is intended only to be illustrative of an approach.

* By 'difficult' is meant cases where there has been some amount of judicial disagreement, either inside the Court of Appeal, inside the Lords, or between the two. It is a way of measuring the idea of the 'voluntariness' of a judicial decision, in that the result cannot be totally determined by the law, inasmuch as at least one pair of judges have decided differently.

material before a judge, he is not only free, but forced, to give a decision that will have ideological undertones. There is no such thing as a 'neutral' decision in these circumstances.

Consider, for example, a decision often taken as evidence of the Conservative bias of the Lords, in a case on the 1971 Race Relations Act. The court was required to determine whether a prohibition on discrimination in facilities that provided a service to 'any section of the public' included a private club. The judgement was criticised for using a restrictive definition that curtailed the reach of the Act. It has often been asserted that they should instead have extended the scope of the legislation. Perhaps they should. But had they done so, they would not have been acting neutrally, but demonstrating another ideological bias. Wherever choice exists, the choice made will be representative of some set of values. Neutrality in any absolute sense is hardly to be obtained.

Judges' values and court decisions

We shall finish this chapter by discussing the way in which judicial political values, often conservative in a general sense, slip into the system via structural weaknesses in the law.

The following are the most important aspects of law that involve a judge's private ideology in his legal decisions:
1. The interpretation of statutes where they are unclear.
2. The inclusion within statutes of concepts which call for judges to decide an essentially unknowable thing; i.e. what a reasonable man would do, or whether a minister 'is satisfied that', or whether (more rarely) something is 'in the public interest'.
3. Statutes that require the judge himself to use discretion with little in the way of guide lines. Typically these are family law cases where the judge must decide himself what is in the interest of the child.

Statutory construction

This is the most important, because the most frequently found, of these situations. When a statute is unclear in what it requires a court to decide, the judge must find some way of removing what is unclear. Although there exist a host of rules for statutory interpretation, they provide little real help. Like 'Interpretation Acts', they are best seen not as telling judges how to decide, but how to express what he has decided.

Basically what judges have to do in such a situation is to try to work out what Parliament really intended when it passed the Act. They are allowed access only to the text of the Act, and may not even consult what was said in the relevant parliamentary debate, which hardly makes the job easier.

Although some of the difficulties of discovering parliamentary intent are pragmatic, in that it is probable that Parliament had some intention relevant to the case and expressed itself badly, most cases are not like this. The worst problems of statutory construction arise because no one ever thought of a particular problem at all during the legislative phase, and there is no intention to discover. And, of course, the whole idea of Parliament's intention is often metaphysical – who is Parliament? The best approximation is probably that 'Parliament' means the draughtsmen who composed the text and the secretary of state.

These combined pragmatic and logical difficulties mean that where lack of clarity exists in a statute, the judge may resolve it only by setting himself in Parliament's place and deciding what he would himself have intended to do about a problem had he been a legislator. Indeed, this is precisely what judges are told to do by the Swiss rules for interpretation, which gain at least in honesty over our legal system.

Other rules of interpretation, notably the 'plain words' rule, help to point out a further essential weakness in the structure of statute law. One must follow the literal meaning of a statute unless to do so would either be clearly unjust or lead to a situation Parliament would not have intended. This is tantamount to saying that not only must the judge use his own initiative where there exists a lack of clarity, but also that it is up to him to decide when there is a lack of clarity. Statutory lack of clarity is not a practical problem that can, hypothetically, be got round. The judgement of when a statute requires interpretation is itself a political judgement; the law reports are full of cases where a statute that is the very model of linguistic clarity is deemed to require interpretation not because it is hard to see what Parliament *said it intended* but because a judge was unable to believe that it *could have intended* that thing.

It is in the decision to use such interpretative powers that political ideology can most often be seen to invade judicial impartiality. Consider the two following examples of statutory interpretation. The first demonstrates a conflict between judges where there does appear genuine uncertainty about the meaning of a phrase. In the second the conflict is really not about verbal confusion but about whether Parliament could possibly have meant what it said.

In *Suthendran* v. *Immigration Appeal Tribunal* the Lords had to decide the meaning of a clause of the 1971 Immigration Act, Section 14(1), which allows an alien 'who has a limited leave' to stay in the country to appeal against a decision of the Home Office not to extend that appeal. Suthendran, having entered as a student with a 'limited leave to stay' while he underwent a training course, defied the terms of his leave, took a job, and overstayed his permit. Various efforts were made, by him and by his employers, to get his leave extended and to get him a work permit, though none of these actions were taken until his original one-year permit had expired. He appealed against the Home Office's refusal to let him stay and originally his appeal was upheld but later was rejected by the Immigration Appeal Tribunal on the ground that the Act clearly only granted the right of appeal to those who *have*, not to those who *no longer have*, 'a leave to stay' and Suthendran's appeal had not been lodged until some time after his permit had expired.

Is the Act unclear here? Can one say that 'has a leave to stay' automatically includes those who 'have had' but do not now have a leave to stay? The Lords were divided three to two on the issue, the majority denying Suthendran's appeal and upholding the Home Office's right to deport him. Divorced of context it might seem that the debate is trivial but the political context introduces on both sides of the case important reasons for finding one way or another. The minority were worried at the potential injustice of the 'literal reading', for it would allow the Home Office to win dubious cases by delaying their decision on a request to remain until the original leave had expired and thus save themselves from a potentially embarrassing appeal. The majority felt it necessary to stick to the literal words of the Act. Although they did not say so, there was a political reason here too, in all probability. The reason is demonstrated by a case going on in the Court of Appeal at almost the same time; if an alien manages to remain in Britain for five years, he wins an automatic right to permanent residence. The court clearly feared that by indefinite delay and by using up all the various rights of appeal given in the Act, an alien could prevent himself ever being deported.

The majority in this case were 'strict constructionists'. Lord Simon, one of the majority, said, for example:

'Parliament is *prima facie* to be credited with meaning what it says in an Act of Parliament . . . The drafting of statutes, so important to people who hope to live under the rule of law, will never be satisfactory unless the courts seek . . . to read the statutory language . . . in the ordinary and primary sense which it bears in its context without omission or addition.'

He goes on to admit that this must not be done were it to produce injustice but that 'it would be wrong to proceed on the assumption that the Secretary of State would act oppressively'.

The minority simply invert this last argument. Lord Kilbrandon: '. . . faced with two interpretations of this somewhat perplexing statute, . . . neither of them altogether convincing, I prefer that which . . . at least avoids giving a statutory sanction to a possible injustice which I do not believe Parliament would knowingly have countenanced'. One thing is certain: no decision in this case would have been neutral, and nothing, other than a private feeling about what one would have done as a legislator oneself, can solve the problem presented.

Although in the American context one is used to the idea that strict constructionists are conservative, no simple lining up like that is possible in this country because strict construction may on occasion require the more liberal of two possible readings. The next case demonstrates this, for three of the judges – Wilberforce, Dilhorne and Kilbrandon – heard both cases. Whereas Dilhorne was a strict constructionist and conservative in the Suthendran case, in *Davmond* v. *SW Water Authority* he insisted that the words of the Act could *not mean* what they said and again produced a conservative judgement. Wilberforce, in the minority on Suthendran, now turns into a strict constructionist, to render a liberal judgement.

Mr Davmond complained that he ought not to be required to pay a sewerage charge in his water rates because he was not connected to mains drainage. The statutory clause in question provides that water authorities can fix such charges 'as they think fit' and Dilhorne says: 'This section is silent as to the persons from whom water authorities can obtain payment of their charges.

177

I find this most astonishing.' After insinuating that the government deliberately left this section unclear so as to avoid controversy in Parliament, Dilhorne goes on to say that it is unthinkable that the intention was to allow water authorities to tax anyone in the UK, and proceeds to demonstrate that Parliament could only have intended to make those pay who actually benefit from a service. In so doing he rejects the argument, persuasive to Wilberforce and Diplock in the minority, that as local authorities had *always* had the right to pay for sewerage from a general rate, Parliament could not be seen as intending to remove this vital public health power from the new authorities, unless they said so. This second case, like the first, demonstrates that statutory interpretation necessarily involves private belief. How else could a judge first decide whether a clause was in need of interpretation and then go on to interpret it?

Inconclusive concepts

A second structural weakness of law is that statutes often require judges to interpret such notions as 'reasonable care', or others that, though having the appearance of 'hard law', are in fact empty. A good example is the task set by the law on obscene publications, where the jury has to decide whether a magazine 'has a tendency to deprave or corrupt'. In public law the vital questions refer to a minister's judgement of a factual situation. Courts may hold a minister to be acting *ultra vires* where a statute empowers him to act 'if he is satisfied that' something is the case. The judge has to decide whether the minister considered anything he ought not to have considered, or failed to consider what he ought to have done. By their own testament, judges *may not* replace the minister's judgement with their own – they are entitled only to decide whether or not the minister *could* be satisfied of something.

Now these examples are even more pernicious than statutory interpretation because they pose problems only soluble by the judge in fact doing what he is supposed not to do – replacing a minister's judgement with his own. The Tameside case is the most recent important public law example of this test. The 1944 Education Act authorises the secretary of state, where he is satisfied that an education authority is acting unreasonably, to instruct them to desist. The House of Lords then had a double inference problem: what constitutes 'unreasonable behaviour' by an LEA, and could the minister be satisfied in this case that these constituent elements existed?

The case centred round the cancellation or postponement by a newly elected Tory education authority of detailed comprehensivisation plans due to go into effect in September 1976, the authority not being elected until the spring of that year. In particular the controversial point was whether or not the hastily reintroduced assessment procedures for the grammar school places that would now exist would be fair, given the shortage of time, and the possibility of a withdrawal of co-operation by teachers angry at the abandonment of the plans.

The Lords unanimously argued that the word 'reasonable' must be taken very extremely – it did not refer to mistaken behaviour but only behaviour so guaranteed to create chaos that no reasonable education authority could possibly undertake it. On these grounds it was further argued that the Secretary of State, who only had 'to be satisfied' that the authority was acting unreasonably, could *not* have been considering the situation correctly, because there were no grounds on which he could possibly believe Tameside's new plan to be literally unreasonable in this way. This, despite the fact that the authority in the end had to plan on doing the assessment of several hundred children, for only 200-odd places, in a few weeks, with a team of only a few teachers not joining the strike; and where, though there was testimony by some experts that it was possible, there was testimony by others that it was not.

Not only was the decision in the Tameside case conservative but it was conservative *because* the Lords had no choice but to put themselves in Mr Mulley's place. The only way they could possibly come to the conclusion that he was misdirecting himself in law was by considering the evidence available to him (and, actually, evidence *not* then available to him) and deciding that *they* didn't think the authority was acting unreasonably.

This, naturally, is not the only case raising similar problems. In the past the courts' tendency has been to treat ministers' statements that they were satisfied with something as sacrosanct except when there was objective evidence that they had cheated. So in the classic case of *Podfield* v. *Minister of Agriculture*, in the mid-1960s, a minister required to use his discretion in allowing or refusing a special investigation into the Milk Marketing Board was held to be acting *ultra vires* in refusing an investigation only because he had stupidly written a letter admitting that his action was dictated by party-political motives. However, over the last decade courts have increasingly felt able to say that a minister *could not* be satisfied, while at the same time insisting that they were not applying their own reasoning but objectively testing the minister's process of reasoning.

There are other structural weaknesses of this sort. Often statutes as well as common law rules involve the idea of 'reasonable behaviour', or rest on what a 'reasonable man' would do in some situation. For example, one branch of family law entitles a court to dispense with the consent of a parent to the adoption of his child where that consent is 'unreasonably' withheld. On this criterion the Lords, in a case in 1976 concerning a homosexual father, felt entitled to ignore the father's objection to the adoption of his son. Though he wished only to be allowed to visit the boy for a few hours a week, in the mother and stepfather's home, they argued that no *reasonable* father could fail to agree that a homosexual has nothing to offer his son. Certainly a conservative judgement by much modern opinion, but what could the court do but consult their own ingrained prejudices? Who else has a better right to have their prejudices consulted, after all?

Discretionary judgements

In a vein generally similar to the case considered above, one must separately add those cases where the courts are not so much called upon to vet another's decision as to make their own first-order decision. The second example is again taken from family law but only because it is an area where cases most ripely demonstrate the inevitability of judicial ideology having a role. The first example is more directly political than the second.

It is no dramatic case of the overthrow of a parliamentary statute by a powerful and independent judiciary. Merely the 'automatic' application of a written law in a civil case against a mere local authority. In 1979, elections to the former Greater London Council were won by the Labour Party which campaigned on one issue above all others: it would introduce cheaper fares on London Transport. It was therefore a manifesto commitment. As soon as possible after their election they introduced an extensive flat-rate policy of cheaper fares under the general label of 'Fare's Fair'. To cut the fares they had to increase rates, the property tax on London residents. The GLC did this by telling the London borough councils to apply a supplementary rate. Most obeyed without question, and public transport fares in London dropped dramatically, though rates did go up. One Conservative borough council rebelled and appealed to the courts. The case did not come up until the London Transport Executive, under the instructions of the GLC, had completely restructured its transport plans and fare structures to fit the Labour Party manifesto.

When the borough council's case came to the High Court it failed, but they went on to the Court of Appeal under the presidency of Lord Denning. It upheld the appeal on an interpretation (ultimately accepted by the Law Lords) of one word in the governing Act, the 1969 London Transport Act. This had a phrase which said that the LTE, under conditions set by the GLC, must organise the metropolis's transport 'economically'. Nobody in the country knows what, if anything, that was really supposed to mean. Most probably it was there as a caution against rampant inefficiencies. However, the courts saw it as very simple. It meant that London Transport must be run at least on a break-even basis. It could not adopt any policy known ahead of time to be sure to incur a deficit, even if the relevant political, elected authority asked it to do so and guaranteed to make up the deficit by a grant, financed from local taxation, which they had every right to levy. Whether or not such a policy is just, sane, politically admirable or whatever is no decision for us to make. But no more is it a decision for eight senior lawyers to make. This one decision had immediate and direct effects on a travelling population of nearly ten million people, involving, in the estimate of the transport experts, an average fare rise of 150 per cent, in a world where almost no mass public transport system breaks even and during a period when it would throw a large number of newly-employed transport workers out of a job in a city which already had more than 300,000 on the dole. Right or wrong, this was an enormous power to be exercised by an odd interpretation of one word.

But cases of less public importance can also reveal the extent of the power wielded by judges through their interpretations. In one typical family law dispute a father wanted custody of his daughter, the girl's estranged mother having died. He could offer a home with a perfectly adequate income, a wife (the daughter's stepmother) and a stepsister for the daughter, with a generally suitable background in terms of parental and sibling age. But he was challenged by his wife's mother, the girl's grandmother, known to the social services as bitterly opposed to the father and determined to make the child hate him. The father, on the other hand, was accepted as doing his best to help the daughter continue loving her other relatives. The job of a judge in such a case is to choose whatever is in the child's best interest. The High Court and the Court of Appeal both decided the grandmother should have custody because the stepmother, now in her late twenties, admitted having been promiscuous as a teenager. Although most readers will agree with the social services report in this case, firmly on the side of the father and stepmother's right to custody, no one can complain that the judges unfairly exercised a biased opinion. Yet again they were given no choice but to rule as their private attitudes required because there *is* no other solution.

Instead of this harrowing family law case we might have quoted a more traditionally 'political' example from, say, the Restrictive Practices Court, where judges are required, off their own bat, to decide whether some complicated trade arrangement is or is not in the public interest. We chose the family case only because it has an immediate subjective meaning for most of us. The problem remains the same in that judges are required to decide what is or is not in X's interest, in a political system that supposedly decides 'interest' questions through a pluralist electoral representative system. It is hardly surprising that they consult their private views and decide, in the family case, that grandmother should have custody, and in restrictive practices cases readily accept high unemployment rates. Still, if Parliament insists on judges answering problems that legislatures and executives fight shy of, they can only blame themselves if the answers are not always to their taste.

Judges' attitudes and their political role

How far may we expect the same problems of subjective interpretation to affect the new, more overtly political, areas now under judicial scrutiny? As we have seen, these include many facets of central–sub-central relations which would previously have been settled by negotiation, as well as, notably, trade unions and industrial relations. Major Conservative legislation of the early 1980s has created a whole corpus of new law in this area. It is of course no accident that new restrictions on trade unions, such as the prohibition of secondary picketing and the obligations to ballot their membership through a secret vote before undertaking strike action were imposed as laws and given to the courts to enforce. By so doing the government intended to distance itself from actual enforcement of its constitutional victories over the trade unions, and give the provisions the aura of non-political technical expertise which judges enjoy. Does this not mean, however, that they are in danger of being converted into front-men for the Conservative Party in a much more immediate sense than has been evident before?

Two points should be made in this regard. First, judges were far from seeking the political power thus acquired. Before the legislation of the 1980s some judges in the lower courts and notably Lord Denning in the Court of Appeal, were clearly trying to tighten the law on secondary picketing (the right of strikers to penalise companies not party to the original dispute, so as to put pressure on their main opponent). The House of Lords, however, resolutely upheld union immunities on appeal.

In enforcing the new restrictions in the 1980s, the courts have certainly not acted to reduce their impact. In imposing financial penalties on SOGAT 82, a print workers' union in dispute with Rupert Murdoch, owner of *The Times*, over his dismissal of many of their members, the Court of Appeal did not take into account, for example, that Murdoch had deliberately split up his newspaper's holdings into separate companies. By picketing his distribution company (engaged exclusively in distributing *The Times* and its companion newspapers), SOGAT 82 were only technically engaged in illegal secondary picketing; they were actually carrying on their primary dispute against *The Times* by one of the few means at their disposal. Courts have emerged as strict constructionists on the union legislation. If they have not sought to mitigate their consequences they have not sought to extend them either. This rather passive interpretation of their role has paid off in terms of avoiding the overt hostility of trade unions; as noted in Chapter 4, these have concentrated on political support for the Labour Party, in hopes of getting the legislation modified, rather than on the tactic (counter-productive electorally) of attacking the courts which apply it.

In the less constrained field of central sub-central relations the courts record has been rather mixed, sometimes upholding the government and sometimes Labour authorities. Judges' caution over these increasingly politicised cases perhaps gives a clue to their more general attitudes: like all courts they often have to rely on private values to make decisions because the law is actually silent on what the decision should be. In the absence of any clear public opinion they will be likely to hand down judgements reflecting their own class and career socialisation. This may on occasion be more conservative than the majority view in the population, though often as we have seen it merely reflects popular conservatism. Where they can see a real political conflict arising, or for that matter where there is enough public debate for there to be a clear majority opinion, they are unlikely to go against it. The US Supreme Court (often analysed in similar terms) has been called 'the least dangerous branch' of government. The House of Lords is no different. Perhaps this is why the two most brilliant and strong-minded men since the war to be appointed young to the Lords, Patrick Devlin and Alfred Denning, both felt so ineffectual that they resigned, Devlin to write and lecture, Denning to head the lower-ranking Court of Appeal where he could at least try to influence legal thinking with vigorous dissents. Neither had the freedom to be effective in the highest court of the land.

Chapter 9
Coercive powers: the police and military

In the last few chapters we have examined various bodies and institutions in the British political structure which function autonomously of national government. Sometimes these directly hinder the implementation of central policies and thus contribute to the fragmentation discussed in Chapters 1 and 2. Sometimes they distance themselves quite carefully from overt political matters, like the English courts, but make autonomous decisions affecting a wide range of life. In these cases they may not increase fragmentation but they certainly contribute to the loose-jointedness of the system.

All the institutions examined up to this point have claims to some kind of representative role, alternative or supplementary to that of the British Parliament and government. Local authorities have elected councils, the European Community has its directly elected Parliament, courts are invested with legal authority, many quangos and interest groups have elected spokesman. The police and the military, who are discussed in this chapter, could on the other hand be dismissed simply as bureaucracies with little discretion or ability to pursue independent policies. Such an impression is strengthened by the fact – remarkable in a world where two-thirds of the countries are subject to recurrent military coups and half the rest are run by a bureaucratic and secret police apparatus – that the British police and military forces have never tried to take over, or even directly threaten, the civil government.

There is indeed a significant absence of this type of political ambition among police and military leaders. This is not to say that they do not have an important political role or make important political decisions. To a large extent, as with judges, these result from the failure of other authorities to make sufficiently detailed rules about the matters on which they have to act. As we saw in Chapter 8 the law is far from clear, even after court rulings (and these, after all, are given only after a case is raised – the matter may previously have lain obscure for many years). Police are bound to make their own interpretations. Given the immense mass of law that purports to regulate our lives, and their limited material and manpower, the police are also bound to set priorities: to decide what shall be given most priority and enforced most strictly, and what shall be left to enforce itself, if it can.

The constitutional position of the police

The late 1980s are a difficult time to write about the police in Britain. Their constitutional position is being called politically into doubt as never before, largely as a result of objections to their role in the 1984–85 miners' strike, when they were organised very effectively in support of the Government. Apart from this general problem, three major statutory changes were enacted between 1984 and 1986 that may have wide-ranging consequences. One of these sets up an independent Crown Prosecution Service taking the decision of when to prosecute out of the hands of the police. A second act, the *Public Order Act 1986* is the most far-reaching legislative overhaul of criminal law dealing with public disorder since the 1936 Act was passed in the face of fascist and communist clashes on London streets. Finally the *1984 Police and Criminal Evidence Act* goes further towards codifying police powers of arrest, search, seizure and detention, and interrogation, and the associated suspects' rights, than has ever been attempted in Britain.

The problem is that the first two changes did not even come into effect until late 1986, and the third has been in operation only from 1985. Consequently we can only really speculate on what impact they will have. It must be admitted that the overall impact could in the end be very slight – a typical cosmetic trick of British politics. The reforms are discussed in the last section of this chapter, on police powers. Otherwise we discuss the police as they were in 1986 and have been for many years. The constitutional position of the police in Britain has been in one sense simple with only one important Act governing them; but in another it has been extremely complex; they have no clearly-defined role, and the mechanisms of political control over them are few and ill understood. The current structure and constitutional position of the police derive from the Royal Commission on the Police, which sat between 1961 and 1963. Most of its recommendations were put into the 1964 Police Act. Apart from the change in treatment of complaints against the police instituted by the 1976 Police Act, there has been no important legislation since 1964 (and before then there was hardly any legislation at all).

The 1984 Police and Criminal Evidence Act, which also alters slightly the provision for complaints against the police under the 1976 act, is the only serious exception to this. Far-reaching though the 1984 act may prove to be, it does not affect the general constitutional position of the police, the structure of the service, or the all-important role of the chief constable. One reason the 1984 act is important is that even if it changes little of substance, it at least gives a *statutory* backing to what has been largely a common-law matter to date. Even now the law on policing is scattered in hundreds of precedents, by-laws, and conventions accreted over time. So much is this so that it is extremely difficult to give any simple straightforward account of the powers, roles and duties of the police and of the way they are controlled. Even to attempt to do so can be misleading, because the very confusion and uncertainty about the matter is itself an important fact about our political system.

To make a really simple start we can say that there are four important types of actor involved in the system. These are: the Home Secretary (and Scottish, Welsh and Northern Irish Secretaries within their areas), the chief officers of

each of the police forces, the other officers of the forces, and the Police Authorities. One thing we can be sure of is that the really important entry in this list
is the chief officers, the chief constables of the police forces outside London and
the commissioners of the Metropolitan and City of London Police Forces – to
which we must add the head of the Royal Ulster Constabulary in Northern
Ireland. Their importance arises from the fact that (by tradition, common law,
and now by statute) they are the only police officers who in any way interact
with the political elements, the Home Secretary and the corresponding
regional Secretaries, and the Police Authorities. They also have total and sole
command of all other officers in the police service.

The chief constable is wholly responsible for all operational, administrative,
disciplinary and logistical decisions in his force. He cannot be given an order by
any political authority on any such matter. (The position of the commissioner
of the Metropolitan Police is somewhat different, as the police authority
in his case is the Home Secretary himself; in theory the Home Secretary may
have some slight power to give him orders, but in practice we can treat him
as substantially in the same position as a chief constable. This also applies for
the Royal Ulster Constabulary.)

The chief constable (and no other officer) is, however, 'responsible' to his
Police Authority. The meaning of this responsibility and accountability will
take us some time to analyse satisfactorily. The Police Authorities have the
same structure now for every police force outside the metropolis, consisting
of two-thirds of councillors from those local authorities covered by the force,
and one-third from magistrates in the area. Before the 1964 Act there were a
variety of police authorities depending on the sort of police force, i.e. county,
borough or city force, and it is sometimes argued (for example by Sir Robert
Mark, the ex-commissioner of the Met.) that they exercised much more
detailed control than do the new Police Authorities. As well as being responsible to the Police Authorities, chief constables can be required to give reports
to the Home Secretary or corresponding regional Secretary on any matter; the
Home Secretary or corresponding regional Secretary can give certain orders
to the Police Authorities, and has an ultimate influence on them by determining their grant from the Exchequer, and by failing to recognise a force as
efficient.

There is much disagreement on the extent to which central government controls and influences local police affairs, though such disagreement is probably
more a matter of what sort of local autonomy one regards as important, rather
than differences of opinion over facts. One can, quite legitimately, portray central government as having crucial power. For they, through Her Majesty's
Inspectors of Constabulary, must check the efficiency of police forces. They
also have considerable control over the funding of the constabularies. Manpower targets, for example, are not solely a matter either for the chief constable
or the Police Authority. The Home Secretary and his regional colleagues can
affect such matters considerably, both indirectly and by fiat. General questions
of the nature and abundance of police equipment are also most directly
decided by the Home Office, or regional offices.

This question of relative autonomy in different spheres of policy-making was well demonstrated by the urban riots in Liverpool, Manchester and London in the summer of 1981. As soon as they broke out, MPs were demanding action and explanations from the Home Secretary. It was he who announced, rapidly, decisions about buying and authorising more effective riot control equipment. The central government was quite rightly seen as the overall authority for the range of tactics available for deployment and for the general police strategy to be adopted. But when it came to the level of just how streets were to be policed, given the existing material, of whether a 'low profile' or 'intensive policing' was to be adopted, neither the Home Secretary nor any other political authority was involved.

The range of strategies adopted by chief constables during these few weeks is the best measure of immediate police autonomy; the ultimate role of the Home Secretary and his regional counterparts in deciding how in the future similar situations should be handled, is the best indicator of a different sense in which the police are not independent.

Operational control of the police

This bald and deliberately simple setting out of the system we are to analyse, immediately demonstrates the typically British indirectness and pluralism of authority and power in the system – it is indeed reminiscent of the political system for controlling education in Britain, and for good reason. If there is any central ideological thread running through the history of British policing and education, it has been fear of allowing the central government to have any political control of the area. In the case of the police, the fear has extended to local political control. To judge from senior police officers' views, it is now local political control they dislike even more than central. Privately (and some-times publicly) chief constables express very scathing views of the calibre and political judgement of local councillors, which is one reason why the Police Authorities tend to be so difficult to analyse. The other is that they do so little of significance in any case.

It would be a mistake to assume that senior police officers are all alike, or that they necessarily share a closely knit ideology. Their perceptions of their role, duties and responsibilities vary a good deal. Perhaps more important, their perceptions of police tactics and strategies vary, and this leads to huge differences in policing policies even in situations where their political and social values may be identical. The former chief constable of one West Country force, for example, is known as the darling of the National Council for Civil Liberties because of his commitment to something called 'community polic-ing'. This same concept is often on the lips of a Midlands chief constable, a young man known principally for his experience in counter-terrorist policing, who is the archetype of a neutral professional only concerned with the tech-nicalities of his job. The chief constable of a major northern city is a funda-mentalist Christian, known for giving speeches about the need to restore moral values to our society, who gave up 'soft policing' during urban riots only after he felt (soft) measures had failed. The deputy commander of the Metropolitan

Special Branch publicly opposes any increase in police powers to deal with terrorist threats, because he thinks his job is to police society rather than to reorganise society to make policing easier.

These differences come about partly because policing *is* a technical professional matter, and because professional values vary with the different experiences and problems which police officers have faced. The whole doctrine of the 'professional' nature of police work is complicated and potentially dangerous. If one accepts the 'professional' thesis there is no good argument for political control. But who is to judge when some decision is a professional matter?

Even the examples given above over-simplify the variety of our police system, for not all forces are territorially organised in the way so far assumed. There are other police forces such as the British Transport Police with a very wide jurisdiction stretching throughout the United Kingdom. The Department of Defence has its own civilian police force for guarding such key points as research establishments. The lines of political control over such bodies are extremely hard to define. The most obvious example of a centrally controlled and politically highly relevant body with a police function is of course the security service and its more public counterpart in the Special Branch of the Metropolitan Police (about 500 highly trained men, operating within local forces over the whole of the UK). Here even more than in other areas of police work it is difficult to find out enough to draw firm conclusions about power, control and police ideology. Certainly the wide deployment of the 'national' forces of police, supplemented by bodies such as Customs and Excise and Immigration Control, give the central government more potential to act directly at local level than is generally admitted. In terms of numbers on the other hand the 'national' police are eclipsed by the local forces. In discussing police work in general one must therefore focus on the latter, since they deal with the overwhelming bulk of cases.

The Royal Commission on the Police of the early 1960s profoundly shaped the nature of the service today and left one problem unresolved, the consequences of which are still with us. The most important practical consequence was the power the resulting Act gave to the Home Secretary to enforce mergers between police forces, which has drastically reduced their number, massively increased their size, produced much greater uniformity and rendered more serious the problem of political control. Before the amalgamations forced through by Roy Jenkins as the Labour Home Secretary in the mid-1960s there were over 150 separate and independent police forces in England and Wales outside London, many of them very small indeed, covering small areas. They tended to be highly individualist, with characteristics suiting the difference between, say, a sprawling, almost deserted rural county or a physically compact and densely populated urban centre. The Royal Commission evidently did not object to this, for it recommended as the best size for a force something in the region of 500 officers.

There are now only forty-nine forces outside London; the biggest is the West Midlands Constabulary, a force of 6500 officers, policing both Birmingham and rural areas miles from its centre. Partly as a result of the original amal-

gamations, and partly because of the subsequent local government reorganisation, these forces now cut across local authority lines, with no simple identity
between them. Thus problems of co-ordination occur between, for example,
police forces and social services, one of which may be organised on a metropolitan
basis, the other around district councils. Forces like the Thames Valley Police
bear no relationship to any administrative or traditional community at all. The
political consequence is clear: the old watch committees for forces like, for
example, the City of Leicester police were staffed with councillors from that one
council, and were aware of the city's problems as a unit, able to help and, if
necessary, influence the chief constable to create a policy for an area for which
they were already collectively responsible. The council members of the Thames
Valley Police Authority are drawn from a whole series of different councils, have
no permanent political unity or other collective responsibilities, do not know each
other and are correspondingly both unable and perhaps unwilling to exercise the
same sort of detailed control. It is in this sort of context that the potentially
uncontrollable power of chief police officers becomes a serious problem.

Although it is not usually presented in this way, it can be argued that the
current structure of the police service is a compromise between efficiency, supposedly served by amalgamations and greater size, and the need to keep the
police independent of the central government. For the 1962 Royal Commission
had, somewhat unusually, a minority dissenting report, in which a very distinguished lawyer, Lord Goodhart, argued forcefully for a total change in the
nature of the police service. Goodhart wanted a single national police force,
directly under Westminster control. This was, and still is, opposed as being
too dangerous an instrument. One chief constable recoiled in horror at what
he saw as a massive force of 120,000 men under the control of one super-chief
constable. His argument was that the power of a chief constable was much too
great to put such a force in any one man's hands.

So it would be, but that was never what Goodhart, or other civilian advocates of the idea, had in mind, and the assumption that such would be the
political shape of the force tells us a good deal about the actual police situation.
The chief constable in question did not see himself as too powerful, though
he commands a force which accounts for nearly one-fifth of those men and
resources. His fear is unrealistic, though explicable on different grounds – such
a force could not have the political independence, and therefore would not
have the power, he enjoys. The point is that only by making the central state
directly command the police force can it be politically controlled.

This is highly relevant at a time when the different police forces are being
increasingly co-ordinated informally, largely through a non-accountable body –
the Association of Chief Police Officers. This has led to the spread of uniform
practices in areas such as public order generally and in information processing
(there is now a central police computer), all leading to easier deployment under
central guidance as in the 1984–85 Miners' Strike. Few probably would dispute
the need for modernising procedures and effectiveness in this way – the question
is, however, if the separate forces are to some extent to be nationalised and put at
the disposition of the government, should they not also be accountable to Parliament? If not, there is an increasing danger of their acting in an arbitrary, and even

a partisan way, in support of an already strong Executive. Goodhart's plan would have given Britain a politically accountable force *with* whatever benefits there may be in size and uniformity. But it would do so at the cost of the hallowed British tradition of the impartiality and political independence of the police, assumed to be safeguarded by their division into local forces. Thus the scene is set to investigate the two vital questions that are so little understood or discussed when the political role of the police is considered in this country. The questions are first, just how accountable or responsible are the chief constables; and second, what is meant by the police being politically impartial in our society?

Police accountability

Accountability is at best a complex matter, and the complexity allows simultaneously for chief constables believing quite sincerely that there is a great deal of accountability to the political rulers of society, and for many others to believe there is virtually none. Two things are clear. Both the Home Secretary and, to a more limited extent, the Police Authorities may demand reports from chief constables about matters arising under their command, and indeed each chief constable has a duty to report about his force to his Authority every year. Only the Home Secretary (or the regional Secretaries) may demand reports on 'operational' matters, and the annual report to the Police Authority is under the chief constable's discretion. He can (and they sometimes do) refuse to divulge to his Authority information expressly requested, such as the size of the Special Branch component of their force. Whatever the Home Secretary demands as information can be made the subject of questions and debates in Parliament. Although there are problems, it is probably true that political authorities can extract enough information from the police after the event. At least, the Home Secretary can, and often does, while the Police Authorities may be able to, but hardly ever do. It seems common ground both to the police and to academic critics that the Police Authorities have in practice been either extremely passive or assertive in a party–political and left–ideological sense. In each case they have made very little use of even those powers they have under the 1964 Act, despite the expectations and intentions of the Royal Commission.

If the ability to find out what someone is doing after he has done it (and if you know what to ask about in the first place) is accountability, then there is a considerable degree of accountability by the police service in Britain. For example, the 1981 national enquiry into the West Yorkshire force for its failure to catch a murderer, the 'Yorkshire Ripper', over a period of years, strongly criticised its procedures and produced major operational changes inside the force. But, as a distinguished constitutional expert once said, 'What we really mean by accountability is the power to say "Tell me what you are doing, and stop doing it".' There we have a problem, because no one seems empowered in Britain to utter the second half of the sentence. The only actual control over what the police do, as opposed to what they tell you about what they are doing, is the law: if a chief constable breaks it the courts exist, as they do for any citizen. Also a rampantly inefficient chief constable could be dismissed on the Home Secretary's order.

It may be difficult at first to see why this situation should not be enough. Policemen find it very difficult indeed to see why it is not adequate. Why should anyone control the chief constable in 'operational matters'? The problem is that under 'operational control', which sounds an anodyne matter of technical expertise, lie at least two major discretionary powers, the exercise of which involves fundamental policy questions which would appear, at least on the surface, to be more naturally the scope of democratically elected politicians than appointed and autonomous police chiefs.

The discretion arises from two obvious facts: the police do not have the men or resources to patrol everywhere fully, to investigate all crimes fully, or indeed completely to carry out all of their legal duty to 'cause the peace to be kept and preserved, and prevent all offences against the persons and properties of Her Majesty's subjects'. Choices have to be made about the distribution of these resources, and the choices will affect the lives of Her Majesty's subjects. Should major police resources be put into a campaign against drunken drivers at Christmas time? Should vandalism in huge anonymous council estates be a major concern, even if this may mean less protection against serious theft for richer sections of a city? Should pornography be swept off the streets, prostitution be kept tightly within the law, should a lot of effort go into investigating possible subversives in trade unions? Whatever answer one chooses to give to such questions, it is hard to believe that they are not just as important, and just as clearly political or policy questions, as questions about how social service department resources should be spent. While no one would believe that the Director of Social Services in a local authority should have uncontrolled discretion, the doctrine of operational autonomy gives the chief constable the sole responsibility for answering such questions.

The second area of discretion covered by operational autonomy is both more important and more unusual. Almost alone among western democracies, England and Wales have up to now entrusted to the police the business of criminal prosecution in most, though not all, criminal cases. The usual pattern is to have an independent civilian officer either, as in Europe, a member of the judiciary or, as in North America, an elected politician, who decides when and whom to prosecute, and for what. With certain exceptions where the case must be referred to the Director of Public Prosecutions (DPP), the police themselves have been the prosecuting authority in England and Wales, which means that discretion as to whether or not to bring an alleged offender to court lay with the chief constable. The occasions when the DPP or the Attorney-General must give permission for a prosecution are important in the sense that they cover major crimes – murder, cases involving the Official Secrets Act, etc. – but these are comparatively few in number and probably of little overall impact. It is noteworthy that this pattern is not found in Scotland, where a judicial officer, the Procurator Fiscal, acts as does the juge d'instruction in France or the District Attorney in America.

This discretion too is vital; it is no part of the law of England that all offenders must be prosecuted, so again the legal duties of policemen have not removed policy discretion. For it is policy discretion that matters here. Were we only talking about prosecuting decisions in individual cases, decisions about whether or not the evidence is strong enough to give a good chance of conviction, it might matter less. We are considering, however, whole policies on what sort of crimes and what sort of offenders should be prosecuted whenever possible, or when it might be better to make extensive use of cautions, or indeed to ignore some offences completely.

A real example concerns juveniles. Should the police try whenever possible not to prosecute juvenile offenders, should they prosecute only for a second or subsequent offence? Should they prosecute all juvenile offenders? In one police force in the mid-1970s four adjacent divisions systematically used different policies of this sort on juvenile offenders, according to the preferences of the divisional commanders to whom prosecution policy decisions were delegated by the chief constable.

It may be a good thing to have variety and experiment in prosecution policy, and varying circumstances may make it advisable to enforce laws differently even in contiguous neighbourhoods. But who should make such decisions? Elected local politicians, or independent policemen?

It is this sort of subject matter inside the label of operational autonomy that makes it clear that the English police service is *not* fully accountable in vital ways, but forms independent baronies each able to construct and apply its own policies. Naturally there are many other such areas of autonomy, some more obviously of political relevance. The power to ban marches of political extremists has been shared, for example, between chief constables and Police Authorities and the Home Secretary, but no ban could be imposed without a chief constable asking for it. Then, clearly, it is an operational matter whether or not to provide police protection for a march, how to react to violence during a demonstration, and so on.

Police impartiality

If the police are constitutionally able to make policy in this way, if they are free from political control in carrying out their job to a degree greater than most of our institutions, how do they justify this? What major value in society is upheld by this autonomy?

An answer to this involves a discussion of three concepts: the policemen's notion of political impartiality; their understanding of the nature of the law; and their idea of the link between the police and the citizen. In short, we must come to grips with the typical police officer's view of the political role of the police.

It has always been a tradition in Britain, since the days when Peel persuaded a reluctant Parliament to let him set up the metropolitan constabulary, that the police should not be agents of the government, or even of the state as such, but should impartially uphold the law. Where conflicts have a clear political aspect it has always been seen to be of prime value that the police should not take the government's side, and should not be seen to do so. The contrast is often drawn with France, where the Minister of the Interior has frequently used the police to help his government in a clash with some opposing sector of society. In contrast we have British examples like the Home Secretary during the General Strike of 1926 trying to prevent the use of the police in any way that might make them seem to be on the side of the government against the unions. It is ironic that political thinkers on the left and right naturally assume the police are an agent of the state which upholds the government against those challenging its authority, while the agent in question does not agree and seeks to avoid this role.

Senior police officers traditionally dislike anything which involves them in such clashes. When the incoming government in 1979 proposed to make secondary picketing illegal, chief constables and Home Office officials were desperately keen that the criminal law should not be used, because they did not want their officers involved in disputes with unionists and thus appearing to 'take sides'. The industrial disputes of the 'Winter of Discontent' before that election were, it is argued by some, made worse by the unwillingness of the police to take any action against pickets who broke the then existing law, again because of the need to be seen as impartial. This was obviously not the case during the miners' strike of 1984–85 when the police were co-ordinated nationally in vigorous action against picketing and in support of the National Coal Board and of the government without apparent opposition by chief constables to this role. The riots of 1981 and 1985 have also typed police as the major defenders of established authority, as did the use of police power during the Wapping newspaper dispute in 1986–7.

While police officers in command positions have at least in the past sought to avoid protecting the government *per se* they have had a totally different attitude to the idea of upholding the law. This they have seen as sacrosanct, however little they think of the politicians who create it. It is this notion of the law as an absolute which must be upheld and protected, which justifies the absence of political control. In this perspective, not only is there no need for detailed control (because no political decisions are seen as involved in upholding the law), but detailed control is unacceptable. The law is pure, politics dirty, and the police serve the pure law, not the potentially corrupt politicians. The image of impartiality in upholding the pure law that the police believe they have is of practical value to them. Police officers are well aware that they can only uphold the law with at least the passive acceptance of the population; and such acceptance, so the argument goes, is dependent on the image of impartiality.

The police as a pressure group

This argument, firmly believed by most senior policemen, is long-standing, and obviously has much truth in it. In the last decade, however, there has occurred a new development in the police image of themselves and of their relationship to politics. To a considerable extent they have been thrust by the Thatcher Governments into the front line of potentially explosive disputes (like strikes and riots). Increasingly, senior policemen are becoming more vocal in public about policy matters; they too are becoming political actors and propagandists, though they would probably not accept that label. And, as part of the same development, they are beginning to assert a special relationship between themselves and the people and a special knowledge of the public needs. Sometimes, indeed, they claim what amounts to a superior role in interpreting what the public wants, compared with politicians.

Much of this development can be attributed to one man, Sir Robert Mark, the controversial Commissioner of the Metropolitan Police in the mid-1970s, whose book *In the Office of Constable* is the only serious and thoughtful work by a senior police officer on the role of the police. Until he took over the Met. and started appearing on television and writing in the papers, there had been an unspoken rule that, as a corollary of their political independence, senior police officers would never make public their beliefs and arguments on policy.

The beginning of this new openness in entering public controversy was Sir Robert's Dimbleby Lecture on BBC TV in 1973. This caused a furore because he attacked, amongst other targets, what he described as 'crooked lawyers', who fabricated alibis for criminals. It was all part of a general campaign to shift the balance in favour of the prosecution in criminal trials, a campaign that has been pushed hard by the police ever since. Afterwards many other chief constables entered the public arena, trying to move public opinion and to bring, in this way, pressure to bear on governments for reform. Now Sir Robert has retired the most consistently outspoken campaigner for strengthened police powers in many situations, but especially in public order, is the Chief Constable of Greater Manchester, James Anderton. But many more engage in public discussion, to the point that local politicians often complain bitterly at what they see as a usurped role.

It is not clear how effective such political involvement is; very little has been done by governments in response to police officers' demands. The police failed to prevent the passing of the 1976 Police Act, which set up an independent review board of laymen to investigate complaints against the police and to decide on disciplinary matters, a right previously exclusive to chief constables. Although this was the only controversial matter on which the Association of Chief Police Officers was unanimous for twenty years, and though it was opposed fiercely and publicly, it went through virtually unchanged, and Sir Robert Mark resigned rather than accepted it in the Metropolitan. In his book, as in public and private comments by other chief constables, there is a feeling that the police are 'the people's police', that they owe a primary obligation to the interests and demands of 'the people' which transcends that of any duty to the government. This is accompanied by a firm belief that policemen, by virtue of their daily contact with the population, know better than the politicians what it is the electorate really want in matters of social control. This belief, coupled with a deep suspicion of politicians of all colours, both justifies what they regard as a basic constitutional principle of police independence, and makes it seem all the more important.

Whether there really is such a basic constitutional principle is doubtful. As a principle it is perhaps enshrined in the 1964 Act, but previous precedents are rare and odd. The oldest actual precedent, on which most of the argument for autonomy depends, is a 1903 case in which the courts ruled that a police officer cannot make a local authority responsible for his acts, as he is not a servant of the local authority. It is argued almost from this sole precedent that if the local authority is not liable in civil damages for an officer's acts, it cannot be in control of him either. The argument is particularly anomalous because for a long time the Crown could not be held liable for acts of public servants, but no one ever suggested that civil servants should be independent of the Crown in carrying out their duties. Of course, with the British constitution mere duration of a practice is enough to make it a constitutional convention, but in this case sustained debate on whether it really is a principle would be less odd than asking if the independence of the judiciary is a basic constitutional provision.

Military aid to the civil power

There has been no incident since the early years of the century in which British soldiers have been used against British civilians in mainland Britain, But there is a more or less regular army detachment at Heathrow Airport, the SAS (Special Air Service) were used to break the siege of the Iranian Embassy in London in 1980, which led to several deaths, and armed soldiers have been present at a series of other incidents. Even where violence does not occur, troops are indispensable to the government for internal duties. It was the army that provided fire-fighting services when the fire brigades went on strike in 1978, the army that cleared up refuse in Glasgow when a strike by dustmen caused a health and safety hazard. The army has either been called in for, or on call for, running services in transport, electricity and docking at various times in post-war Britain. Army officers are now regularly trained in crowd control, and soldiers exercised in how to deal with riots and urban terrorism. And there is Northern Ireland, where British troops have been in a war situation since 1968, with numbers varying between ten and twenty thousand posted there at any one time. No one can join the British army without having to face the certainty of patrolling the streets of Belfast at some time, which will put him in risk of his own life, and leave him authorised to use deadly violence should an (entirely probable) situation so require it.

How important is the internal security role of our armed forces, and what is the legal framework for their use in such a role? Comparisons between France, Germany and Britain underline a rather important point; under its military budget France fields 76,400 gendarmes, equivalent to 33 per cent of its non-conscript troops, while the German BundesGrenzPolizei, again part of the military budget is 20,000 strong. These parliamentary forces, trained and armed as soldiers, do not exist in Britain – which into the bargain has a police service with no great capacity, training or resources for the use of extreme violence in a systematic way. (Apart from the fact that all French police are armed, there is also the CRS (*Compagnies Republicaines de Securité*) which numbers nearly another 20,000.)

Nor are France and Germany unusual; most countries have some form of disciplined armed force they can call on to deal with major disturbances without having to go all the way to using regular military. But Britain, which traditionally does not trust the government to dispose of coercion (hence the localisation and autonomy of the ordinary police), has never had such a force. Consequently, when situations occur beyond the scope of the police, the army has to be used.

The legal situation when troops are used to control civilian events is confused in the extreme. Traditionally troops were only used in a riotous situation, under the control of a local magistrate, and after he had read a proclamation as required from the 1714 Riot Act (hence 'reading the riot act'), which had the effect of making those taking part guilty of a felony. This Act was repealed in 1967 when the old felony/misdemeanour distinction was abolished. Under section three of the Criminal Law Act 1967, which repealed the 1714 Riot Act, it is now lawful to use such force as is reasonable to suppress a riot.

The trouble is that no one knows exactly what this means. The presence of a magistrate, and his command to troops to fire on a crowd, for example, is required by military law, so that an officer who gave such an order off his own bat might be court-martialled. But it is *not* required by common or statute law; an officer in a position to use force to prevent a riot and who did not do so might be at fault under ordinary law and, more to the point, if a magistrate ordered firing, the officer complied, people were killed and later a court decided that the amount of force used was excessive, the fact that the officer was obeying the magistrate's order would probably *not* be a defence to a murder or manslaughter charge. The general doctrine in question is that where troops are giving aid to the civil power it may not be inaccurate to describe the legal rights and duties of a soldier as being no more than those of an ordinary citizen in uniform.

This all seems to mean that if the government uses troops to control civil disturbance it can rely on no special legal protection for them, and there is no way that they can transform the situation into one where anything but the most extreme caution needs to be used. Nor can they make life easy for the soldiers in question, who are accordingly always unwilling to be involved in such a situation. On the other hand, there is no constitutional restriction on when, how, where or why the government does use troops. As part of the Crown prerogative the Cabinet can order the troops to go into any situation whatsoever, and do anything — so long as what they do is to uphold the law and does not break the law.

That is the situation on mainland Britain, but not, it appears, in Northern Ireland, for both Parliament and the courts. In Northern Ireland different codes prevail which give more freedom to the military, stemming from a tradition of almost continual civil disturbances and buttressed by emergency powers granted not only by British governments but by the devolved Northern Irish Parliament (1922–72) and the nineteenth-century Irish courts.

Police powers

There are two rather different tasks we set the police service. One is the detection and control of crime in a general sense, and principally involves individual threats to property and person. This is the stuff of police thrillers, detective stories and so on. The other, much less politically neutral, is the maintenance of public order. Although there is little evidence that police activities in this area are in fact now more common than at many other times in the past, the public visibility of this side of police work has been very high in the last ten years. The urban riots of 1981 and later, the policing of political protests, and above all the involvement of police in industrial disputes, especially the 1984–85 miners' strike and the violent picketing of Rupert Murdoch's new printing plant at Wapping in 1986–87 have caused a greater degree of political controversy than the police have had to face for a long time. In particular these have increased the demand for more direct political accountability. Although a future Labour Government is unlikely to carry out some of the demands of its members – banning the police from all industrial disputes is one of the most dramatic – police activity in controlling picket lines has made them more controversial. One survey of Labour Parliamentary candidates reports 78 per cent in favour of direct political control of police operational decisions. However, reforms legislated in the last few years may go some way to defusing these feelings.

One of the major problems about this sort of public-order control work until now has been the haphazard and ill-designed nature of the legal tools available to the police. Until the passage of the 1986 Public Order Act, which has only just come into operation, the powers of the police rested on a combination of a relatively old statute, the 1936 Public Order Act, and a host of rather ill-defined common-law powers developed in an *ad hoc* manner over the years. The new Act does not seriously pretend to alter powers in any dramatic way, but does seek to make them much clearer, and better designed to fit the realities of street police work in highly conflictful situations. It is sorely needed, and though not popular with the political left and civil libertarians, may prove as much in the interest of protesters in the future as of the police.

One reason for suggesting this is that a clear delineation of powers will prevent the expansion of common-law powers that tends to occur in crisis situations. For example, during the miners' strike the police essentially invented for themselves a legal authority, supported by the Attorney General in the Commons, which appears to have had no prior legal history at all. This was the power to stop coachloads of picketing miners miles away from the site of any picket line and turn them back. This was done by a crude extension of the common-law right of a police constable to arrest someone he believes to be about to commit a breach of the peace. As far as anyone had understood before this, the arrest power could only be used if the breach of the peace was imminent, immediately in the view of the constable. In this case miners were effectively being arrested because they might, miles and hours away, do something. Never properly tested in the courts, the police were able to do this precisely because there was no determinate version of their authority. Similar inventions of authority ought to be much harder in the future. The new Act takes the old, vague and little understood offences of riot, unlawful assembly and affray, and replaces them with five much more tightly defined offences: riot, violent disorder; affray; causing fear or provocation of violence; and causing harassment, alarm or distress. A second section of the Act spells out and slightly increases the power to restrict or prohibit public processions and requires notification of them. Taking a broad coverage, the Act also collects together racial hatred offences, and even football hooliganism offences. Thus it gives a unified general codification of a set of powers intentionally tailored for the modern task of public order. Nothing in the Act will prevent the police using their powers in ways that some will find politically biased, but no Act could do that. At least the police will not have to use blunderbuss charges ill-fitted to their unenviable tasks.

Of course the real fear many have of police power has never been so much their power to arrest, as what happens after arrest. Unlike the United States, whose constitutional Bill of Rights has been interpreted by the Supreme Court to give criminal suspects clear formal protection from police intimidation, no British citizen has had any real statutory protection since the police forces were first organised. Such protections as exist, for example the right to be told that one need not answer police questions, the right to see a solicitor or have a friend informed of one's arrest, have rested on 'Judges' Rules'. These rules and directions were put together entirely by the judiciary, had no binding force, were very widely disregarded, and at best were interpreted in vastly different ways in different places. Furthermore very basic powers, as for example the right of a police officer to stop and search someone on suspicion were either common-law based, contained in a mass of different specialised legislation, or simply varied from place to place. The Metropolitan Police, for example, could stop and search for stolen goods under a 1839 act; this power was also enjoyed by police in Birmingham, Manchester, Liverpool and Rochdale, but nowhere else! Similar uncertainties and randomness existed for gaining warrants to search premises, for arrest in general and so on.

What is potentially the biggest reform in police power this century was passed to deal with this situation in the Police and Criminal Evidence Act 1984. The Act, parts of which are only just coming into force, is a good example of the bipartisanship that sometimes still occurs in British politics. Its origin lies in a Royal Commission set up by a Labour Government in 1977. The bill itself went through two Parliaments, because the election of 1983 required its reintroduction in the next Parliament, giving time for thousands of amendments to be debated and for intense lobbying by all sides.

Obviously no details can be discussed here. The Act's main value lies in codifying what are basically the best practices from the past and applying them uniformly across the land. The Judge's Rules are now replaced either by clauses in the Act itself, or by elaborate Codes of Practice for police officers attached to the Act. A breach of one of these codes will now automatically constitute a disciplinary offence by a police officer in a way that ignoring Judges' Rules never could be.

In general the rights of suspects will now be on a much surer footing. One imaginative aspect of the Act demonstrates this. As soon as the Home Office has finished experimental trials, the government is committed to requiring that all police interrogations be tape recorded – one copy of which will be part of the unofficial record going to the prosecutor and court, and with full rights for the accused and defence to hear the tape. If anything can put a stop to the widespread tendency of the police to invent confessions, this should, and the resulting increase in confidence should spill over to criminal processes in general.

The final great reform of the mid-1980s came about as a result of the same Royal Commission. As we have noted, police in England and Wales have always had the duty not only to detect crime and charge suspects, but also to decide whether or not to prosecute, and to take charge of the prosecuting process. Except for a few very serious crimes, where the Director of Public Prosecutions either had the duty or the power to step in, this meant that prosecution policy could, and did, vary at the will of the chief constable for the area. One consequence of this has been the prosecution of a very great number of cases where the evidence was too weak to gain a conviction. In 1978, for example, 50 per cent of those pleading not guilty to criminal charges were finally acquitted in court. This may speak very well to the fairness of criminal courts, but raised very serious questions about police use of their powers. Given the enormous damage to anyone's life of facing a criminal charge, allowing the police to prosecute anyone they choose to charge with a crime has for long given England an unsavoury reputation in criminal justice.

The police did not in fact have to prosecute even when they thought someone was guilty – they had the power to issue a formal caution instead, which many experts believe had as much deterrent power. They did not do this as often as they could, by any means. One estimate suggests that around 46,000 cases a year were prosecuted which could have been cautioned, and should have been on the basis of guidance issued by the Director of Public Prosecutions. Another study claimed that another 46,000 non-cautionable cases were prosecuted when the evidence was too weak even to try to get a conviction.

The obvious step has now been taken. From October 1986 there has been an independent Crown Prosecution Service throughout England and Wales, based on area offices each with a Chief Crown Prosecutor and a staff of legally-trained civil servants, the entire service coming under the Director of Public Prosecutions. From now on the police will only be able to charge, and then the decision of whether to prosecute, and for what, will be in separate hands, as it has always been in Scotland under the Procurator Fiscal. There are critics of the system, inevitably. The Royal Commission had wanted independent regional services rather than a national one. Others believe the new service will work too closely with the police and will not have the desired effect. If this is so it will reflect the consensuality of British administrative political culture, but there seems no good reason to second guess a system that works well elsewhere.

Overall then Britain stands at the beginning of a new era, not only for police enforcement of criminal law but for most other aspects of their relationship with the public. Their precise standing in relation to the government of the day is also more debateable than it was in the past, and changing fast; it is not clear whether old self images of impartial arbiters between populace and government, or new ones as defenders of the traditional order against anarchic or radical challenges, will in the end win out. As with all the changes we have reviewed in this chapter, it will take years before it is clear what real difference has been made by the reforms of the mid-1980s.

Chapter 10
Britain and the world: foreign and defence policy

In the immediate aftermath of the Second World War, Winston Churchill observed that Britain's international interests lay in three interlocking 'circles': in Europe, in the Empire and in the Atlantic 'special relationship'. Since 1945 – with all-party support – the strategy underlying Britain's foreign policy has been to maintain British influence in all three 'circles'. This strategy, moreover, has had some tactical successes. Successive governments – with Foreign Office assistance – have been remarkably adept at extricating themselves from a series of difficult crises as a result of actions which have rightly occasioned a degree of self-congratulation. What both politicians and bureaucrats have failed to recognise, however, is that tactical success has masked strategic failure: Britain's foreign policy strategy has in reality been damagingly *overextended*, both economically and politically.

This overextension has been due to the continued (and mistaken) belief held by the framers of UK foreign policy that Britain can still play a great power role in the international system. The irony is that relative economic decline in the post-war period has made this role impossible to sustain and the very attempt to sustain it has further hastened decline. In spite of the limited strategic reappraisals which followed the Suez debacle in 1956 and the decision to withdraw from East of Suez in 1967, foreign policy-makers have still not managed to devise a strategy and role for Britain that is commensurate with its depleted resources. Indeed, it is testimony to the collective failure of imagination of government, bureaucracy and electorate that, even after 25 years, Dean Acheson's aphorism remains remarkably apt: Britain did indeed lose an Empire yet it has still not found a role.

In order to substantiate these claims, the chapter reviews post-war developments in each of Churchill's three 'circles'. It seeks to show how the balance of emphasis accorded to the circles has changed over time and how the requirements of one circle have frequently conflicted with those of another. The first section examines the origins of the 'special relationship' and reviews the problems posed for Britain's future defence policy which have arisen from the breakdown in the post-war social-democratic consensus over the last 10 years or so. The second section analyses the retreat from Empire and demonstrate how the continued pursuit of a residual imperial role has inhibited the development of a foreign policy more in keeping with Britain's loss of status as a great world power. The third section reviews Britain's increasing involvement in the European circle and examines the way in which its Atlantic and Imperial commitments have not only impaired its ability to act as a 'genuine-partner-in-Europe' but also had a disruptive effect on the development of the European Community. The final section examines some of the main features and problems of Britain's contemporary defence policy.

The Atlantic 'special relationship'

The 'special relationship' with the United States – the centrepiece of Britain's post-war defence policy – was of obvious importance both during the Second World War and at the 'post-war settlement' conferences at Yalta and Potsdam in 1945. Even in the wake of victory, however, there were significant tensions between Britain and the United States: the British were outraged by the ending of collaboration in atomic research engendered by the McMahon Act of 1946; the Americans were wary that British imperialism might enjoy the same sort of post-war revival that it had experienced after 1918. The tensions were soon overcome, however, by the emergence of a greater, *external* threat. During 1947 and 1948 Stalin tightened the Soviet grip on eastern Europe by ensuring that favourably-disposed regimes achieved power in Poland, Hungary, Bulgaria, Rumania and Czechoslovakia; the electoral success of the French and Italian Communists and the growth of Marxist-inspired insurgencies in Greece and Turkey suggested a worrying increase in Communist influence inside the western sphere of influence; and the Berlin blockade of 1948 hinted that Stalin might be contemplating overt aggression against the West. All these developments served to reinforce the growing perception inside British and American foreign policy-making circles that the security and material interests of the two countries strongly converged. The result was an increase in Anglo-American *military collaboration*, both in the Third World and – primarily – inside Europe.

In the context of the *Third World*, the Truman Doctrine – that the US would support any 'free people' struggling against Communism – was the symbolic acknowledgement that the United States was prepared to assume the role of primary protector of the global interests of Western capitalism; with Britain henceforward taking a secondary, supporting role.

The doctrine was never as all-embracing as it sounded, but it did lead directly to the United States taking over from Britain the responsibility for the survival of non-Communist regimes in Greece and Turkey. It also produced, in the late 1940s, an informal Anglo-American agreement to pursue 'parallel policies' in the Middle East in the defence and promotion of Western oil interests.

The Korean War of 1950–53 was the first major test of the special relationship as a counter to the global encroachment of Communism and although the costs involved were considerable, the Western Powers were in the event broadly successful in containing Communist expansion within their preferred defence perimeter. However, despite both the collaboration in Korea and the pursuit of 'parallel policies' towards the Middle Eastern oil-producing states in the early 1950s, the special relationship – at least as far as the Third World was concerned – suffered a serious blow with the 1956 Suez crisis, when American diplomatic and financial pressure effected a rapid and ignominious withdrawal of the British Expeditionary Force. Thereafter, a greater degree of cynicism and suspicion entered into British and American assessments of each other's Third World entanglements. Even though Harold Wilson provided token military assistance to the Americans during the Vietnam war in the 1960s, the equivocal character of British support did little to restore the notion that the special relationship had any real meaning in the context of either British or American dealings with the Third World. Indeed, during the 1970s, the whole idea of a 'special relationship' in the context of the Third World seemed increasingly irrelevant.

With the electoral victories of Mrs Thatcher (in 1979) and Mr Reagan (in 1980), a greater degree of correspondence between British and American Third-World policies re-emerged. The evidence seems to suggest, however, that this policy convergence has largely consisted in the British following in whichever direction the Americans have already decided to go. Under the Thatcher Government, Britain's policy has largely been confined to diplomatic backing for whatever position the United States chooses to adopt in its defence of Western global interests: thus, for example, Britain's support for the American invasion of Grenada in 1983; its continued reluctance to apply economic sanctions against South Africa; and its active connivance in the American 'reprisal' raid against Libya in April 1986.

While Anglo-American *military* collaboration in the Third World has all but disappeared over the last 30 years, the special relationship has continued to flourish – at least in British eyes – inside NATO, the West's device for deterring Soviet aggression in Europe. It is inside NATO, moreover, that clear evidence of Britain's 'overextended' foreign policy can be discerned. Although notionally a defensive alliance among *sovereign states of equal status*, NATO was from the outset an essentially hierarchical organisation with the United States at the apex, Britain (and France, before its effective withdrawal in 1966) immediately below it, and the remaining members at the base. The Americans and British (and French) derived their predominant position partly from their greater military capability at the inception of the alliance, and partly from their disproportionately large contributions to NATO's budget. In 1950, when Britain still ranked as one of the countries in the world with the highest income per capita, such a disproportionate contribution could reasonably be justified; as Britain has slowly descended the economic league table, the commitment has made less and less sense. Of course, Britain has benefited from the security which its extra financial contribution has provided, but while the benefits of 'additional security' cannot be gauged, the costs of making that contribution – in terms of resources not devoted to domestic industrial investment – have undoubtedly been considerable.

Quite apart from its disproportionate contribution to NATO's conventional forces and to its budget, however, Britain has also, since the mid 1950s, been committed to a nuclear capability within NATO. Publicly, Britain's possession of an independent nuclear force has always been justified on the grounds that, over and above the effects of the American nuclear umbrella, it constitutes an additional deterrent to Soviet conventional or nuclear aggression in Europe. On this account, the independent deterrent has effectively proclaimed to the Soviets:

Even if you do not believe that the United States would really risk a nuclear attack on itself simply in order to come to the aid of Western Europe, you would be well advised not to try anything because we Europeans will definitely use our nuclear weapons if we have to.

This public explanation has masked a rather more curious, political motive behind the acquisition and maintenance of Britain's bomb. This is simply that first Attlee, then Churchill – and then every British Prime Minister since – seem to have regarded the possession of nuclear weapons as a *necessary* condition for Great Power status in the post-war world. It has thus been argued that in order to make its counsel heard in Moscow and Washington, London has to possess nuclear weapons; with all the attendant costs – over and above those of maintaining conventional forces – that have thereby been incurred.

What is particularly disconcerting about this view is that the possession of nuclear weapons is also seen as *sufficient* condition for Great Power status. Britain's relative economic decline in the post-war era has effectively eroded any claim it might have had to such a status; a nuclear capability can never compensate for the fundamental loss of international influence that accompanies economic decline. The irony – noted earlier – is that in their attempts first to acquire a nuclear deterrent, and subsequently to maintain its technical credibility, successive British governments have pursued a resource allocation strategy that may in some measure have contributed to the very economic decline which has rendered the possession of the deterrent superfluous.

All this is not to deny, however, that the independent deterrent may be necessary for other reasons. It is possible that by maintaining its nuclear forces, Britain demonstrates a degree of commitment to the defence of western democracy which is essential if the United States is itself to remain committed to the NATO alliance. There has always been a strand of American strategic opinion that has advocated a principally European defence of Europe; there is thus always the concommitant danger that if the Europeans – and especially the British, given their historical role within NATO – seem unprepared to shoulder their share of the defence burden, the United States will effectively withdraw from NATO and leave the Europeans to face the Soviet threat alone. This possibility has been intensified by the current willingness of the USSR to trade concessions with America to promote a full international settlement.

For many Europeans, of course, American withdrawal might be no bad thing. The left in Europe has always argued that 'the Soviet threat' was a diversionary creation anyway, of capitalist elites who needed to distract the attention of their domestic populations away from the true class enemy within. Advocates of European nuclear disarmament also argue that while Soviet adventurism in the immediate post-war period was perhaps likely because the lines of partition between East and West were at that time uncertain and relatively fluid, in the intervening years the lines of partition have hardened substantially, which enormously increases the costs of Soviet aggression and accordingly reduces its probability.

Not surprisingly, those strategists who believe that there always has been, and still is, a Soviet threat to Western Europe take a contrary view. They acknowledge that there is no *direct* evidence of Soviet aggressive intent (there wouldn't be, would there?) but point out that this is so precisely because of the continued existence of the NATO deterrent. There is, they suggest, an abundance of indirect evidence which demonstrates that wherever the costs of aggression have not appeared to be too great the Soviets have been quite prepared to use the military instrument in order to defend or expand their sphere of influence; thus Hungary in 1956, Czechoslovakia in 1968, Afghanistan in 1979. If the Soviets do not have long-term aggressive intentions towards the West, ask NATO's proponents, why does the Warsaw Pact need three times as many tanks as NATO in the European theatre? Why has the Soviet navy massively expanded its presence in the Indian Ocean and the Pacific since 1970, making use of its new-found bases at Aden and Cam Ranh Bay? Why does it provide covert – and sometimes overt – support to almost any insurgent group which opposes the incumbent regime in Third World countries that are at present in the Western sphere of influence?

These questions are not only deliberately rhetorical; they are also in large measure unanswerable empirically. The truth is that we simply do not know whether there is a Soviet threat to western Europe. We do not know whether it is the existence of NATO since 1949 that has deterred Soviet aggression or whether Soviet inactivity in western Europe has been the result of self-restraint or lack of interest. And we do not know – indeed, we cannot even make a genuinely informed guess – what would happen in the long-term if NATO were to be disbanded as a result of an American withdrawal.

The Empire-cum-Commonwealth

It is in relation to Empire and Commonwealth policy that the 'overextension' of Britain's post-war foreign policy has been most apparent. Consider the position in the early 1950s. Although HMG had divested itself of responsibility in India (in 1947) and in Palestine (in 1948), the British Army of the Rhine was busily protecting West Germany from Soviet conventional assault; the RAF was assembling a nuclear strike force capable of providing an independent deterrent against a possible Soviet attack; a large expeditionary force was fighting in Korea in support of the US policy of 'containment'; guerrilla insurgencies (or, depending on point of view, liberation struggles) were being suppressed in Kenya and Malaya; British garrisons in Suez, Aden and Cyprus – stationed there to protect British 'strategic interests' – were coming under increasing indigenous pressure to leave; colonial administrators throughout British Africa were finding it increasingly difficult to subdue local nationalist pressures for constitutional change; and the Royal Navy still operated a *Pax Brittanica* in the Persian Gulf and Indian Ocean. For a Great Power, recently victorious in a world war, such widespread commitments and responsibilities seemed entirely acceptable. For a small European power, which had had to sell off virtually all of its overseas assets in order to finance that world war; which, since 1946, had been able to pay its way only in virtue of an enormous American loan; which was experiencing endemic balance of payments crises; whose protected imperial markets were crumbling in the face of foreign competition; and whose economic growth rate was lagging woefully behind its international competitors, the commitments – with hindsight – were ludicrous.

Yet it was only after the Suez crisis in 1956 (when Britain, with France and Israel, took over the canal zone in order to topple the Nasser regime in Egypt) that a serious strategic reappraisal of Britain's global over-commitment was undertaken. The fact that Britain, together with France, was obliged abruptly to withdraw its (militarily successful) expeditionary force as a result (principally) of American pressure, marked a watershed in Britain's foreign policy. After Suez, politicians of all ideological persuasions came to recognise that Britain was no longer quite the Great Power that she had been at Yalta: Britain could no longer compete with the two superpowers in the race for global influence.

The response of the newly-installed Macmillan Government was to encourage (or at least acquiesce to) the indigenous 'wind of change' that was already blowing through the Empire. Beginning with Ghana in 1957, the long-established pretence of 'preparing indigenous populations for self-government before we can grant independence' was abandoned. A series of acts of decolonisation – in Africa, the Caribbean and the far east – followed, so that by 1970, all that remained of the Empire were a few small dependencies scattered around the globe. (Even Rhodesia – the illegal creation of a small minority of recalcitrant white settlers – was satisfactorily disposed of after the Lancaster House agreement on Zimbabwe in 1980). The final part of the retreat from Empire was completed following the 1967 decision of the Wilson Government to withdraw British forces from East of Suez. The decision, taken primarily on the grounds of essential cost-cutting, was not reversed by the incoming Heath Government and by the end of 1971, British forces had withdrawn from both Aden and Singapore; the Indian Ocean was left to the Soviets and the Americans.

Given that it had taken Britain over two centuries to assemble its imperial possessions, the dismemberment of the Empire was accomplished with remarkable rapidity. For Britain, however, the 15 years of 'overextended' expenditure between Suez (when it was recognised that the global role could not be sustained) and the withdrawal from East of Suez (when the global role was effectively ended) still represented a significant additional drain on the Exchequer; at a time when Britain's relative industrial decline was continuing apace. The drain was compounded, moreover, by the costs imposed upon the domestic economy by the sustained attempts between 1945 and 1968 to maintain the Overseas Sterling Area and the reserve role of sterling. The whole idea of the preservation of sterling as a reserve currency was always bound up with Britain's supposed 'Great Power' status: it was consistently assumed that as a Great (capitalist) Power, Britain must have a high-status currency commensurate with its dominant international political role. From the point of view of the domestic economy, however, it was most unfortunate that successive British Prime Ministers through to Harold Wilson (in his first period of office at least) felt impelled to pose as the leaders of a still-great power. The attempt to preserve sterling's international value and status was a major contributory factor to Britain's continuing Balance of Payments crises of the 1950s and 1960s; crises that provoked domestic 'stop-go' economic policies which were inimical to the long-term health of the British economy (Ch. 1).

During the 1970s, Britain's involvement in the Empire 'circle' was commendably limited. The Commonwealth, although composed largely of regimes sympathetic towards Britain (the colonial administrators had always taken care to leave the right people in charge at the time of decolonisation) had never become the sort of surrogate Empire for which the more ardent imperialists had hoped; becoming instead a vehicle through which the 'new' Commonwealth could claim special aid concessions from the old imperial country. The aid thus provided, however, was by no means burdensome; Britain's strategic involvement in the Empire-cum-Commonwealth had been trimmed down to match its reduced capability. In addition, by way of a replacement, the construction of a new 'European' role for Britain seemed to be well under way.

This cosy state of affairs was not to last however. In 1982, Mrs Thatcher – in defence of the principle of sovereignty – launched her South Atlantic campaign. Whatever the rights and wrongs of the conflict, two aspects are abundantly clear. First, the military campaign was brilliantly conceived and executed; the repossession of the Falkland Islands was – like decolonisation and the withdrawal from east of Suez – another 'tactical success'. Second – and more disturbing – it meant that the UK embarked on a long-term (and long-distance) military and financial commitment which it could not really afford. Britain had ceased to maintain a presence in the Indian Ocean in the late 1960s because it could not justify the expense in the face of competing defence and social welfare demands. It was decidedly odd that, almost 20 years later, a small and increasingly impoverished west European power was prepared to allocate a significant proportion of its limited financial resources to the preservation of the rump of its imperial possessions. Overextension in the Empire Circle had, in the 1980s, reared its ugly head once more.

The shift towards (Western) Europe

After Suez, it was increasingly recognised that the strategy of maintaining Britain's influence in all three of Churchill's 'circles' was impossible to sustain given Britain's diminished and diminishing resource base. As Britain's involvement in the Empire gradually declined with decolonisation, so its interest in the European circle grew; beginning with Macmillan's unsuccessful attempt to join the EEC in 1961–63 and culminating in Britain's accession to the European Community in 1973. What has created considerable difficulties with this strategic shift, however, is that successive governments have simultaneously attempted both to maintain the 'special relationship' and to retain a foothold of some sort in the Empire/Commonwealth circle. While the shift to Europe has tended to reduce the problem of overextension, the retention of the Atlantic and imperial connections has at the same time damaged Britain's relationship with Europe and prevented it from effectively performing the predominantly European role which successive governments since Macmillan's have attempted to pursue. Before assessing the extent of this damage, however, it is necessary to examine three major factors which underpinned the shift towards Europe.

Given the continuing strength of the 'special relationship', a necessary – though by no means sufficient – condition for Britain's entry into Europe was always American approval. Indeed, immediately after the war, the Truman administration encouraged the then Foreign Secretary, Bevan, to take a leading role in stimulating political and economic co-operation and integration in Europe; in 1945, a strong, united Western Europe that would act as a bulwark against Communist expansion was inconceivable without British participation. What the Americans failed fully to appreciate, however, was that Britain could not simultaneously lead European unification and maintain its imperial links. In the aftermath of the war, the imperial bonds were far too important emotionally to permit their dilution with European entanglements. As a result, the UK did not participate in the 1950 Schuman Plan and the process of functionalist economic integration in western Europe proceeded swiftly – and successfully – without British involvement. The United States, however, had remained favourably disposed to British entry into Europe throughout the post-war period; it regarded Britain's economic integration with the rest of Western Europe as the natural corollary to Britain's military role in the European wing of NATO.

A second reason behind Britain's shift towards Europe was that during the 1950s it became increasingly clear that the Commonwealth was not an effective instrument for maintaining British influence around the world. Suez itself had seriously damaged Britain's relations with the 'new' Commonwealth. Indeed, the Indian Prime Minister Nehru was so outraged by the British action that, in tandem with Ghana's Nkrumah, he began a series of diplomatic initiatives which were to culminate, in 1963, in the creation of the Non-Aligned Movement. After 1960, the position worsened further: in 1961, in the face of strong British resistance, South Africa was expelled from the Commonwealth; in 1965, Ian Smith's UDI created an illegal and racist regime in Rhodesia which the British government did little – effectively – to undermine; and in the same year, the Immigration Act introduced strict controls on the entry of 'new Commonwealth' – that is, black – citizens into the UK. All of these developments steadily eroded Britain's standing in the eyes of 'new' Commonwealth leaders and in consequence British politicians saw less point in allowing Commonwealth ties to act as a brake on the increasing British desire to achieve accommodation with Europe.

A third, and perhaps the major, reason underlying the strategic shift to Europe was the apparently autonomous change in the pattern of Britain's trade which occurred after 1960. As Table 10.1 indicates, UK exports to the EC countries increased from 20.9 per cent in 1960, to 29.3 per cent in 1971, and to 43.8 per cent in 1983. Given that Britain's main trading interests were becoming more concentrated there, it is perhaps not surprising that during the 1960s and 1970s the leaders of all three major political parties began to stress Britain's role as a primarily European power; increasingly, this was where the UK's main material interests were located. Combined with the promise of the higher growth rates which the Six had achieved during the 1950s and 1960s, the economic logic of

Table 10.1 Percentage of British exports to and imports from EC countries

	British exports to EC as % of all British exports	British imports from EC as % of all British imports
1935–38	21.7	18.6
1948	16.7	13.1
1954	21.5	18.4
1960	20.9	20.2
1971	29.3	29.9
1979	41.8	43.1
1983	43.8	45.6

All figures include West Germany, Italy, France, Belgium, Netherlands and Luxembourg (the original 'Six') and Ireland and Denmark (which joined, along with the UK, in 1973).

Source: *Annual Abstract of Statistics* (HMSO: various years)

closer British co-operation with Europe pointed strongly towards a determined effort to enter the EC.

Yet, somehow, British leaders (with the notable exception of Edward Heath) have never appeared to be really committed 'Europeans'. In part, this has been the consequence of purely domestic pressures inside Britain: the retrospective referendum on EEC membership in 1975 was Harold Wilson's device for appeasing the left wing of the Labour party; the repeated efforts to 'renegotiate the terms of British membership' and the megaphone haggling over the size of the British contribution to the EEC budget have both reflected inter-party squabbles at home. As noted earlier, however, much more serious both for the community itself and for Britain's position within it, have been the confounding effects of the continuing Atlantic and imperial commitments. Three examples serve to illustrate the problems thus encountered.

The first of these concerns the circumstances surrounding Britain's first application to join the European community in 1961–63. De Gaulle's attempts after 1958 to inhibit the supranational momentum of the EC, and to keep it more as an association of sovereign states, had squared very well with Macmillan's conception of what European co-operation should be about. As a result, in October 1961, Macmillan entered into a series of negotiations aimed at securing Britain's entry into the new, more 'Gaullist' community; approaches which were welcomed by De Gaulle who was hopeful of building a genuinely European security community independent of the United States, as well as a less supranational economic one more suited to his liking. Negotiations continued for over a year – with apparent success – but, in late 1962, the 'special relationship' interposed itself. The American government cancelled the Skybolt missile system which Britain had contracted to buy. De Gaulle apparently regarded the cancellation as a great opportunity to develop Anglo-French nuclear collaboration and for the UK to reduce its military dependence on the United States. The British, however, failed to seize the opportunity. De Gaulle's hopes were dashed when, in December 1962, Macmillan accepted Kennedy's offer of Polaris as a replacement for Skybolt. It is possible that Macmillan's acceptance was simply the excuse for which De Gaulle had been waiting in order to veto the British application. It is more likely, however, that the decision to accept Polaris convinced De Gaulle that Britain's Atlantic ties were stronger than any emergent commitment she might have to Europe. In any event, the special relationship had for the time being succeeded in preventing the UK from moving any further in the European direction now publicly favoured by its leadership.

A second area in which the Atlantic relationship has confounded Britain's links with the rest of Europe has been the British government's strong support for the American bombing of Libyan cities in April 1986 (after discovery of links between the Libyan government and terrorist attacks on American troops in Europe). This drove a further wedge between Britain's Middle Eastern position and that of her European partners. Considered in isolation, this particular divergence of European opinion over the Middle East might not have been too serious. What is important, however, is that it provided yet another example of Britain's determination to pursue an independent foreign policy – regardless of the consequences – at a time when EC leaders were desperately trying to use the development of a *common* European foreign policy to stimulate further integration.

It is in this context that a third example of the way in which Britain's extra-European commitments have prevented her effective 'Europeanisation' assumes relevance. In addition to her Atlantic ties, Britain's residual *imperial* pretensions and responsibilities have also had a damaging effect on the construction of a common foreign policy. Britain's continued insistence that *it* knew what was best for its former imperial possessions, for example, created difficulties in the negotiations over Lome II, the trade and aid package negotiated in the late 1970s between the European Community and the ACP group of Third World countries. Similarly, the Falklands campaign – undertaken without formal consultation with the rest of Europe, yet demanding their formal acquiescence – caused some resentment in the Community as a result of the tensions which it created between the Nine and their Latin American trading partners. Finally, the decision by European foreign ministers in 1980 to recognise the PLO as the legitimate representative of the Palestinian people – an essential step if they were to act effectively as mediators in the Arab–Israeli conflict – was unilaterally reversed by the Foreign Secretary Howe in October 1986 when two PLO negotiators (having earlier been expressly invited to talks in London as part of a wider, Community initiative) were refused entry to Britain.

It is hardly surprising that these demonstrations of British 'independence' have met with considerable disapproval in Europe. The British affect to be 'genuine Europeans', but they are unprepared to compromise their freedom of action if either Atlantic or residual-imperial commitments make competing demands. In taking this stance, moreover, Britain has inhibited the growth of an informal common European foreign policy and thereby damaged the further development of the Community itself.

Defence policy

The underlying aim of a defence policy is to provide its domestic population with a realistic sense of security. Since the late 1940s this aim has been satisfied in Britain principally through NATO, a defensive alliance which has itself contributed to the British sense of security partly through the *punishment* threat inherent in the American 'extended nuclear deterrent', and partly through the '*denial* deterrent' represented by NATO's conventional forces stationed in West-Central Europe. In spite of the apparent success which NATO has enjoyed in this context for almost 40 years the *management* of British defence policy has been made increasingly difficult in recent years by the need to devise an overall political strategy which simultaneously encourages the Americans to remain committed to the defence of Western Europe yet which also prepares for the possibility that the United States – for whatever reason – might withdraw in the future. Given that defence expenditure has had to compete with a wide range of rival domestic priorities, the efforts of the British defence establishment have to date been largely successful; the US *is* still committed to Europe, yet at the same time Britain also possesses the skeleton of a defence force that is capable of being expanded in an emergency to offer some sort of minimum protection of Britain's vital interests without American assistance. (Though how long this skeleton will survive is another matter; see below).

This rather delicate compromise has been effected by deploying British defence forces in a manner which not only meets a wide range of contingency needs but which also demonstrates Britain's strong commitment to NATO: the Royal Navy plays a crucial role in NATO's contingency plans for protecting the Eastern Atlantic in the event of future hostilities in Western Europe; the 55,000-strong British Army of the Rhine (BAOR) constitutes a central pillar in NATO's efforts to prevent the Soviet bloc from making easy territorial gains in the European theatre; and Britain allows the Americans to use bases in the UK without which the US would be unable to support its conventional and nuclear deterrent forces in Europe. In addition to those NATO-centred commitments, Britain also possesses a nuclear 'insurance policy' in the form of Polaris (which the Warsaw Pact has to consider as an 'additional decision-centre' in its assessments of the likely costs and benefits of aggressive adventurism in Western Europe) and conventional forces capable both of defending the homeland itself and of participating in limited outside-area operations (such as the retaking of the Falklands in 1982) where such action is deemed necessary.

The central tenet of NATO's military strategy since the organisation's inception in 1949 has been a preparedness to employ nuclear weapons against an aggressor in the event of either a nuclear or a conventional attack on any of the signatory nations. During the 1950s and early 1960s the guiding principle in this context was '*massive retaliation*'; an incursion by Soviet bloc countries into, say, the Federal Republic of Germany would be met with an all-out nuclear attack on the aggressor's population centres and military installations. The doctrine was intended to signal to the Soviet Union and its allies that any attempt by the Warsaw Treaty Organisation (WTO) to take advantage of its clear numerical superiority over NATO in conventional forces would be suicidal. While 'massive retaliation' had the considerable advantage of being relatively low-cost, (NATO did not need to build up its more expensive conventional forces to match those of the Warsaw Pact), doubts about its credibility gradually increased. Would the

Americans really engage in a massive nuclear strike against the Soviet Union – and thereby invite a commensurate Soviet attack upon the US itself – merely because the WTO had engaged in a conventional assault on West Germany?

Increasingly unconvinced that the threat of massive retaliation was credible in Soviet eyes, NATO leaders, in December 1967, formally shifted the basis of their strategy to 'flexible response'. With this new doctrine, NATO leaders effectively declared that their response to any future aggression would depend upon the exigencies of the situation at hand. A conventional attack might be met with a conventional response, but equally it might elicit the use by NATO of battlefield nuclear weapons, or even provoke a limited strike against the aggressor's population centres. Although it was implied that NATO would endeavour to ensure that its response to aggression would not provoke an escalation into all-out nuclear confrontation, the doctrine was also intended to introduce into Soviet calculations an unacceptably high degree of uncertainty as to what the West would actually do if the Soviet Union did decide to use force in order to achieve its presumed goal of dominating Western Europe. However, while the introduction of flexible response undoubtedly improved the credibility of NATO's nuclear deterrent by maximising Soviet uncertainty, it also led to an increase in the range of hardware that NATO had to acquire in order to maintain that improved credibility. A graduated, minimally escalatory response to Soviet aggression was only possible if there were several gradations of response available to NATO decision-makers; unfortunately, 'gradations' meant more and different types of weapon system which in turn meant higher costs.

The doctrine of flexible response has in all probability been more credible, more realistic and less dangerous than 'massive retaliation'. It has nonetheless been strongly criticised on the grounds that it increases the chances of a graduated escalation into all-out nuclear war: A attacks B with conventional forces; B responds with a tactical nuclear offensive against A's battlefield forces; A responds with a nuclear strike against B's military bases; B engages in selected nuclear strikes on A's cities; and so on. The danger, it is argued, is that flexible response increases the chances that the nuclear threshold will be crossed, and once it *is* crossed, an escalation into an all-out nuclear exchange rapidly follows. Accordingly, it has been suggested that NATO should move to a 'No first use' (NFU) position. This would take the form of a guarantee (though we don't know whether anyone would believe it) that NATO would only use nuclear weapons if one or more of the signatory nations had already been subjected to a nuclear attack. In these circumstances, given the Warsaw Pact's long-standing and pronounced conventional superiority in the European theatre, NATO would be obliged to devote considerably more resources to strengthening its conventional capabilities in Western Europe. And unless defence budgets were to be increased in all member countries of NATO, such a transfer of resources could only be achieved at the expense of other elements in NATO's overall strategy. Not surprisingly, therefore, 'No first use' – despite its attraction as a conciliatory gesture – has for the time being been shelved. Nonetheless, a modified version of NFU – 'no *early* first use' – continues to feature in the continuing policy debate about NATO's future strategic doctrine.

Regardless of the specific strategic doctrine which underlies NATO's posture towards the Soviet bloc, however, British defence planners in the late 1980s and early 1990s are confronted with two serious and continuing sets of problems. The first of these concerns the implications of the Labour Party's shift towards a non-nuclear defence policy for Britain.

Until 1980, Britain had a largely bipartisan foreign policy. This is not to suggest that Her Majesty's Opposition was unprepared to engage in the most strident criticism of the incumbent government's foreign policy, but that the strategic decisions taken by one administration would not explicitly be reversed by the next. In the last decade or so, however, British politics has witnessed something of a breakdown in the post-war social democratic consensus, with the Conservative Party under Thatcher moving to the right and Labour, under Foot and subsequently Kinnock, moving to the left. During Mrs Thatcher's term of office, the shift to the right has not produced much trauma as far as the functioning of the NATO alliance is concerned. Indeed, the 'special relationship' has undergone something of a rejuvenation.

The longer-term implications of the shift to the right, however, could be less desirable. It can reasonably be argued that, as a distinctly second division side in economic terms, Britain can no longer afford the luxury of a continually-updated independent deterrent. Yet present Conservative policy is strongly committed – whatever the financial burden – to the acquisition of Trident as a replacement for our increasingly outdated Polaris submarine force. (No one asks what Britain will do when 'Star Wars' becomes technically feasible and the Americans ask if we'd like to buy it). While the shift of the Conservative Party to the right can in no sense be construed as a *direct* threat to NATO, it does constitute a reinforcement of the tendency of British governments to spend more on hardware than the economy can really afford. And unless the defence budget is to be substantially increased, cuts in Britain's conventional capabilities would appear to be the necessary corollary of maintaining continually-updated independent nuclear deterrent.

The most serious problem for NATO as it is currently constituted, arises not from British overextension but from the threat and/or reality of a radical Labour Government. Labour's current defence policy foresees British unilateral nuclear disarmament and the removal of all American nuclear bases and forces from British soil. It also asserts that under Labour Britain would assume a non-nuclear role within NATO. There is no telling what the United States' response to such a dramatic course of action would be, but – as noted earlier – it is quite likely that the Americans would simply withdraw their extended nuclear deterrent and leave the Europeans to provide for their own defence themselves. Labour's implicit riposte is that an American withdrawal would enable NATO to be transformed into a *conventional* West European alliance, well suited to opposing a conventional Soviet attack. Quite apart from the enormous extra cost which such a strategy would entail, however, a purely conventional NATO would be highly vulnerable to any threat of 'nuclear blackmail' which the Soviet Union might, at some later date, choose to pose. And here, of course, we are back to the unknowable; how likely is it that at some future date the Soviet Union *would* use threats or nuclear blackmail against Britain? Is there, or is there not, a Soviet threat? We simply do not know.

211

Even if Labour won the next election, however, all the signs are that the Labour leadership, at least, is shifting the basis of its policy platform towards the electoral middleground. Although Neil Kinnock is a unilateralist of long standing, it is likely that once in power, he would not carry through Labour's present 'official' defence policy to its full extent. The dismantling of Polaris and Trident would almost certainly go ahead. Cruise missiles, because of their emotive connotations, would in all probability be decommissioned, if not already bargained away by the US in negotiations with the Soviet Union. But because of the enormous – and dangerous – uncertainty that would surround an American withdrawal from NATO, it is likely that Kinnock in power would seek to persuade the US to remain within the alliance. Notwithstanding the added impetus which the 1986 Libyan crisis gave to demands for the removal of American bases from Britain, a Kinnock Government would probably not require the removal of the remaining armoury of submarine- and aerial-launched missiles that the United States currently has stationed in Britain. There are enough clever politicians in the present Shadow Cabinet to find an appropriate excuse for reversing the conference resolution on a non-nuclear defence policy. Whatever Labour's 'real' intentions are, however, one thing is certain. The acquisition of Trident proposed by the present Conservative administration represents a direct continuation of the costly and overextended European defence policy that has been pursued by successive British governments since nuclear weapons were first acquired in the mid 1950s.

The second major problem confronting contemporary defence policymakers is the seemingly inexorable rise in costs – over and above 'normal' inflation – which makes the provision of a balanced defence force increasingly difficult. The problem stems in part from technology. In order to match the technical improvements which Warsaw Pact forces enjoy, NATO defence planners are obliged over time continually to upgrade the technical quality of their own weapon systems. In order to illustrate the consequences of this continual upgrading, an analogy is often drawn between weapon systems and cars. The unit cost of a Rolls Royce is obviously greater than that of a Mini. Thus, if Soviet bloc forces deploy the weapon-system equivalent of Rolls Royces, then in response NATO is obliged to replace its current generation of 'Minis' with Rolls Royces; with an inevitable increase in costs. The crucial point is that defence costs tend to rise faster than the rate of inflation. Moreover, while rises in unit costs can in principle be offset by increases in productivity, the speed of technological change – which results in shorter production runs – means that there is probably a limit to the extent to which improved efficiency can compensate.

Confronting this problem in 1979, the NATO countries agreed to increase defence spending by 3 per cent per year in real terms. Mrs Thatcher's Government – almost alone among the NATO allies – has adhered closely to this commitment and as a result, British defence spending increased by 25 per cent in real terms between 1978–79 and 1985–86. With this increase in spending, Britain has (just) been able to sustain its conventional commitments inside NATO and to maintain its independent deterrent. However, increasing domestic pressure for more expenditure in non-defence areas has meant that the Thatcher Government's commitment to the '3 per cent solution' has now been abandoned. With unit costs likely to continue increasing in the future – despite improved defence procurement procedures recently introduced – any future British government is likely to be faced with some very hard choices over defence policy. Whether it is the Conservatives (committed to Trident), the Alliance (committed – possibly – to Polaris) or Labour (committed to strengthen NATO's conventional forces with the resources released by scrapping Polaris and Trident) who are in power, cost pressures may well force a fundamental strategic choice between Britain's NATO-centred *maritime* commitments in the Eastern Atlantic and its *continental* commitments in West Germany. Unless such a choice *is* made, Britain may be unable to carry out either role effectively. The unfortunate Catch-22 is that abandoning either its maritime or its continental commitments would undoubtedly increase the likelihood of an effective American withdrawal from NATO, yet such a withdrawal would make it even more imperative that Britain retained both a significant naval presence in the Eastern Atlantic *and* a conventional presence in continental Europe. As a nation in relative industrial decline, Britain can perhaps no longer afford to 'carry two rifles instead of one' in the defence of Western Europe, as it has since 1945. The problem is to determine which rifle – if any – should be dropped, and if the answer is 'neither', then the only solution is an ever-increasing defence budget with all the domestic political and economic costs which that entails.

Summary and conclusions

British foreign policy in the immediate post-war years was predicated on the assumption that Britain was still a Great Power which possessed both the capability and the responsibility to undertake a major role in world affairs. The overextended foreign policy strategy that was consequently pursued did not prevent successive governments from achieving a string of tactical successes in very difficult circumstances. But it undoubtedly diluted the strength of an already weakening economy. With the strategic reappraisal that followed Suez, the extent of Britain's overcommitment was reduced through decolonisation and withdrawal from East of Suez. Two serious problems, however, have remained. In the first place, overextension has continued with the NATO commitment to provide both a conventional defence of Western Europe and a continually updated independent nuclear deterrent. Secondly, Britain's 'Europeanisation' – the substitute role for the loss of Empire – has been distinctly half-hearted. While Britain's overall foreign policy in the post-war era has shifted *towards* the European 'circle', Britain has still not moved *into* it. Yet, in the long run, it is as a European power – acting in concert with the rest of Europe – that Britain is most likely to find a world role commensurate with its material interests and capabilities.

Chapter 11
Characterising British politics

Delusions of grandeur, overextended commitments, internal conflicts, disarticulation or sheer fragmentation of decision processes, are all aspects of British politics in the 1980s which have emerged from the foregoing analyses. It is important to put these assessments in historical perspective, by way of acknowledging the extent to which they are given a negative cast by a growing consciousness of economic and political decline. What are seen in the 1980s as overextended commitments were in the '60s and even '70s seen as reassuring proof of Britain's central place in the world. What is now seen as conflict was then regarded as a rather healthy tradition of two-party adversarial politics, giving electors clear-cut choices which they lacked in coalition systems. Failure to adapt was viewed as stability and continuity, and fragmentation as democratic pluralism.

It is important to realise that perceptions of British politics have changed, and no doubt will change, radically. This chapter reviews the various characterisations that have been made since the 1960s. Such characterisations are not simply descriptions of course, though they are that too. But they also contain reflections on the British political experience, diagnose what is wrong and suggest remedies for putting it right. Each interpretation is not only a characterisation of the past but also a prescription for the future. It is appropriate therefore to conclude this book with an assessment of the strengths and weaknesses of each, and of their suggested or implied remedies – finishing with our own (appropriately modest in view of the way so many others have been overtaken by events).

Events and characterisations

Until the early 1960s, conventional wisdom had it that Cabinet government, in conjunction with the two-party system, worked rather well. Over succeeding decades serious doubt developed about its efficacy and responsiveness. The gaps between the traditional picture of how things are done and the actual ways in which they are done – discussed at various points in earlier chapters – fuelled various new analyses of how the system operated.

Economic decline stimulated much rethinking. Rather than an absence of new ideas, the danger is one of confusion between the sheer numbers of re-interpretations and associated diagnoses on offer. Confusion is compounded because the different accounts highlight very diverse aspects of the situation and propose very different – and often conflicting – remedies' for what they see as major political weaknesses.

We begin by comparing and evaluating some of the more popular and influential of the new interpretations and contrasting these with evidence accumulated from our detailed analyses. After this review we present our own conclusions, which provide a more complex and (we hope) more balanced account of the main trends in contemporary British politics.

The traditional view

Two distinctive political parties holding a virtual monopoly of electoral votes and exchanging governmental power smoothly and peacefully dominated British politics from 1945 to 1974. During the earlier part of this period, the two-party system did seem to guarantee good government. Party discipline in the Commons, Cabinet government, and the doctrines of individual and collective responsibility, together solved the problem of combining popular accountability with efficient administration. A permanent, incorruptible and able Civil Service imposed coherence on policy choices and supplied technical advice, while ensuring that the actual machinery of government ran smoothly.

Within this system interest groups were not disruptive since they enjoyed close working relationships with civil servants, trading support and technical information for concessions on the detailed administration of policies affecting them. No organised interest was totally ignored and a neutral Civil Service held the balance between them. Local/central relations took care of themselves, with limited and benevolent central direction matched by local compliance.

Public records now reveal that relationships were never as tidy or smoothly regulated as in the idealised picture. Uncertainty, confusion and downright chaos were present in all governments of the post-war period. Increasingly bold media coverage helped dent the myth of individual and collective responsibility so crucial to any claim that government is accountable for its actions.

By the mid 1960s the growing economic difficulties and failure of attempts to meet them had led to initial doubts about how well the system was functioning. By the early 1980s these had swollen to the extent that a new party emerged to 'break the mould of the old two-party system', as the Social Democrats put it. Even the traditional parties repudiated the 'consensus politics' of the 1950s and seemed anxious to disavow their previous record. Within twenty years, conventional wisdom had passed from almost complete acceptance of the old model to near-unanimous rejection.

As we have shown, the weaknesses of the system cannot be attributed to any one institutional feature, historical event or individual government – although critics have been quick to single out each of these for blame. An analysis of six of the most important accounts of what went wrong shows that each diagnosis has some validity. This should lead us to look deeper and search wider for weaknesses when attempting ourselves to characterise what could be called the 'changing British political system'.

The technocratic critique

The decade following 1960 was dominated by attempts to reform the machinery of government. The mood was predominantly technocratic. By implication, at least, little was wrong with the party and electoral system or with the actual policies of governments. It was assumed that the welfare state and Keynesian demand management were inviolable foundations upon which policy was based. What apparently was defective was the linkage between these and society at large. Thus the Civil Service was branded as old-fashioned and unresponsive. The Treasury, in particular, was considered unable to take the longer view which planning required. Local governments were too small to operate with necessary economies of scale and required amalgamation into larger units. Industry and the unions were basically sound but needed the aid and guidance of a reformed governmental system intent on economic growth. Such assumptions led successive governments to embark on a series of reforms and reorganisations (for details see Chapters 1 and 2). Experience of these showed that reforms were often very difficult to achieve – even internally – witness the weakening of the Fulton recommendations (1968–69) on reform of the Civil Service or the compromises forced on local government reorganisation.

But more importantly, the reforms revealed the fundamental weakness of British governments when they attempted to influence, persuade, cajole or coerce the main economic and political actors in British society. Incomes policies foundered on the rocks of trade union resistance. Price controls were often opposed by industry. Individual firms shied away from anything but a voluntary or highly flexible industrial policy. The Treasury was constantly suspicious of long-term planning or any agency established to promote it. Many local governments showed a marked reluctance to accept central government's *diktats*.

Of course, in theory, British central governments could do virtually anything. Party discipline, Cabinet and unitary government should ensure this. Perhaps successive governments' reliance on administrative reforms shows that they too believed the myth. More fundamental changes in polity and society were considered unnecessary. But as the individual chapters of this volume have shown, both British government and British society are much more fragmented than either the traditional view or the technocratic critique would have us believe. Administrative reform has been piecemeal at best and has certainly failed to make any discernible improvement in the quality of economic policy.

Although characteristic of the late 1960s and early 1970s under Wilson and Heath, the influence of the technocratic diagnosis has not entirely waned.

Further tinkering with the 'machinery of government' was planned in the early 1980s by all the main parties and a number of other bodies too. While some reforms may be useful (and any breach in official secrets is likely to promote accountability and responsiveness), it is not necessarily the case that these go hand in hand with enhanced efficiency. Change itself may be initially disruptive and is in any event likely to be less far-reaching than planned, owing to the entrenched opposition it will provoke. The major obstacles to growth lie in the power relationships inside and outside government, rather than in the administrative structure itself.

The corporatist thesis

If the problem lies in the independent power of societal groups, which governments cannot effectively coerce, perhaps these should be drawn into the process of negotiation and consultation instead? As we have seen, in the traditional view this was already happening. All significant organised groups stood in a close relationship to civil servants, feeding in advice and offering support in return for sympathetic application of relevant programmes.

We have seen, however (Ch. 2), that this symbiotic relationship does not exist for all groups and that in particular the trade unions get pushed to the periphery of Civil Service consultations, besides having repugnant policies imposed on them by governments. This tendency to dictate to interest groups reflects the British tradition, reinforced by the Thatcher administrations of strong autonomous and rather aloof government, which knows better than anyone else what to do in the national interest.

As this fails to elicit the necessary compliance from organisations which are too strong to knuckle under, an obvious solution is to treat these as equals and buy or win their support. This would involve mutual concessions, on the part of government as well as of the other participants, but it would be worthwhile in return for effective and workable agreements. Governments were driven to such negotiations in the 1970s, with the Labour Government's social contract with the trade unions in 1974–78, when the government traded legal concessions and price restraint for limits on wage increases.

The corporatist thesis (strictly speaking the 'societal' or 'liberal' or 'neo-corporatist' theses) sees such negotiations as increasingly necessary and increasingly prevalent in modern societies. The independent power of labour and business organisations renders their agreement indispensable to any effective economic policy, so there is really no alternative to recognising their autonomy and bidding for their support.

In the British case such mutual recognition is often described as 'tripartism', a form of 'societal corporatism' which emphasises the need for co-operation between government and the peak associations representing both sides of industry, the TUC and the CBI. This will be brought about by growing recognition of common interests (e.g. the benefits of greater prosperity). While some disagreements will remain, these can be limited to specific policy details. In particular the organisations involved in the negotiations have to set aside fundamental disagreements about ultimate goals in order to arrive at agreed solutions to individual problems. In this process of negotiation all three par-

217

ticipants must have influence on the development of policy. The government cannot expect to dominate and coerce, since this would simply mean that the other groups would feel no obligation to recommend acceptance to their members. Such acceptance is of course a crucial part of the arrangements. There is no point in leaders making agreements if their members do not accept them. It is here that corporatism or tripartism as a description of what is actually going on reveals a fatal flaw. It is only too obvious in the British case that organisations cannot bind all their members and that 'peak associations' such as the TUC and the CBI are particularly weak in that respect.

To some extent, however, the weakness extends to all the functional groups representing economic interests. Even a powerful individual union such as the Transport and General Workers' finds it difficult to control its individual sections, while these in turn find it difficult to exact compliance from committees of shop stewards in individual factories. (Such committees in many cases were in fact promoted by communists or other left-wingers to strengthen grass-roots representatives against the official union leadership.) On the other side, even the powerful financial interests of the City of London are divided by sharp conflicts of interest. So there is little chance of finding a set of generally supported top level representatives with whom to do business.

To the extent that corporatism identifies a growing tendency for societal interests to build themselves into organisations with a permanent bureaucracy and some kind of representative leadership, it is undoubtedly right. It is also correct in its recognition of the power of such groups. This is what has driven governments from time to time into seeking some accommodation with them. On the other hand, the diagnosis is surely over-optimistic in assuming that leaders can control their members more effectively than the government itself can, through legislation or other means. (Neither government nor group leaders are *very* effective.) Corporatism also assumes the existence of enough agreement on fundamentals to provide a basis for constructive negotiation, whereas it is the creation of such a consensus that is the root of the problem. If sufficient agreement existed in the first place, negotiations would probably be unnecessary, as what the government did would attract support in any case.

Government overload

One of the dangers of negotiating with interest groups is the tendency for governments to trade permanent concessions – enhanced legal privileges in the case of unions, subsidies in the case of business – for temporary support for an incomes or prices policy lasting only a year. Further long-term concessions are then exacted when the agreement comes up for renewal.

The trade-off is even worse for government if the rank and file refuse to keep the agreement. In any case the attempt to placate societal interests has been seen by some political scientists as a major cause of government weakness. The government, they feel, has become increasingly 'overloaded' with demands from all sections of society from unions to motorway protesters, from local governments to Welsh Nationalists. Faced with this barrage from a society holding unrealistic expectations of government, politicians have attempted to please everybody but have really succeeded in pleasing no one. In taking on an inflated set of responsibilities to meet or head off popular demands they have outpaced their financial and manpower resources. An over-extended administration is necessarily less efficient, and its failings add up to an impression that government is in perpetual minor crisis. More public services are delivered but their quality has declined. Higher civil servants are so strained by their extended responsibilities that the increased numbers of policies are less well co-ordinated and it becomes difficult to distinguish between matters of higher and lower priority. The government, in its efforts to accommodate competing claims, constantly changes its mind, modifies programmes or even completely reverses its general strategy. Fundamental to the overload thesis is the assumption that British society is too pluralistic – that there are too many channels of influence exploited by interests with independent bases of political power. By implication, it is not the political institutions or machinery of government that are primarily at fault, although they may be less adequate as a result of strain.

There are points at which this interpretation fits our earlier analysis. As the 1960s and 1970s wore on, so governments appeared increasingly under siege and unable to produce satisfactory policies. The Conservative Governments of both Heath and Thatcher hived off many trading activities and abolished some quangos without noticeably reducing government responsibilities.

On the other hand, there is little to indicate that popular or group demands in Britain *are* particularly voracious. Indeed, all the evidence is that ordinary electors have very modest expectations and simply look to the government to stop things getting much worse rather than taking on vast new commitments (Ch. 4). There is also no evidence that government has been particularly accommodating or responsive to organised groups, except for limited and exceptional periods (notably 1974–78).

The case of the lobby against motorway extensions and the administrative handling of its objections is instructive. There has been statutory provision for public inquiries into the line of new roads since the Trunk Roads Act of 1936. Until the late 1960s there were relatively few inquiries, and these were peaceful; the need for new roads were generally accepted. As the basic network was completed, however, and environmental concerns came to the fore, there was an increase in the number of inquiries into new schemes, many of which became extremely acrimonious. The Ministry of Transport responded to this development by restricting the scope of inquiries and giving only grudging and limited concessions to the objectors. For example, they tried to exclude discussion of the need for a road, and restrict arguments to whether it should take the proposed line. In general the Ministry was as obstructive as possible. At the inquiry of 1976 into the widening of the A1 at Archway in North London, an objector was first promised a line-by-line derivation of a cost benefit table, then told that such calculations did not exist, then offered information which would enable him to do the calculations himself – information which was never in the end supplied.

This hardly looks like government bending over backwards to meet group demands and overloading itself with new programmes in the process! Rather the situation is the familiar one of a ministry fighting to preserve existing responsibilities in accordance with a fixed departmental view. The example is particularly piquant as the pressure group demand in this case was for government to disengage rather than to expand, and the representatives of government rejected the opportunity.

All the stresses and strains which the government machine increasingly experiences can as convincingly be attributed to its own difficulties in making and implementing effective policies as to having external demands imposed upon it. As pointed out in Chapter 2, British central government lacks any central co-ordinating body. The main decision-making body, the Cabinet, has little control over other institutions, which as a result tend to pursue their own policies and interests without regard to overall priorities. In an increasingly complex modern society, this is bound to show up in inconsistencies and policy muddles. The cause lies not so much in the range of government responsibilities as in the way they are handled.

Conviction politics

Can the gap at the centre be made up by strong political leadership, with a clear sense of where it wants to go and enough firmness and determination to impose its will, using the existing institutions and processes of British politics (punitively and coercively if necessary), to weaken the adversaries of progress and reform? Something like this is the underlying diagnosis of the Conservative Governments of the 1980s under the leadership of a self-proclaimed 'conviction politician' – Margaret Thatcher. It must certainly be granted that her Administrations have done more to change British society and politics and to alter the direction of the economy, than any others since the post-war Labour Governments led by Attlee.

In this view, central institutional reforms are unnecessary as existing structures give adequate powers of control. Negotiations with societal interests such as unions, local authorities and business, simply get in the way of effective decision-making. If these resist they can be restricted by legislation enforced through effective mobilisation of courts and police, and reinforced by populist appeals to the electorate on the theme of 'who governs Britain?'. The shedding of many government activities through privatisation helps disengage the government from direct participation in society, reinforcing its aloof image as ultimate guardian of the national interest, while on the other hand giving a new impetus to the private sector of the economy whose vigorous growth is the only way to avert decline.

Flaws in this argument have emerged in many of the preceding pages. The economy has certainly been redirected toward the provision of services and finance, but nothing has been done to hinder the decline of the manufacturing base, the de-industrialisation of areas outside the South-East of England, or to reduce large-scale unemployment. Relative to Germany and Japan, or even Italy and France, Britain still seems in decline – notwithstanding recent increases in productivity in some industries. The lack of investment in either research or new technology remains low, while investment in defence is too high. Privatisation seems capable of enriching shareholders and financial institutions, and spreading housing and property ownership, but irrelevant to the more urgent problems of the economy.

The attempt to 'give unions back to their members' by legislating for internal secret ballots was an astute and popular move which seems likely to stick. There is no guarantee, however, that popular involvement in union decision-making will always strengthen governments' hands in dealing with them. Union members are just as likely as their leaders to pursue sectional wage claims when the economy is picking up; indeed, leaders highly dependent on popular approval may be even less likely to deliver the goods in corporatist-style negotiations than they were before. But with popular support, strategically placed unions *are* obviously in a good position to blackmail governments in support of intransigent claims. Thatcherite victories in this version of the 'class war' may thus be short-lived, and depend more on oil revenues, now running down, and on contingent unemployment and depression, than on the government's real power.

A facet of Thatcherism is to ignore problems of institutional co-ordination as irrelevant. In areas where the government has been unable to coerce other bodies effectively, such as sub-central government, few of its declared objectives have been achieved, while tactical victories like the abolition of the GLC and metropolitan counties have been elevated to strategic significance. What the attempt to dictate and coerce *has* done, however, is to increase conflict and bad feeling at many levels of society, which is also reflected in a real hostility between the parliamentary parties.

Adversary politics

This has reinforced a tendency already evident since 1964 for governments to switch economic and other policies markedly with a change in party control. Some observers have asserted that this adversarial tendency is itself the major weakness of British politics. Strong party discipline in combination with periodic elections ensures dramatic changes in policies with each change of government. In such an environment the longer-term structural adjustment needed to adapt the British economy to technological and trading changes is impossible. Related arguments posit the existence of a 'political/business cycle' – or the tendency for governments to reflate the economy before elections to enhance their popularity. This school of thought stresses the extent to which the particular nature of British two-party politics aggravates the tendency towards party division found in all democracies. For in Britain the two major parties provide stark ideological contrasts and once in power they feel obliged to carry out the sometimes radical promises contained in party manifestos. The fact that electoral considerations oblige governments to reverse or modify these policies in the period preceding general elections only serves to add more confusion.

No doubt there is something to this general thesis and we have referred both to party reversals of policy and adversary politics several times during this book. Clearly the Alliance was persuaded that the argument is valid, their major rallying cry being the alleged capriciousness of the old two-party system together with the 'unfair' electoral system which polarises Labour and Conservatives and heavily penalises moderate third parties. However, on its own the adversary thesis is simply not sufficient to explain the trials and tribulations of British governments. Failure in policy implementation cannot be related to electoral calculations or to the rigidity of a first-past-the-post two-party system. Party competition as such has little to do with the machinery of central government, where the failures in policy implementation have their origin.

The radical alternative

Perhaps party programmes *should* translate more effectively into government actions – thereby guaranteeing responsiveness, at any rate, and possibly improving the prospects for implementation?

A final diagnosis of the British political predicament, which stresses the potential of party as a co-ordinating and driving force, emanates from the radical or 'hard' left – particularly from sections of the labour movement. Simply stated, this dismisses the constraints imposed by societal pluralism, the nature of the party system, or the complexity of administration. Instead, the blame for social and economic malaise is placed squarely on the shoulders of unresponsive and weak Labour Governments. (From a different perspective this is of course not unlike the Thatcherite diagnosis that firm leadership has been lacking.)

The left take it for granted that non-Labour governments, the Civil Service as at present constituted, and capitalism, will in combination always guarantee economic decline and deepening inequality. Financial interests are maximised under a regime which allows free investment abroad, and they have an ultimate influence over the other institutions by threatening a run on the pound. Only Labour can save British industry from stagnation through lack of investment, by forcing fundamental reforms based on a planned and directed economy.

The Labour Governments of 1964–79 and 1974–79 failed because they vacillated in the face of the City, the Civil Service and international financial pressures. The same can be expected from a government with similar attitudes under Neil Kinnock. A revamped party supporting a Labour Government committed to radical change, and held steadily on course by intra-party democracy, is the only hope for the economy, and for Socialism. This critique is interesting because its very existence testifies to the breakdown of any earlier liberal consensus. To a greater extent than earlier interpretations, it combines a clear-cut programme for action with an (unflattering) description of the present situation.

The success of the programme, if it is ever tried, will rest heavily on the validity of the description. A first assumption is that Labour could be elected on such commitments. This is problematical. As we have seen (Ch. 4), electors are repelled by the prospect of change unless it confers immediate benefits. Extensions of government control, rather than guaranteeing these benefits, tend to disadvantage Labour when they become foremost in a campaign.

Hence a programme of full-blooded socialism, far from catapulting Labour to power, would result in a further loss of Labour support, probably to Social Democrats and Liberals.

The radical reply to this is first, that electors would react differently if given a real choice rather than the marginally contrasting alternatives which are all they have been offered before; second left-wingers argue that electors are misled about their real interests through the biased presentation and comments of the media (radio, television and newspapers).

This is ground already covered in Chapters 4 and 5. Media commentators and reporters are undoubtedly more sympathetic to moderate and widely agreed policies, involving limited change, than they are to sweeping proposals for radical action. Hence they have given a better hearing to social democrats – within the Labour Party and outside it – than to the representatives of the left. Of course this tendency cuts both ways; support for moderation has also resulted in less sympathetic treatment for free marketeers, monetarists and extreme nationalists within the Conservative Party.

Nonetheless, neither Socialists nor extreme Conservatives have been denied a hearing and the former particularly have succeeded in establishing themselves as newsworthy. So their statements and policies have been relayed to the audience in no more distorted a form than happens with other political groups. Given a necessary minimum of information, electors are quite capable of relating policies to their own concerns and evaluating them in the way described in Chapter 4. Since evaluation is based on policy emphases made by the parties at a very broad level, subtleties like the tone of surrounding media comment will simply get lost. The existing situation does offer electors a chance to evaluate all the major alternatives. Given their suspicion of change, they *are* likely to vote against extreme left-wing policy, but this reflects their own preferences rather than any media bias.

Quite apart from its unrealistic view of electors, the radical diagnosis also discounts constraints on government action identified earlier, and in particular those stemming from the autonomy and considerable power of extra-governmental institutions – from pressure groups (Ch. 2) and courts (Ch. 8), to 'other governments' (Chs. 6 and 7). These cannot simply be swept away. Possibly Britain could leave the EC, but the government would have to go through a complicated disaffiliation procedure first, and would still have to face internal bodies with substantial delaying powers and obstructive potential in various areas. There is no reason for considering a left-wing government better equipped to deal with failures of implementation due to internal and societal opposition, than any other kind of government. Indeed, the inference is that obstruction at all levels would be greater under a government trying to put through radical socialist policies. Whatever the innate merits of a socialist programme, one thing that would count against it is precisely the long period of delay and uncertainty before it would be implemented and the consequent effects on the currency and economy. This assumes, of course, that the programme *is* practicable, given the existence of multiple power centres in British politics and society.

Constraints on government decision-making

It is the existence of diverse groups and institutions, all with independent standing of some sort, which we have identified as the most striking feature of British politics. It is their obstructiveness which subverts the traditional picture of British government as centred on a supremely authoritative body, the Cabinet, able through its command of Parliament and the Civil Service to do practically anything. Similarly their presence casts doubt on technocratic solutions which simply create new co-ordinating or planning procedures. Without effectively subordinating the separate ministries and 'other'governments, new procedures cannot of themselves ensure effective implementation. Corporatism and tripartism similarly fail to reckon with the inability of central representation to guarantee membership compliance. Yet these institutions have shown, under Mrs Thatcher, that they cannot simply be coerced without producing unforeseen and economically counterproductive consequences.

Given the spread of responsibilities among a variety of institutions, the overload thesis appears simply misplaced. There *is* no tightly organised government structure taking on increasing tasks which in the end overstrain it. Responsibilities are accumulated by separate departments and quangos without much reference to each other or to popular demands. Overlap between departmental responsibilities, and failures to resolve them, cause confusion and delays, but these are due to the inability of the centre to assert itself sufficiently, not to central overload. This is a weakness which remains unaffected by the presence or absence of adversarial parties.

All the accounts we have examined fail, crucially, to take cognisance of the loose-jointedness of the political system as a whole, the autonomy of its component parts, and the external and internal constraints these impose on decision-making. In this section we examine the constraints revealed by earlier analyses before attempting our own overall characterisation.

Internal constraints

We have already detailed the existence of independent 'departmental views' of government policy, and the freedom which 'advocacy politics' give ministries and other government institutions to advance their own goals within the administration. As noted in Chapter 2, clashes also occur between civil servants and ministers within departments. If the minister agrees with Cabinet policy he may find himself fighting his own civil servants to get it accepted. At the same time, opposition will mount from other departments on joint working committees. The Cabinet itself may not be particularly united, and factions may form along ideological lines which spill over into the parliamentary parties. If the policies affect quangos and sub-central government, other centres of criticism and obstruction may form.

As central government lacks an extended local administration of its own, it depends on councils and authorities for the implementation of most programmes. Hence the attitudes of local officials and their national associations, perhaps even more than those of elected councillors, become crucial to effective promotion of policies. As Chapter 6 amply demonstrated, local representatives are only formally subservient to the government. In practice they can deploy many resources of expertise, information, control of manpower, etc. against their legal masters. They are often motivated to do so by belonging to a party opposed to the one(s) controlling government.

Local governments do not impinge only at the level of field administration. Collectively they account for about a third of total public expenditure. As targets for such expenditure form the main reference point and instrument for the whole of the government's macro-economic policy, local bodies are inevitably drawn into argument about priorities. If cuts are made they must be imposed against strenuous opposition. Although their power is essentially one of reaction against government policy, rather than the creation of a line of their own, their ability to delay or modify centrally imposed policies can be considerable.

Such power also belongs to judges – partly by default as we saw in Chapter 8. Their ability to assess the propriety of ministerial actions under various statutes adds another element of uncertainty to the general political situation and opens up another course of action to those opposing government policy. The judges favour the *status quo* and so tend to rule against 'other governments' taking on more powers. The *status quo*, however, also covers the existing rights and privileges which have been upheld by courts in recent years in contradistinction to government attempts to restrict them.

Under stress of economic crisis it is unlikely that any central government can rest content with existing relationships. It is bound to try to change them in some way to promote greater efficiency. Hence judges' attachment to established rights and disinclination to challenge any powerful existing group by no means favour, and may actually hamper, government plans. The same to a lesser extent can be said of the police and army, whose aim is often to avoid being branded as agents of the government.

It is, of course, usually the interest groups, and particularly trade unions, which are popularly regarded as the main challenge to government. The trade unions can exercise considerable constraints over policy. The TUC prevented legislation based on the Labour Government's White Paper on industrial relations, *In Place of strife*, being enacted in 1969 and turned the Conservative's 1971 Industrial Relations Act into a virtual dead letter by refusing to co-operate with its administration. Subsequently, under the social contract, they won the repeal of the Industrial Relations Act (and its replacement by the Trade Union and Labour Relations Act of 1974, and the Trade Union and Labour Relations (Amendment) Act of 1976), the passage of the Employment Protection Act 1975 and the Health and Safety at Work Act 1974. At the same time, certain individual trade unions in key strategic industries, notably the miners in the winter of 1973–74 and transport and public sector workers in the winter of 1978–79, have managed to restrict the effectiveness of governments' voluntary or statutory incomes policies. This hardly means that the trade unions are the dominant force in British politics. After the election of 1979, the trade unions were consulted very little and the government pushed through new Acts to restrict picketing and limit their other immunities. Nevertheless, trade unions can certainly inhibit government action, although the extent of their influence depends partly on the party in power and, probably more significantly, the level of unemployment. It also depends crucially on the state of unity among trade unionists themselves; as we have seen, they are often internally divided between powerful individual unions and between the official leadership and 'unofficial' shop-floor committees inside unions.

The influence of industry and commerce is at least as strong in Britain as that of labour, although the way it is exerted is less obvious. Within business there are also divisions. The interests of finance and industry, manufacturing and retail, nationally based and multinational firms, and large and small companies, often diverge. This prevents unanimous representations being made to government. On the manufacturing side the CBI has close contacts with the Civil Service and one or two notable successes in influencing policy. For example, the 1975 Industry Act, based on a very radical Labour Party policy document, was almost totally emasculated due to some extent to pressure from the CBI in particular and business in general. Much of the manufacturing sector's power, however, is less direct. Here the top one hundred UK companies account for 40 per cent of sales, capital expenditure and exports; over a third of employment; and 75 per cent of outward investment. This concentration means that the decisions of these companies are vital for the future performance of the British economy and, therefore, for the prospects of the government in power. In a very different sense the government must take account of these companies' views and interests because they play such a crucial role. In other words, the constraint they exercise is largely, although not exclusively, structural.

The power of financial interests – that is, of the City, the banks, insurance companies and pension funds – is even less direct, although it is becoming better documented. Insurance companies and pension funds have increasingly large equity holdings in British industry, while merchant banks often control the voting rights attaching to such shares. At the same time the important position of the City of London in world financial markets means that their activity has a crucial influence on the British balance of payments through the so called 'invisible exports' – made up of insurance premiums, broking commission, etc. All this imposes another structural constraint on government which can be very restrictive, as in the period between 1974 and 1977 when the government's freedom of manoeuvre in economic areas was effectively lost through a near-permanent 'run on the pound' in the money markets. As a somewhat jaundiced Jim Callaghan said, with only limited exaggeration, at the 1976 Labour Party Conference: 'An unwise resolution, an ill-judged statement can knock £200 million off the reserves in a minute or add 20p to the price of goods in your shopping basket.' No government can ignore the political implications of such power. In addition, the finance sector has now evolved direct contacts with the Treasury through the Bank of England and more recently through its developing trade associations. Such representations ensure that in some cases the influence of 'the City' is overt and direct. Though again we have noted the internal divisions which prevent financial representatives, unlike those of industry, even joining together in the same peak organisations.

None of this should imply that the power of business is overwhelming, although there is a tendency to ignore its influence. All we are arguing here is that industrial and financial interests act as a constraint on government, and like the trade unions, restrict its autonomy. At the same time we must not ignore examples of other interest groups and policy networks constraining government in other fields of policy-making – for example, the National Farmers' Union in agriculture, the British Road Federation in transport and the British Medical Association in health and welfare. Governments do not make policy in a vacuum; they are influenced and restricted in their decisions by many societal forces.

External constraints

Most analyses of the British political system treat it as though it were a discrete system and not part of an international political and economic order. There are, however, obvious external constraints on government action which are worth considering briefly at this point.

As we saw in Chapter 6, the relationship between the EC and British government is not a simple one. The Commission is vested with authority which is independent of the national governments but it is still tied by decisions taken by the Council of Ministers. In the Council of Ministers the British, in common with all members, can usually veto decisions. Nevertheless, membership of the EC has restricted the autonomy of British governments in a number of ways.

Our earlier analysis indicated that Britain has become deeply enmeshed in the EC although the extent of involvement differs in various policy areas. As the EC is a political organisation, decisions taken by the Council of Ministers inevitably involve compromise and concessions. So, for example, the British may have to make concessions on farm prices in order to protect the interests of their fishermen. At the same time, the British government and its legislation is subject to rulings of the European Court. Indeed, the Court has the power to determine the constitutionality of British Acts of Parliament. In both these ways the autonomy of the British government has been reduced by membership. Britain has also to reckon with the fact that trade in the Community is increasing and its economic success depends heavily on tariff decisions made by the Commission and Council of Ministers.

Perhaps the greatest constraint on central government stems from the structural reality that Britain is a trading nation dependent on exports and imports for its economic survival. Like all advanced industrial countries, Britain has been buffeted by the instability and unpredictability of the world economic system over the last fifteen years. Fluctuations in oil prices, world interest rates and in the general level of trading in the world economy, have had profound effects on British domestic policies. Until the advent of North Sea oil, Britain was in a particularly vulnerable position. Low productivity and growth constantly exposed the economy to balance of payments and currency crises, and will presumably do so again as oil prices and reserves decline.

Up to date, these forces were most evident during the life of the 1974–79 Labour Governments when the major factor shaping economic policy was the falling value of the pound on the world's money markets. The continuing crises led eventually to the International Monetary Fund requiring the government to pursue even more cautious fiscal and monetary policies which had widespread repercussions for public expenditure and thus a wide range of social programmes. Unfortunately, Britain remains in a less than ideal position as an international trader.

Fragmentation – a jigsaw without a picture?

The evidence points to a variety of groups, interests and organisations all exerting considerable influence over policies but divided internally and externally. Government decision-making is severely circumscribed by their activities. Most exercise a negative or veto power: they can constrain the alternatives considered by governments or open for them to pursue. They can even prevent a government carrying out a policy to which it is committed. But they cannot substitute their own policies. On the whole they can only react to central suggestions or policy imposition.

All this limits the scope for real change. Governments whose policies are often thwarted appear as decreasingly in control of events. Decision-makers in general seem both to themselves and to others as merely responding to political and economic forces they can do little about.

This situation, of course, is hardly confined to the United Kingdom. All modern industrial states face problems of adaptation and control, and at least two of the interpretations discussed earlier (corporatism and overload) have been applied to a number of other governmental systems. However, Britain seems to be experiencing especially difficult problems – in part because of secular economic decline, but also (and relatedly) because of the particular nature of its political system.

Briefly the British state (i.e. British governments in general) seems weak in comparison to governments in comparable countries. As a result it is poorly equipped to engage in the kind of highly positive intervention which the vast changes wrought by economic and technological developments have made necessary in recent years. The large number of goods and services provided by government and public utilities (over 40 per cent of gross domestic product) does not contradict this point. Public spending patterns are only one indicator of the extent of government influence and power. Others include the extent to which, historically, the agents of central government have managed, controlled, coerced and influenced economic and social forces. Developments in Britain which seem to have limited their role drastically can be summarised as follows:

1. The eighteenth and nineteenth centuries saw the emergence of a set of institutions: a strong executive, a unitary system of government and highly centralised political parties dominated by London-based élites. The strength of these institutions, and the unity of the élites, produced the impression of a strong centralised state, especially as for most of this period economic liberalism was proving so successful and the society was unusually homogeneous and secure from outside threats. Crucially, élites found it unnecessary to establish strong linkages with economic and other groups in society, either to speed industrialisation or to maintain order (in contrast with post-Tokugawa Japan, Bismarck's Germany, or even the Third

Republic in France). And when linkages were established it was on an *ad hoc*, functionally fragmented, basis, lacking co-ordination or general policy direction.

2. The relative independence (or autonomy) of local government, unions, business, police, courts and so on, can be traced to this period. As can the assumption in British political culture that 'governments know best' or that professional civil servants and London-based politicians and parties can solve society's problems. And so they could and did during the nineteenth century – usually by delegating power to lower level authorities. When industrialisation produced a more reformist Liberal Party and a new social-ist party, they too took on the attitudes to governing of the established élites. Hence neither the politicians (old or new), nor the civil servants, perceived any need to move into society to negotiate support, to build a consensus, to create hierarchical relationships incorporating economic inter-ests (in particular) into decision-making structures.

3. The advent of total war, the emergence of a powerful labour movement and serious economic dislocation in an increasingly changing and unpre-dictable world, did of course force governments to intervene more and more in economics and social life. Chapters 2 and 5 especially have documented the extensive nature of such intervention, involving close contacts between affected interests, lower authorities and central government. However, intervention seems to have taken on particular forms which limits its effec-tiveness:

    (a) It often consists of *ad hoc*, unco-ordinated action inspired by a particu-lar problem or policy.

    (b) Intervention is also functionally differentiated and fragmented, i.e. in-dividual firms have access to the Ministries of Trade and Industry on a piecemeal rather than a systematic basis.

    (c) Individual local government departments often have strong links with Whitehall, but few horizontal links at the grass roots. Corresponding horizontal links at the central level are (historically) also weak. Home Office/police relations are similarly fragmented. A corollary here is that peak associations and their equivalents have developed similarly. Peak associations have always had a very generalised representative role but few close working relationships with individual members.

    (d) Underlying this particular form of contact and strengthened by it is an active distaste of governments and administrators for systematic and detailed intervention. Hence great discretion is accorded lower level authorities – whether they be police, army, judges, local authorities, quangos, various organised interests, or corporations – to implement policy in functionally distinct areas.

    (e) The distaste for detailed intervention has both produced and been jus-tified by an adherence to simple, general solutions to economic and social problems. Such solutions have been patterned on the free trade and non-interventionist policies which worked so successfully in the nineteenth century. The most obvious successor was Keynesian macro-economic planning. Precisely because this rested on central manipulation of finances without any detailed follow-up, it was universally accepted for thirty years. Contemporary successors are monetarism (restriction of public expenditures without detailed follow-up) and block privatisation. Adoption of such 'unitary' panaceas which will transform problems through generalised central action, are understandable given the formidable political problems involved in strengthening vertical and horizontal linkage. But they are not really a substitute.

(f) Hence as pressures have increased, successive governments have found themselves obliged to confront individual lower level groups and authorities, often in ways leading to serious conflict, especially as the political opposition tends to back those resisting central direction. Examples are the confrontations with both unions and local governments in the early 1980s. Governments lack both the central co-ordinating structures and institutions and the vertical authority structures which strong peak associations disciplining their members could provide. The result is a continuing sense of political crisis and confrontation. This was the great paradox of the first two Thatcher administrations: detailed, interventionist policies but no ideological concern to provide investment and resources to ensure the policies were successfully implemented.

(g) This accepted, new corporatist arrangements have been tried (NEDC, planning agreements in industrial policy), if not always successfully. And peak associations are constantly exhorted by government to exert greater influence on members. The London-based media play an important part in this process, always favouring consensus-building options to ones involving confrontation.

Developments in the post-war period

Against this background post-war developments fall into an entirely understandable pattern. With the first limited attempts by governments to manage aspects of social change on a permanent basis, during the 1930s and 1940s a fragile consensus with the leading economic and political actors of society was established. The Labour triumph of 1945 precipitated a flood of social and economic reform which led to a greatly enhanced role for government at all levels.

Crucially, however, amid the frenzy of activity associated with the Second World War and its aftermath, little in the way of permanent or fundamental changes in the role of the state occurred. The machinery of government remained virtually unchanged. Vertical linkages between central officials and the leading economic and social groups in society remained weak. And when new linkages were forged they tended to be between central government and business and labour élites who, as we have noted, often had little contact with or control over their own members. The institutions of the state itself remained fragmented. The judiciary was fiercely independent; the police remained largely under local control. Local governments, in spite of being given vast new responsibilities, were controlled indirectly by statute and through the purse-strings. Central government did not impose its own agents (such as prefects in France) on the system. Finally, important divisions within central government, and particularly between the Treasury and the spending departments, persisted.

So, in spite of greatly increased public expenditures (and the higher public expectations of government which they brought), British politicians continued to depend on remarkably undeveloped institutions of co-ordination and control. It was almost as if the pulling of levers in Whitehall and Westminster was all that was needed to operate the new system. Keynesian demand management with its emphasis on macro-economic policy almost certainly reinforced such views. To reform the economy, detailed, micro-intervention was unnecessary. All that was needed was a change in public expenditure or in fiscal and monetary policy and all would be well.

The workings of this type of attitude can be illustrated by an example from the late 1970s when it was increasingly obvious that general fiscal manipulation was inadequate, partly because the collapse of large enterprises like British Shipbuilders and British Leyland (cars), with vast social consequences, had to be averted by direct subsidy. At this point one of the larger British car-hire firms – like most large institutions a traditional purchaser of British cars – passed under the control of foreign interests. No particular notice of this was taken either in Whitehall or in the media. Yet it was highly likely that foreign control would be quietly followed by purchase of cheaper cars abroad after a year or so. Where French administrators would have been concerned to ensure that French control and purchasing policy remained, the British apparently did not even consider the loss of a small but steady market share for their manufacturing industry.

Similarly, when the government invested close to £100 million to set up a car manufacturing firm in Belfast in the early 1980s, they apparently left total operational control in the hands of the American founder and were taken by surprise by his bankruptcy in 1982. The firm had not been monitored even to the extent that administrators knew of its month by month economic prospects.

Perhaps surprisingly, at least until the 1960s, Labour Governments were as prone to see the world in general terms as were Conservative. In the context of relative economic prosperity and a broad acceptance of the traditional view of the constitution and party system, it is perhaps not surprising that politicians of all shades broadly agreed that the system worked. Why, after all propose a stronger state, more planning, co-ordination and control when Britain was widely recognised as stable, efficient and politically mature?

When, during the ever-intensifying crises of the 1960s and 1970s, governments did attempt reforms and greater control, the fragile consensus with interest group leaders quickly evaporated. To their great consternation governments discovered that unions, local governments, industrial corporations and others could act independently. Nothing better illustrates the structural problems of British governments than the continuing struggle to control public expenditure. In this area successive governments have fallen foul of both internal weakness and external constraints. The absence of success eventually led the Thatcher Governments to impose draconian solutions such as 'fining' recalcitrant local governments and the imposition of a pay and working conditions settlement on the teachers in 1987. These and similar measures have often produced more problems for government than they have solved.

British policy in Northern Ireland can also be understood within this general argument. Until the beginning of the present troubles British administrations virtually ignored the internal government of the province. Certainly the linkages with the Northern Irish Parliament and Government were tenuous; what they did was an Irish affair. Following the Assembly's demise, London had no alternative but to govern directly, but in a context of virtually no historically established linkages with Northern Irish society. The devolved administration of Northern Ireland, Scotland, and increasingly Wales, reflects the absence of such links.

A fragmented British political system?

If the British state is fragmented and weak, so too it might be claimed are the administrative and governmental arrangements of most states, especially under the stresses to which they are subjected in an increasingly interdependent and unpredictable world. The difference lies in the long-standing recognition of such weaknesses elsewhere, in contrast to the traditional characterisation of Britain as politically stable and efficient. This view, which we examined at the outset of the chapter, saw the two-party system in conjunction with Cabinet government as a uniquely effective method of governing. Clearly such a claim is not appropriate for the 1980s or 1990s. Indeed in functional terms a number of other countries appear to operate political systems better suited to the modern world than the British. Most of these – France, Germany, Sweden, Japan, the Netherlands – are 'democracies'. But each has political arrangements considered alien to the British way of governing. It is testimony to the present bankrupt state of the British system that there are serious proposals to incorporate some of these alien features, including proportional representation; multi-party and coalition governments; federalism and regionalism; open government; and corporatist arrangements in industrial and economic policy. It is also significant that many of Britain's more successful competitors do have relatively strong central state institutions or (equally important) decision-making structures built more on consensus and co-operation than on conflict and confrontation.

We should not infer from this some blueprint for the reform of British government. It is one of the merits of the explanation in terms of fragmented centres of power, and lack of central co-ordination, that simple one-factor solutions to British problems are ruled out. Any attempt at change will in any case be undermined by the opposition it provokes from various interests and groups. Even such a minor institutional adjustment as Welsh and Scottish devolution was defeated in the late 1970s, despite the fact that the country had lived with a much more thoroughgoing devolution of power to Northern Ireland for half a century. When the central government could not get its solution accepted in this case, it is unlikely to muster enough support for more serious changes in power relationships, especially if it tries to impose them unilaterally.

The most likely outcome in the near future is an uneasy, shifting equilibrium as governments experiment with institutional changes, negotiate with societal interests, and try to back this up by imposing key policies. Some such combination may work if it is accompanied by a willingness to establish permanent administrative relationships with individual organisations in particular sectors. The breakdown of class barriers noted in Chapter 4 may aid an attempt to build up consensual working relationships. The attitudes of the general population are positive and encouraging. In the end, however, the traditional, recently reinforced, aloofness of government may prevent this happening; and whatever general form of economic management happens to be in force during future economic upturns could serve as a fresh justification for avoiding detailed intervention. We have already seen this happening as 'privatisation' is credited with regenerating the British economy irrespective of world recovery and oil revenues.

There is certainly some merit in avoiding ill-advised and hasty institutional changes. It may be that some of the alternative arrangements we have reviewed are inappropriate for Britain. Some may even constitute threats to long-established individual freedoms, for greater administrative and economic efficiency is unlikely to be achieved without sacrifices in terms of other societal values. A fragmented system does after all have some beneficial effects. Centralised police and military coercion is difficult to achieve with a fragmented structure. And the relative independence of lower level governments and policy networks does provide a bulwark against the emergence of a centralised, strong and unresponsive élite.

But, as was pointed out earlier, fragmentation does not guarantee effective popular control. Instead, it puts a great premium on the *negative* or *reactive* power of various organisations. Unfortunately there is no magic formula which can produce both popular control with participation, and efficient and responsive government.

What is important, however, is that British élites and public recognise the fragmented and often inefficient nature of the present political system. The serious problems that have plagued successive governments since the 1960s – regional disparities, poor economic performance, sour industrial relations, racial unrest and a state of near civil war in Northern Ireland – remain with us and are unlikely to be resolved in the foreseeable future. Reforms are, therefore, urgently needed. Moves in the direction of greater accountability and participation may actually increase fragmentation; while moves towards centralisation or a corporatist consensus may undermine popular control. This is the central and possibly irresolvable problem of British politics over the next decade.

References and bibliography

As each chapter summarises a variety of findings and discussions, and also reports original research, we have not deemed it necessary to clutter the text with detailed references on each point. Generally these have been given only when another author was directly quoted, where a table was based upon particular references, or where a whole section of the discussion was based on one book. The purpose of this note is to give detailed references for the main sources for each chapter. Generally these divide between broad treatments which provide a good overview of a particular topic, and detailed studies on which we have relied for supporting evidence. Books with broader coverage are generally listed first under each heading.

Place of publication is London except where otherwise stated.

Economic difficulties and central decision-making (Chapters 1 and 2)

On economic decline, see **David Coates** and **John Hillar** (eds) (1986) *The economic decline of modern Britain: the debate between left and right*, Wheatsheaf.

S. H. Beer (1965) *Modern British politics*, Faber, is a good general background to policy-making in British central government, though inevitably dated by now.

A. H. Birch (1964) *Representative and responsible government*, Allen & Unwin, deals with many of the problems of accountability and answerability that crop up throughout the discussion, again from an earlier perspective. A more up-to-date account is **J. J. Richardson** and **A. G. Jordan** (1979) *Governing under pressure: the policy process in a post-parliamentary democracy*, Oxford, Martin Robertson.

On 'Whitehall' specifically is **G. K. Fry** (1981) *The administrative 'revolution' in Whitehall*, Croom Helm. On the Cabinet, see **Peter Hennessy** (1986) *Cabinet*, Blackwell, Oxford. For views of the role of Prime Minister, see **Anthony King** (ed.) (1985) *The British Prime Minister*, Macmillan.

Budgetary processes are reviewed in **A. Wildavsky** and **H. Heclo** (1974) *The private government of public money*, Macmillan.

Views from the inside, based on personal experience, are given in **R. Crossman**

(1979) *The Crossman diaries: selections from the diaries of a Cabinet minister*, ed. A. Howard, Magnum; **G. Kaufman** (1980) *How to be a minister*, Sidgwick & Jackson; **W. Rodgers** *et al.* (1980) *Policy and practice: the experience of government*, Royal Institute of Public Administration, London.

General surveys of pressure groups are **R. Taylor** (1980) *The fifth estate: Britain's unions in the modern world*, Pan; **R. Undy, V. Ellis, W. E. J. McCarthy** and **A. M. Halmos** (1981) *Change in trade unions: the development of UK Unions since the 1960s*, Hutchinson; **W. Grant** and **D. Marsh** (1977) *The Confederation of British Industry*, Hodder & Stoughton; **G. K. Wilson** (1977) *Special interests and policy-making*, Wiley. On the role of the City see **M. Moran** (1984) *The politics of banking*, Macmillan.

On 'planning' see **A. Budd** (1978) *The politics of economic planning*, Glasgow, Fontana; **J. Leruez** (1975) *Economic planning and politics in Britain*, **Martin Robinson, M. Shanks** (1977) *Planning and politics*, Allen & Unwin; **D. Foley** (1963) *Controling London's growth*, Los Angeles, University of California Press.

Government and Parliament (Chapter 3)

The most comprehensive coverage of Parliament is **Philip Norton**'s *The Commons in perspective*, Blackwell (1985). There is also:

P. Norton (1978) The Organization of Parliamentary Parties in S. Walkland (ed.) *The House of Commons in the 20th Century*, Clarendon Press, Oxford.

J. Schwartz (1981) Exploring a new role in policy-making: the British House of Commons in the 1970s, *American Political Science Review*.

J. Schwartz and **J. Lambert** (1972) The voting behaviour of British Conservative backbenchers in S. Patterson and J. Wahlke (eds) *Comparative legislative behaviour: frontiers of research*, New York, Wiley.

J. A. G. Griffiths (1974) *Parliamentary scrutiny of government Bills*, Allen & Unwin, is illuminating on the extent of Parliament's legislative powers.

The major work on dissent in the parliamentary parties during the 1970s is **P. Norton** (1980) *Dissension in the House of Commons 1974–9*, Oxford University Press; this also summarises earlier work and gives more extended references. For an analysis of private members Bills see **David Marsh** and **Melvyn Read** *Private members bills*, Cambridge, 1987.

For divisions on moral legislation see **D. Marsh** and **J. Chambers** (1981) *Abortion politics*, Junction Books. Ideological lines of dissent over the post-war period are traced by **S. E. Finer** and **H. Berrington** with their associates (1961 and subsequent dates) *Backbench opinion on the House of Commons*, Oxford, Pergamon.

The major works on Select Committees are **A. Robinson** (1978) *Parliament and public spending*, Heinemann: and **D. Englefield** (ed.) (1984) *Commons Select Committees*, Longman.

On information flows between governments and Parliament see **D. Englefield** (ed.) (1985) *Whitehall and Westminster – Government informs Parliament*, Longman.

Parties, electors and social structure (Chapter 4)

A critical treatment of the British parties is **S. E. Finer** (1980) *The changing British party system 1945–79*, American Enterprise Institute, Washington DC. Party relationships and the internal balance within the major parties themselves have changed so rapidly in the 1980s that the best guide to the current situation are reports in *The Times*, *The Guardian*, *The Independent*, *The Sunday Times*, *The Observer* and *The Economist*.

Election issues and party strategies are systematically reviewed in **I. Budge** and **D. J. Farlie** (1983) *Explaining and predicting elections*, Allen & Unwin. A detailed account of party activity in each campaign is provided by **D. E. Butler** and associates (various dates), *The Nuffield general election series*, Macmillan, the latest is with **D. Kavanagh** (1988) *The British general election of 1987*, Macmillan.

Party election manifestos are analysed in **Ian Budge**, **David Robertson** and **D. J. Hearl** (eds) (1987) *Ideology, strategy and party movement* (Cambridge University Press), Ch. 3. See also **Ian Budge** and **D. J. Farlie** (1977) *Voting and party competition*, Wiley, Ch. 11. The latter also measures the effects of issues, class, religion and region on individual voting for elections up to 1974. The authoritative account of national voting in the 1970s is **I. Crewe** and **B. Sarlvik** (1983) *Decade of dealignment*, Cambridge University Press; this traces the declining influence of party loyalty and class affiliation on voting. For the 1983 election see **A. Heath**, **R. Jowell** and **J. Curtice** (1985) *How Britain votes*, Oxford, Pergamon. A critical re-analysis of the relationship between class and voting is **Mark Franklin** (1985) *The decline of class voting in Britain*, Oxford, Clarendon Press.

The major study of class structure and class mobility in contemporary Britain is **J. Goldthorpe** *et al.* (1980) *Social mobility and class structure in modern Britain*, Oxford University Press. For political effects see **D. Robertson** (1984) *Class and the British electorate*, Oxford, Blackwell.

Regional variations in class structure are explored in **I. Budge** and **C. O'Leary** (1973) *Belfast: approach to crisis*, Macmillan, ch. 8. Regional influences as a whole are assessed in **I. Budge** and **D. W. Urwin** (1966) *Scottish political behaviour*, Longman; **W. L. Miller** (1980) *The end of British politics? Scots and English political behaviour in the seventies*, Oxford University Press; **I. Budge** and **C. O'Leary** (1977) 'Permanent supremacy and perpetual opposition in Northern Ireland', in **A. Eldridge** (ed.) *Legislatures in plural societies*, Durham, N.C., Duke University Press; **K. Morgan** (1970) *Wales in British politics*, Cardiff, University of Wales Press.

For electors' values see **I. Budge** (1970) *Agreement and the stability of democracy*, Chicago, Rand McNally; **L. Moss** (1980) 'Some attitudes towards government', Birkbeck College, London, and various surveys reported in *The Times* (London) 26–28 June 1980; **J. Dennis** *et al* (1971) 'Support for nation and government among English children', *British journal of political science* **1**: 254–8.

For electors' reactions to the economic situation the best source is **J. Alt** (1979) *The politics of economic decline*, Cambridge University Press. *Family expenditure survey* and *Social trends*, both published annually by the H. M. Stationery Office, give valuable information on living standards.

The mass media (Chapter 5)

General overviews of the media include **Jeremy Tunstall** (1983) *The media in Britain*, Constable, and **Alastair Hetherington** (1985) *News, newspapers and television*, Macmillan. For the debate on bias see the **Glasgow University Media Group's** *Bad news*, Routledge (1976); *More bad news*, Routledge (1980); and *Really bad news*, Writers and Readers (1982); **R. Worcester** and **M. Harrop** (1982) *Political communication in the general election campaign of 1979*, Allen & Unwin, and **B. Gunter, M. Sverrevig** and **M. Wober** (1986) *TV coverage of the 1983 general election*, Aldershot, Gower; together with the critique by **Martin Harrison** (1985) *TV news: whose bias*, Policy Journals. For an account of media coverage of elections see **Ivor Crewe** and **Martin Harrop** (eds) (1986) *Political communications: the general election campaign of 1983*, Cambridge University Press.

Sub-central government (Chapter 6)

Books and sources on which the chapter specifically draws are:

D. Birrell and **A. Murie** (1980) *Policy and government in Northern Ireland*, Dublin. Gill & Macmillan.

M. Connolly (1983) *Central-local relations in Northern Ireland*, London, Report to the Economic and Social Research Council (mimeo).

P. J. Curwen (1986) *Public enterprise: a modern approach*, Brighton, Wheatsheaf.

P. Dunleavy and **R. A. W. Rhodes** (1986) 'Funny things happened on the way to central control: the Conservatives and sub-central government', *Social Studies Review*.

M. Grant (1986) *Rate capping and the law* (2nd edn.), London, Association of Metropolitan Authorities.

B. Houlihan (1984) 'The regional offices of the DoE – policeman or mediators? A study of local housing policy', *Public administration*, **62**: 401–21.

N. Johnson (1979) 'Editorial: quangos and the structure of government' *Public administration*, **57**: 379–95.

G. W. Jones and **J. D. Stewart** (1983) *The case for local government*, London, Allen & Unwin.

The Layfield Committee (1976) *Report of the committee of inquiry into local government finance*, Cmnd. 6453, London, HMSO.

R. Parry (1982) 'Public expenditure in Scotland' in D. McCrone (ed.), *The Scottish Government yearbook 1983*, Edinburgh, Unit for the Study of Government in Scotland, pp. 98–120.

Pliatzky Report (1980) *Report on non-departmental public bodies* Cmnd. 7797, London, HMSO.

R. A. W. Rhodes (1986) 'La Grande-Bretagne, pays du "gouvernement local"', *Pouvoirs*, No. 37: 59–70.

R. A. W. Rhodes (1988) *Beyond Westminster and Whitehall: the sub-central governments of Britain*, Allen & Unwin, forthcoming.

P. Riddell (1983) *The Thatcher government*, Oxford, Martin Robertson.

D. Steel and **D. Heald** (eds) (1984) *Privatizing public enterprises*, London, Royal Institute of Public Administration.
S. Young (1982) 'Regional offices of the Department of the Environment: their roles and influences in the 1970s' in **B. W. Hogwood** and **M. Keating** (eds), *Regional Government in England*, Oxford, Clarendon Press, pp. 75–95.

More general reading follows.

The periphery

J. G. Bulpitt (1983) *Territory and power in the United Kingdom*, Manchester, Manchester University Press.
J. G. Kellas (1984) *The Scottish political system* (3rd edn) Cambridge, Cambridge University Press.

Non-departmental public bodies

A. Barker (1982) *Quangos in Britain*, Macmillan.
B. Hogwood and **M. Keating** (eds) (1982) *Regional government in England*, Oxford, Clarendon Press.
R. Klein (1983) *The politics of the National Health Service*, Longman.
L. J. Sharpe (1977) 'Whitehall: structures and people' in **D. Kavanagh** and **R. Rose** (eds) *New trends in British politics*, Sage.
A. Webb, **G. Wistow** and **B. Hardy** (1986) *Structuring local policy environments*, ESRC.
J. Dearlove and **P. Saunders** (1984) *Introduction to British politics*, Cambridge, Polity Press.

Central-local relations

M. Goldsmith (ed.) (1986) *New research into central-local relations*, Aldershot, Gower.
J. Gyford and **M. James** (1984) *National parties and local politics*, Allen & Unwin.
S. Ranson, **G. W. Jones** and **K. Walsh** (eds) (1985) *Between centre and locality*, Allen & Unwin.
R. A. W. Rhodes (1986) *The national world of local government*, Allen & Unwin.

Financial relationships

C. D. Foster, **R. Jackman** and **R. Perlman** (1980) *Local government finance in a unitary state*, Allen & Unwin.
N. P. Hepworth (1984) *The finance of local government* (7th edn), Allen & Unwin.
Paying for local government, Cmnd. 9714, London, HMSO, 1986.

Local political systems

J. Dearlove (1973) *The politics of policy in local government*, Cambridge University Press.

P. Dunleavy (1981) *The politics of mass housing in Britain, 1945–1975*, Oxford, Clarendon Press.
K. Newton (1976) *Second-city politics*, Oxford, Clarendon Press.
P. Saunders (1980) *Urban politics*, Harmondsworth, Penguin Books.
L. J. Sharpe and **K. Newton** (1984) *Does local politics matter?* Oxford, Clarendon Press.

Local government – general

R. Greenwood, K. Walsh, C. R. Hinings and **S. Ranson** (1980) *Patterns of management in local government*, Oxford: Martin Robertson.
B. Keith-Lucas and **P. G. Richards** (1978) *A history of local government in the twentieth century*, Allen & Unwin.
J. Gyford (1985) *The politics of local socialism*, Allen & Unwin.
D. Heald (1983) *Public expenditure*, Oxford, Martin Robertson.
P. Jackson (ed.) (1985) *Implementing government policy initiatives*, Royal Institute of Public Administration.
(Widdicombe) Committee of Inquiry into the Conduct of Local Authority Business, *Report*, Cmnd 9797; *Research Volumes* I–IV (Cmnd 9798–9801), HMSO, 1986.

Britain and the European Community (Chapter 7)

Considering the growing interrelationships here, surprisingly little has been recently written on the subject generally and practically nothing on European institutions in Britain or British institutions in Brussels. The most up to date books are:

M. Burgess (1986) *Federalism and federation in Western Europe*, Croom Helm.
S. George (1985) *Politics and policy in the European Community*, Clarendon Press.
J. Lodge (1983) *Institutions and policies of the European Community*, Pinter.
C. Webb and **W. Wallace** (eds) (1983) *Policy-making in the European Community*, Wiley.

All, however, have become slightly outdated with the passing of the Single European Act and moves towards a free industrial market by 1992.

Courts and legal decision-making (Chapter 8)

The general structure is covered in **R. M. Jackson** (1977) *The machinery of justice in England*, Cambridge University Press; **D. Walker** (1976) *The Scottish legal system* Edinburgh, Green; **H. Calvert** (1968) *Constitutional law in Northern Ireland*, Stevens.
　　B. Abel-Smith and **R. Stevens** (1970) *Lawyers and the courts*, Stevens, covers the legal profession.

J. A. G. Griffith (1981) *The politics of the English judiciary*, Fontana, is a controversial treatment of judges, their background and decisions.

D. Robertson (1982) 'Judicial ideology in the House of Lords: a jurimetric analysis', *British journal of political science* **12**: 1–25 is a first attempt at uncovering voting patterns in the highest court.

T. C. Hartley and **J. A. G. Griffith** (1975) *Government and law*, Weidenfeld & Nicolson, examine the political significance of court decisions.

The police and military (Chapter 9)

R. Mark (1978) *In the office of constable*, Allen & Unwin, examines the system from a policy viewpoint, as does **J. Alderson** (1979) *Policing freedom*, Macdonald & Evans. **G. Marshall** (1965) *Police and government*, Methuen, covers similar ground from outside. **R. M. Jackson** (1972) *Enforcing the law*, Penguin Books, is a helpful survey, now overtaken by events.

J. Lambert (1970) *Crime, police and race relations*, Oxford University Press, foreshadows some questions of great relevance to the 1980s.

There is very little on the internal role of the military, a point which is significant in itself. Some references are made in **R. Clutterbuck** (1975) *Living with terrorism*, Faber. **L. Lustgarten** (1986) *The governance of police*, (Modern legal studies), Sweet and Maxwell/Stevens.

Britain and the world (Chapter 10)

J. Roper (ed.) (1985) *The future of British defence policy*, Gower.

J. Baylis (ed.) (1983) *Alternative approaches to British defence policy*, Macmillan.

J. Burton *et al.* (1984) *Britain between East and West: a concerned independence*, Gower.

D. Dilks (ed.) (1981) *Retreat from power: studies on Britain's foreign policy of the twentieth century*, Macmillan, Vol. 2.

B. Porter (1984) *The lion's share: a short history of British imperialism*, Longman.

E. A. Brett (1985) *The world economy since the war: the politics of uneven development*, Macmillan.

L. Freedman (ed.) (1983) *The troubled alliance: Atlantic relations in the 1980s*, Gower.

Characterising British politics (Chapter 11)

The traditional view is given in textbooks of the 1960s such as the concise book by **G. Moodie** (1963) *British government and politics*, Methuen. Their criticisms point the way to the 'technocratic' reforms of the late 1960s and early 1970s.

Corporatism is discussed generally in **Wyn Grant** (ed.) (1985) *The political economy of corporatism*, Macmillan; **P. Schmitter** and **G. Lehmbruch** (eds) (1979) *Trends towards corporatist intermediation*, Sage. For Britain see **T. Smith** (1979) *Politics of the corporate economy*, Oxford, Martin Robertson; **K. Middlemass** (1979) *Politics of industrial society*, Deutsch; **N. Harris** (1972) *Competition and the corporate society: British conservatism, the state and industry*, Methuen; **R. Taylor** (1978) *Labour and the social contract*, Fabian Society Tract 458.

On 'overload' see **A. King** (ed.) (1976) *Why is Britain becoming harder to govern?*, BBC Publications; **S. Brittan** (1975) 'The economic contradictions of democracy', *British Journal of Political Science*, **5**: 129–59.

Adversary politics are most powerfully condemned in **S. E. Finer** (1975) *Adversary politics and electoral reform*, A. Wigram. See also **A. M. Gamble** and **S. A. Walkland,** *The British party system and economic policy 1945–1983*, Oxford 1984. **A. Wedgewood Benn** (1980) *Arguments for socialism*, Penguin Books, is the radical alternative by one of its proponents. The first Thatcher years are covered in **Peter Riddell** (1985) *The Thatcher Government*, Blackwell.

A comparison with the industrial-institutional development of other countries is implicitly provided in **C. Trebilcock** (1981) *The industrialisation of the continental powers 1780–1914*, Longman. **Peter Hall** (1986) *Governing the economy: the politics of state intervention in Britain and France*, Polity Press.

Notes on contributors

Ian Budge: Professor of Government at the University of Essex. He is the author of numerous books and articles including *Agreement and stability of democracy* (1970) and *Explaining and predicting elections* (1983, with D. Farlie).

David McKay: Senior Lecturer in Government and Director of the European Consortium for Political Research at the University of Essex. His most recent publications include *American politics and society* (revised edition), *Power in the USA* (1987), and *Domestic policy and ideology: presidents and the American state 1964–1987* (1988).

David Marsh: Lecturer in Government at the University of Essex. Among his many publications are *The Confederation of British Industries* (1977, with Wyn Grant), *Abortion politics*, (1982, with Joanne Chambers), and he has edited *Pressure politics* (1983).

Roderick Rhodes: Reader in Government at the University of Essex and joint editor of *Public Administration*. His books include *Control and power in central and local relations* (1981), and *The national world of local government* (1986).

David Robertson: A Fellow of St Hugh's College and a Lecturer in the sub-faculties of Politics and Sociology at the University of Oxford. His major publications include *A theory of party competition* (1976) and *Class and the British electorate* (1983).

David Sanders: Lecturer in Government at the University of Essex, specialising in Comparative Government and International Relations. He has written two books in these fields, *Patterns of political instability* 1981; and *Law-making and co-operation* 1986. He is currently writing an analysis of British foreign policy.

Martin Slater: Lecturer in Government at the University of Essex. He has published articles on French and Italian politics, focusing particularly on trade union politics and labour migration issues.

Graham Wilson: Professor of Political Science at the University of Wisconsin. His publications include *Special interests and policy making* (1977), *Unions in American national politics* (1979) and *Interest groups in the United States* (1981).

Index